D1137979

David Mason – Official Club Historian at Rangers Football Club since 1986, he is one of the most authoritative writers on the history of the club. He has written for various football publications and has appeared on television and radio. He was author of *Rangers: The Managers* and *A Match to Remember*.

Ian Stewart – Author of *My Helicopter Sunday*, Ian is a civil servant who has been a season ticket holder at Ibrox for 25 years. His interest in Rangers Football Club and William Struth has been an obsession and *Mr Struth – The Boss* is the culmination of long hours of research.

MR STRUTH: THE BOSS

David Mason and Ian Stewart

Copyright © 2013 David Mason and Ian Stewart

The right of David Mason and Ian Stewart to be identified as the
Authors of the Work has been asserted by them in accordance with
the Copyright, Designs and Patents Act 1988.

First published in 2013 by
HEADLINE PUBLISHING GROUP

First published in paperback in 2014 by
HEADLINE PUBLISHING GROUP

George Orwell's work reprinted by permission of Bill Hamilton as the
Literary Executor of the Estate of the late Sonia Brownell Orwell

1

Apart from any use permitted under UK copyright law, this publication may
only be reproduced, stored, or transmitted, in any form, or by
any means, with prior permission in writing of the publishers or,
in the case of reprographic production, in accordance with the terms
of licences issued by the Copyright Licensing Agency.

Every effort has been made to fulfil requirements with regard
to reproducing copyright material. The author and publisher will be
glad to rectify any omissions at the earliest opportunity.

Cataloguing in Publication Data is available from the British Library

Paperback ISBN 978 0 7553 6549 4

Typeset in Bell MT by Avon DataSet Ltd,
Bidford-on-Avon, Warwickshire

Printed and bound in Great Britain by Clays Ltd, St Ives plc

Headline's policy is to use papers that are natural, renewable and recyclable
products and made from wood grown in sustainable forests.
The logging and manufacturing processes are expected to conform to the
environmental regulations of the country of origin.

HEADLINE PUBLISHING GROUP
An Hachette UK Company
338 Euston Road
London NW1 3BH

www.headline.co.uk
www.hachette.co.uk

Dedications and Thanks

David Mason

I have been honoured to know a player who began as a foot-balling hero of mine and then became a great friend – Sandy Jardine. His contribution to Rangers as a player and also as a leader of men in the club's troubled times is immeasurable. It was Bill Struth who famously said: 'To be a Ranger is to sense the sacred trust of upholding all that such a name means in this shrine of football.' Sandy epitomises everything that could be expected of a 'Ranger' and it is with great thanks, perhaps on behalf of every fan, that I dedicate this book to him. He has been a constant source of inspiration and he continues to motivate all of those who come within his sphere of influence. Thanks, Sandy!

I would also like to dedicate the book to my father, Hector Mason, in whose footsteps I graciously 'Follow, Follow'. No one could want a greater father.

Finally, thank you to my wife Karen and daughters Laura and Louise, who will be glad to see the cover of my laptop closed!

Ian Stewart

I would like to dedicate this book to a wee boy who sat awestruck in the back room of Dalriada, listening to the stories of Bill Struth and the Rangers being told to him by his Uncle Johnnie. That wee boy was my father Jackie, who in turn passed the faith on to me. He took me to my first match in 1971 and we have had season tickets together since 1987. We have shared so much, good and bad, that I would not have changed for the world. Thank you, Faither.

I would also like to thank my wife Yvonne for putting up with an absent husband for much of the last few months.

Finally, this is for my children Christiane and Janine – two young women of whom I am immensely proud, Andrew – next Financial Director of RFC, Kirstin – make your dreams happen, and finally Iona – the sunshine in everyone's life.

Acknowledgements

It is with great thanks that we acknowledge the assistance and advice we received from a number of parties and organisations, without whom this book would have been hugely incomplete. They include, first and foremost, Rangers Football Club and special thanks must go to Walter Smith, Steven Romeo, Stephen Kerr, Lindsay Herron, Neil Smith, Johnny Hubbard and the many Rangers players who, over the years, have added their own little piece to build the picture we portray here. We are also grateful to James Struth, Hamish Telfer, Gary Havlin, Doug Gillon, Tom Campbell, Alison Muir, Alastair Muir, Hugh Barrow, Graham Sneddon, Neil Stobie, Brian McColl, Matthew McGregor, Robin Paterson and John Beckett for their important contributions.

Perhaps the most valuable assistance came from Anne and Ian Walker to whom we will remain eternally grateful for their quite personal insight and family photographs.

We also acknowledge the assistance we have received from the staff at the Mitchell Library, Perth Library, and the National Library of Scotland. Thanks are also due to DC Thomson, Express Newspapers, Heart of Midlothian Football Club, the *Evening Times*, and the *Daily Record*, per their permission to use extracts from their publications.

CONTENTS

FOREWORD
BY WALTER SMITH

It gives me great pleasure to write this foreword about a man who is a legend in the history of Rangers football club. Bill Struth is one of football's greatest managers and in this year when we acknowledge the achievements of another Ranger, Alex Ferguson, it is nice to reflect on a man who was at the heart of Rangers' success for 34 years from 1920 to 1954. As a young fan, my grandfather would often talk of the Struth era and I grew up with stories of the great Rangers players of the past including Bob McPhail, Davie Meiklejohn, Willie Waddell and Willie Thornton. I had my own heroes from the later Scot Symon period, of course, including the likes of Jimmy Millar and John Greig, but I was raised understanding that Rangers had a great history and tradition.

When I joined Rangers in 1986 I had the great pleasure of meeting many of the men who played under Mr Struth. You could tell that he had an enormous influence upon them and set standards that have largely remained to this day. It seems that when you enter the Main Stand that Struth's influence and to some extent his presence is never far away. When Graeme Souness and I entered the Manager's office at the top of the Marble Staircase we were taken by its history. We knew that Mr Struth was the first in that office and we were keen to ensure that it retained its character.

When I took over the role of Manager, I was well aware of the standards that we had to achieve and the huge responsibility that placed upon me and my staff. Times change, but Bill Struth was benchmark for everything we did and his legacy remains that 'only the best is good enough for Rangers'. It was something I was acutely aware of in my time as Manager.

I know that both David Mason and Ian Stewart have been involved in extensive research for the book over several years and it is good that in the recent turmoil the club experienced that we can look back on a man who was perhaps the most important in the history of the club.

From all I have heard and read, Mr Struth was a great man and Manager and one that I was extremely humbled and honoured to follow.

Walter Smith

PROLOGUE

In the midst of the turmoil that followed the plunge of
The Rangers Football Club into administration on 14 February
2012, the grandiose interior of the historic grandstand of
Ibrox Stadium remained quiet. Inside, a bronze bust in the
image of Rangers' greatest ever manager, William Struth,
stared down from the first landing of the famous marble
staircase, with a cold expression of authority. The sculpture
had been unveiled seven years earlier in tribute to a man who
presided over the club from 1920 to 1954. Such was the esteem
in which Struth was held that a year later, on the occasion
of the 50th anniversary of his death, the club added a further
tribute by naming the B-listed structure the Bill Struth
Main Stand.

Struth's reaction to subsequent events, which culminated in
Rangers' liquidation and relegation to the bottom tier of
Scottish football, can only be imagined. 'He would be turning
in his grave,' offered one of the veteran players who played
under him. 'There would be hell to pay for those responsible,'
said another. Undoubtedly, Struth would have been distraught
and angry at the dramatic events that catapulted the club from
financial meltdown into a downward spiral of retribution and
punishment. However, it can be safely assumed that the mis-
management that led to the collapse of this great club would
never have happened on his watch. Indeed, it is extremely
unlikely that Struth would have stood idly by as it was led to

the slaughter by clubs and institutions acting on a mission of vengeance in the name of 'sporting integrity'.

Ironically, for all that Struth cared for Rangers, he also looked out for the financial wellbeing of lesser clubs. He once said, 'A cheque from Ibrox has often meant sudden wealth to many small clubs. We are pleased that this should be so. It is not just little clubs who count on Rangers and Celtic to help them out. A number of league clubs would have a very thin time otherwise. We always help the smaller clubs whenever possible for friendlies, including paying our own expenses.' He would have viewed the ultimate blood-letting as an act of betrayal.

'If only he were here,' many may have been tempted to venture as if inviting some kind of second coming. However, if Struth could not materialise from the ether, his role in the survival of Rangers in their troubled times was actual and tangible. As the club entered season 2012–13 in the Third Division of the Scottish League, the supporters rallied with season-ticket sales exceeding a mammoth 38,000. Throughout that season, grounds up and down the country were filled to capacity wherever Rangers played and Ibrox repeatedly set attendance records, belying the club's league status.

The league title was secured, of course, but the fans were not drawn simply to watch the team. They gathered in their thousands to demonstrate their loyalty to a club they considered to be a veritable institution – one that was established on the back of the contributions of many great Rangers characters, but none more important than Struth.

Those same fans, steeped in the club's ethos, like generations before them, sang, 'There's not a team like the Glasgow Rangers', and who could deny them? If Rangers was their church, Struth was their god. Indeed, they may even have found solace in his words of wisdom related many years ago, but which are perhaps more appropriate now than at any other time in the club's history. He said, 'No matter the days of anxiety that come our way, we shall emerge stronger because of the trials to be overcome.'

To the fans who have been immersed and raised in the history of Rangers, Struth is a legendary figure. Ironically, most who revere him were born long after his death in 1956, but he is considered the embodiment of The Rangers Football Club. He consolidated the traditions that set this great club apart from others and established the very standards that he expected his charges to adopt. He also set the ideals for all those associated with the club.

No one has ever captured the essence of the club as well as Struth did, and in just three sentences. In a speech he delivered three years before he died, he said, 'To be a Ranger is to sense the sacred trust of upholding all that such a name means in this shrine of football. They must be true in their conception of what the Ibrox tradition seeks from them. No true Ranger has ever failed in the tradition set him.'

However, there was considerably more to Struth's managerial career than a few carefully constructed words can portray. If his success as a manager is to be measured by silverware alone, then Struth's record is quite simply unrivalled. Of the major domestic trophies, Rangers captured 18 Scottish First Division League Championships, 10 Scottish Cup and 2 League Cup victories through the 34 years of his tenure. This record excludes the 6 'unofficial' Southern League Championships, 4 Southern League Cups, the Summer Cup, the Victory Cup, the Emergency War Cup, and the Western

Division Championship, won through the war years, quite apart from the 19 Glasgow Cups and the 20 Charity Cup successes, which were of enormous significance in that era.

Little wonder then that Struth is held in such reverence by the fans, but the players who served under him perhaps knew him best. The testaments of their time at Rangers inevitably dwell on the man they called 'Mr Struth' or 'the Boss'. It was often said that he ruled the club with 'an iron fist inside a velvet glove' but if he was a strict disciplinarian, he was also sensitive to those around him. He cared for his 'boys', as he would call them, and he saw that they stayed in the best hotels, travelled in the best class available and wore the best clothes. Quite simply, he expected them to attain and maintain 'Rangers' standards' and if he gave them the best, he expected nothing less in return. To him, 'Only the best was good enough for Rangers.'

Respect was what he also sought for his players and what he received from them in return. Their respect was such that they were determined not to fail the man they regarded as a father figure. They would never be allowed to get above their station, because they followed his mantra that 'the club is greater than the man'. If anyone dared forget this ideal, they were reminded of it every time they entered his imposing office at the top of the marble staircase – the message was written on a small card strategically placed upon his desk and facing all visitors.

In a society that craves idols, Bill Struth was obviously iconic in his stature and in his words. If any man was greater than the club, it *was* Struth and the idolatry that perpetuates his memory is easily understandable in the light of his achievements with Rangers. But Struth was *not* a god and the fame and adulation masked the frailties that cast a shadow over his private life. Indeed, it is distinctly possible that misjudgements in his personal life were motivational in his professional career, most notably at Ibrox.

Players and associates who knew him talk of a compassionate and imposing man, who gained respect from all those who came within his sphere of influence. In contrast, one of his few remaining relatives who can remember him, coldly commented, 'He was a great football manager,' when asked what kind of man he was.

No matter the trials and tribulations of his personal life, Bill Struth *was* the single most important man in the history of The Rangers Football Club and his achievements will be unequalled. With meticulous research, we have uncovered Struth's roots from the weavers of Milnathort to his birth in Edinburgh and an adolescence spent in the little town of his ancestors, near Kinross. We trace his early interest in sport, nurtured through professional athletics, before being lured into football, initially as a trainer before becoming the celebrated manager of Rangers.

This book is a biographical account of Bill Struth, which also reflects on the impact of the two world wars on football and the key moments in the history of Rangers through the period of his tenure. What emerges is a characterisation of a man who is renowned in Rangers history. What is revealed is that this man *was* a fascinating character whose influence on the development of Rangers is shown to be enormous. The club is indeed greater than the man, but if any single character could be considered to challenge that notion, then Struth would be the sole candidate.

This is the story of Bill Struth.

THE FORMATIVE YEARS

The Struth family roots in Milnathort and Blairgowrie

Bill Struth made his modest entry into the world on Friday, 16 June 1876 at 25 Balfour Street, Leith, described in Cassell's contemporary periodical account of *Old and New Edinburgh* as '. . . a street of workmen's houses'. His father, William, a 'journeyman' stonemason and his mother, Isabella, a domestic servant were from humble backgrounds, but we can reasonably conjecture that the characteristics and aspirations that led Bill Struth to seek high ideals and standards as the manager of Rangers Football Club were instilled in him during his early, formative years.

Although Edinburgh was the city of his birth, Struth had a particularly strong association with the little Kinross village of Milnathort, where he was to spend the later years of his childhood. Both his father and grandfather, also named William, were born and raised in the community, so that was where his ancestral roots lay. Most who lived in the town in the early part of the nineteenth century were weavers. In the fertile soil of the surrounding land lint and flax were cultivated, and these vital raw materials sustained a thriving cottage industry of spinning and weaving in the area. Scarcely a cottage was without its spinning-wheel or a village without its looms, manufacturing tartan shawls and plaids for Glasgow merchants.

Milnathort, as well as being a weaving town, had a long-established corn and flour mill, situated in its centre, and it was here that Bill's grandfather was employed as a miller. Bill's father, who was born in the village in 1853, may have been expected to continue the family tradition and go into the mill, where the employment would be typically steady, but uninspiring. The rewards were not rich and the family's existence at the time would have been little more than meagre.

The relative poverty of the community was in stark contrast to the situation in the great population centres of Glasgow and Edinburgh, which were flourishing in the Industrial Revolution. While these great cities had their own poverty to contend with, they also had a wealthy upper class and this increased demand for the kind of textiles produced by the Milnathort weavers. Ordinarily, such an increase in trade would have been welcomed, but the weavers could not provide the output levels necessary to fulfil the demand.

Moreover, the village could not rise to the challenge by building its own large mills of industrial standard, although there were two smaller mills in nearby Kinross. Despite being located on a trading route, Milnathort was otherwise limited by its geographic setting. The Back Burn, which flowed through the town, was a slowly meandering river that could not deliver the power needed to support a spinning mill on an industrial scale. In contrast, there was something of a boom in towns such as Blairgowrie and Rattray, which were situated on the fast-flowing River Ericht. The river facilitated the construction of twelve mills in these towns, employing over 4,000 workers, largely drawn from the surrounding communities.

Milnathort did not grow to any significant degree and as its weavers struggled to compete, in the second half of the century their trade went into decline. In January 1852, the *Annals of Kinross-shire* reported that there was a 'great depression in the weaving trades of Kinross and Milnathort'. Some of the weavers stayed, but many left to pursue work opportunities elsewhere. Chastened by the downturn, the Struth family decided to leave the village and headed for Blairgowrie. Since there was no previous family association with the town, it is likely that Bill's grandfather was attracted by the opportunity of work for himself and his family. The Struths settled in tenement accommodation in Wellmeadow in the centre of the town, which was close to many of the mills, and that was the start of a new life in a busy little town, with a guarantee of work for the whole family.

The 1871 census shows that all of those of working age in the Struth family had entered the mills. Bill's grandfather had secured employment in a Blairgowrie corn and flour mill just a few steps from their home, and the other family members, including his father, worked in the textile spinning mills. While most of the family laboured in the mills, one rose to the highest echelons of the industry – Bill's uncle James. Starting in the mill as a 'spinning-wheel mechanic', accounts of the time suggest that he had a natural bent for mechanics, encouraged by his employers. He progressed in the textile industry to become chief of Wellington Mill, one of the largest jute industries in Calcutta, India.

Interestingly, Bill almost followed James to India. In an interview he gave to Glasgow periodical newspaper *The Baillie* in 1936, he reflected that when he was 18, he was about to go to Calcutta to work with James, who promised to show him the ways of big business. Sadly, in June 1894, James died at the age of 46, just as young Bill had made all the necessary preparations to leave.

If employment was plentiful in Blairgowrie, the work was hard and the hours long in the mill. Mill workers generally entered employment at the age of 12. They were expected to commence work at 6.30 a.m. and continued until after 7 p.m. in an atmosphere that was far from healthy. Loose fibres in the air made the atmosphere thick, which strained breathing. However, for those seasoned in mill work, it was a way of life that satisfied the aspirations of several generations of families.

There is little doubt that Bill's father could have remained in gainful employment in Blairgowrie for as long as his health held up. However, it seems that he was driven to find a better life than the one apparently ahead of him in the mill. By the time he was 18, William had decided to change direction and seek his fortune away from the town and its mills. He decided that he would uproot, alone, in pursuit of a new life in the capital – Edinburgh. There would be opportunities in the mills lying in the southern fringes of the city, but William was excited by the city's growth and extensive building programme. He left Blairgowrie to head southwards over the Forth to seek his fortune not as a mill worker, but as a stonemason.

William Struth Senior – a new life in Edinburgh

The Edinburgh that Bill's father found when he arrived in the 1870s was a city of excitement. Queen Victoria was at the peak of her reign and the country was riding high on a wave of confidence. The boundaries of trade pushed out further and further from these shores, inspired by Britain's imperialism.

In major cities, great industries had emerged, seizing upon the valuable resources of Lanarkshire and the Lothians, as the fires of the Industrial Revolution took hold. While Glasgow was richer in heavy industrial operations, particularly along the Clyde, Edinburgh had its own industries – distilleries, heavy engineering, and paper mills, mainly along the Water of Leith. In Edinburgh, both the industrial and financial sectors flourished, as the vibrancy of the economy spawned new middle classes and empowered workers, who aspired to improve their lot.

The landscape of Edinburgh was also changing as the medieval Old Town, which surrounded Castle Rock, was transformed and a 'New Town' of fine sandstone buildings grew in the hinterlands. More and more people came to the city from near and far, all in search of opportunity.

The parallels between the young founders of Rangers Football Club and Bill Struth's father are quite intriguing. They were all of similar age, although Bill's father was slightly older, but their motivations in moving to the city were alike and the timing was the same. The Gallant Pioneers of Rangers left the Highland communities of Argyll to seek their fortune in Glasgow sometime around 1870 – about the same time that William made the trip south to Edinburgh, joining the thousands of other migrants who were attracted by the buoyancy of Scotland's two major cities.

When William arrived in the city, he settled among the poorer migrants in the Old Town with its 'grim and sooty' buildings, or Lands as they were called. Scots novelist Robert Louis Stevenson once described them, in his *Edinburgh Picturesque Notes* from the period, as rising like a 'cliff of building which hangs imminent over Waverley Bridge'.

Stevenson had something of a love–hate relationship with Edinburgh, which he called the 'precipitous city'. His views at that time were candid and quite critical. In a letter written to his cousin a year earlier, he said, 'Edinburgh is a very sanguinary shop, and bloodier than ever, you should be glad you are out of it.' It would have been quite a cultural change for a young man from Milnathort.

No matter the degradation of the older parts, the city was an exciting place to live and one that offered opportunity for hard workers. The town's increasing population placed great pressures on the demand for new housing stock to supplement and replace the decaying buildings of the Old Town. Although the New Town was largely completed by the time he arrived, the building boom continued around the city. Showing some measure of ambition and enthusiasm, the young William seized the opportunity and took up mallet and chisel, determined never to return to the mill.

There is little doubt that Edinburgh would have held more appeal than a Perthshire mill town, which once seemed to be his destiny. The attractions were not confined to employment and a few pennies more in his pocket, however – the ladies were plentiful!

Bill's parents – William and Isabella unite

Bill's father took up residence at 17 Bristo Street, in the heart of the Old Town, close to General's Entry, a narrow lane that had gained some fame over eighty years earlier as the place where Scottish bard Robert Burns met his 'Clarinda', Agnes McElhose. If there was romanticism in the air for Burns at that time, Bill's father was also to find love in the dark recesses of Old Edinburgh. The area had become rather squalid since Burns forlornly penned 'Ae Fond Kiss', when his love left the city to return to her husband in Jamaica in a last ditch attempt to save her marriage. But while the bard's memories of Bristo Street would have been bittersweet at the end of his romance, William's story was not one of unfulfilled love. He courted a young girl of similar age to himself, Isabella Cunningham, who was destined to become Bill's mother.

Although Isabella had been born in Polmont, and spent the early years of her life there, the Cunningham family were local to the Edinburgh district. Her father, Robert, was a labourer who originated from Currie and her mother, Helen, came from Dunbar. Isabella lived with her parents, brother and three sisters in Mino Park, just off St Leonard Street, in the southern part of the Old Town, but eventually they took up residence at the Beadle's House at Cameron House Lodge, where Isabella's father was employed as estate gardener.

By the time she had reached her 19th birthday, Isabella had left home to become a domestic servant with the Gentle family, who occupied a residence at 20 Nicholson Street, not far from Mino Park. Significantly, the house was just a short distance from 17 Bristo Street, where Bill's father lived. Isabella's employment was short-lived and she returned to stay with her parents, but she had already met and fallen for the young man from Milnathort. Unlike Burns, who never did capture the fair hand of 'his Nancy', William won Isabella and the couple were betrothed and married in Liberton, Edinburgh on 24 December 1875. Love undoubtedly played its part in the betrothal but necessity was perhaps more compelling – Isabella was three months pregnant when the couple were wed! The pregnancy may well have precipitated the wedding, but we shall never know.

A newborn baby – Bill Struth!

Isabella and William set up home at 25 Balfour Street, Leith – one of several streets built to accommodate the new working class who had come to the city. The house would have been a welcome change from William's lodgings in Bristo Street, at the top of the hill in the dirty Old Town. At the end of Balfour Street was Pilrig Park, where Pilrig House stood – the home of the Balfour family. The commanding residence, which remains today, was once occupied by Margaret Balfour, mother of Robert Louis Stevenson. Stevenson, who was a qualified lawyer and very much part of the affluent middle class, would have visited Pilrig but he would not have moved in the same circles as the young Struth family. Stevenson's preference at that time was to frequent the brothels and public houses of the Old Town!

If the city, though vibrant, was not quite the land of milk and honey that William Struth had sought when he left Blairgowrie, that did not detract from his initial desire to raise his family in Edinburgh. On Friday, 16 June 1876, just six months after they were wed, Isabella gave birth to their first child – William 'Bill' Struth. The baby was born at the couple's home in Balfour Street and the birth was registered at Leith Registry Office on 27 June 1876.

Meanwhile, over in Glasgow, a young football club called 'The Rangers' had vacated their home at Burnbank, with plans to relocate to the former Clydesdale Cricket Club ground at Kinning Park. Three months earlier, one of the club's founders,

Moses represented Scotland against Wales in Partick, Glasgow. It is arguable whether young Bill's father, William had even heard of Rangers at that time, or had any interest in the comparatively new Association game. However, both he and his son would not only learn of the club in the future, Bill would grow up to become perhaps the most important character in the history of The Rangers Football Club.

William and Isabella added to their family during the next three years. Helen was born in 1878 and Robert arrived a year later, at 11 Prospect Street in the Salisbury Crags area of town, near Holyrood. If this was the family home, their stay at the address was fleeting. By 1881, whether through necessity or desire, the young Struth family uprooted and moved back to the centre of the Old Town, setting up home at 7 Drummond Street.

Their home was relatively modern for the area, having been constructed just thirty years earlier. At the end of the street, near its junction with the main thoroughfare of Nicholson Street, was Rutherford's Bar, another favourite hostelry of Robert Louis Stevenson's, although his recollections do not provide a favourable portrayal of a pub that he regularly patronised through the period. He wrote that when he gave the bar his custom, he was the 'companion of seamen, chimney-sweeps and thieves'.

The area has become well known in more recent times. Celebrated author J.K. Rowling reputedly started her first Harry Potter novel as she sat in a café at the corner of Nicholson Street and Drummond Street. None of the Struth family would emulate Stevenson or Rowling with the pen, but Bill certainly went on to achieve his own acclaim in sport several years later.

The move to Drummond Street was perhaps a measure of the family's increasing affluence, as rents in Edinburgh typically increased towards the centre. Certainly, with his apprenticeship served and having attained the exalted position of master mason, William's wages would have risen in tandem with the thriving building industry and the increasing power of the stonemason's union, the United Operative Masons Association of Scotland. Stonemasons were the backbone of the construction industry in Scotland at this time, since most buildings were constructed in stone, not brick. The union won good pay for their members, and a nine-hour day, which was a far cry from the life endured by William's family still working in the mill, back in Blairgowrie.

However, although William had achieved some improvement in the standard of living for himself and his family, it is more than likely that life soon became increasingly difficult on the work front. Following a sustained and prolific period of employment for stonemasons in Edinburgh, the industry plunged into a long period of recession. The downturn was precipitated by the failure of the City of Glasgow Bank, which collapsed with a debt of twelve million pounds in the latter part of 1878. The bank had backed a number of building projects throughout the city and work on these effectively ceased. Stonemasons were already facing some curtailment in employment as many public buildings, including schools, had already been completed and vacant housing levels had risen. The impact of the bank collapse on the building trade was described as 'catastrophic'. The industry was strangulated and lay paralysed for seven years. Trade union historian Raymond Postgate wrote, 'Master builder after master builder was ruined. Employment could hardly be got by any operative: the trade had to try to exist on odd jobs or repairs.'

The strength of the union waned and those masons who were in work, or found employment, had to accept lower wages and longer hours. Inevitably, the Struths would have found the circumstances extremely difficult, but if life was hard for the couple due to the economic downturn in the building industry, they were positively devastated in 1883 when tragedy struck. Their three-year-old son, Robert, fell ill with cerebral meningitis and sixteen days later, he died in hospital. Bill was almost seven years of age when his young brother died.

Information on the family during the following years is scant, although it seems that they remained in Edinburgh. By 1890, however, they had decided to leave the city to return to the country. By then, Bill was almost 14 and had begun to follow in his father's footsteps, pursuing a career as a mason. With the economy recovering in Edinburgh at that time, it is unlikely that the move was hastened by a shortage of work. Similarly, it does not seem that their departure was motivated by any family interests. Had this been the case, they were more likely to have returned to Blairgowrie where William's family remained. Instead, they had decided to move to Milnathort – a return for Bill's father to his roots. While they had some relations in the village, family connections were weak. More than likely, William and young Bill had an opportunity of work in a town they clearly had some affection for. It would be a new way of life for the Struths, who had spent the first fourteen years of their marriage in the hustle-bustle of Edinburgh. For Bill's father, at least, the transition to sedate village life held no uncertainties. For the adolescent Bill, however, life in Milnathort would be a whole new adventure.

The Milnathort years

The family set up home in a two-bedroomed cottage at 21 Hill Street, now known as Victoria Avenue. Hill Street remains largely unchanged from those times, although the little weavers' cottage that the Struths called home has gone, apparently lost in a fire some time ago. The village was a good place to raise a family and it proved a sound move for the Struths, and especially for young Bill. Compared to the noise and hubbub of the city, Milnathort was a sleepy little place, which had changed little since William was born there almost forty years earlier. It did have some variety about everyday life, however, and the Highland Games were held each July. A football team, Loch Leven Rangers, had been established in 1882, playing in blue and white jerseys, white shorts and blue socks. We have no record of Bill Struth having any involvement with this Rangers side, but he said later that he was a founder member and player with another local team – Orwell Thistle.

In later years, Bill recounted the happy days he spent in the village, playing in the countryside and attending the old Orwell Parish Church. In all likelihood, he did not go to the village school but went straight into employment, working alongside his father as an apprentice stonemason. It seems from local accounts that he worked at a builder's yard in Stirling Street. Helen, too, left school at the age of 13 and followed a family tradition by entering the spinning mill. It was not a mill to rival those of Blairgowrie, but she would have endured the same laborious conditions.

Struth never forgot his roots and after joining Rangers he regularly returned to Milnathort to take part in and referee a charity game between local merchants and farmers. Indeed, he donated the jerseys Rangers wore against Moscow Dynamo in 1945 to one of the local sides, Markinch Victoria Rangers. In later years, he would bring some of his stars through to support the local fixture, including icons such as George Young, and, according to the local press, Alan Morton refereed the match in 1936. Struth acted as a linesman. He was proud of his roots. On train journeys that passed through the village, he would tell his players, 'Stand up, lads, and raise your hats to salute my home town.' It was not, of course, but his affection for Milnathort was such that he regarded it as his home town, often creating confusion about his actual origins. The Struth family remained in Milnathort for five years, but the lure of Edinburgh became irresistible – but not for Bill. It seems he had no real appetite for the life of a stonemason – or the city. He had seen his aspirations for a new life in Calcutta collapse. That opportunity had died with James, but he would not cease to pursue a better life away from the hard labours of the mason. He would go to Edinburgh, but his plans were for a new adventure in far off lands.

A new life, and love, in Edinburgh – Catherine Forbes

Milnathort had provided a safe and pleasant environment for young Bill to negotiate the last few years of adolescence and enter adulthood. By the time he returned to Edinburgh, he was 19 years of age and looking for some excitement. He heard that the army were recruiting and on 13 December 1895 he enlisted for the Corps of the 12th Lancers of the Line, a cavalry regiment which had recently established its headquarters in the city. His enlistment papers showed him to be five feet seven inches and 132 pounds in weight at that time. Within three days of joining up, he was transferred to Ballincollig Army Barracks, just outside Cork. It was hardly the life of adventure he sought or expected. The regiment was on duty protecting the Royal Gunpowder Mills in a rather quiet rural setting far from any real action. Within two weeks Struth decided that army life was not for him and he was discharged at his own request.

He returned to the family home at 41 Clerk Street, but his short dalliance with the army suggests that he was unsettled and not completely taken by the idea of pursuing a career as a stonemason. He wanted more from life and looked for new challenges. The family moved to the quiet little Glen Street, at number 3, just off Laurieston Place soon after Bill returned. Although it seems that he was not immediately taken with Edinburgh, the city presented many attractions and opportunities for a young man. He had developed a real passion for athletics, but his desires were to be channelled in a quite different direction – towards the female sex and one in particular, a young girl named Catherine Forbes.

Catherine, or Kate, as she was known, lived at 161 Fountainbridge, just a short distance from the Struth home. She was around the same age as Bill, having been born in Edinburgh's New Town, at St George's, on 10 September 1876, just three months after Bill. Her parents were Alexander Forbes, a stonemason, and Eliza Jane Constant, both born and raised in Cullen in Banffshire. The Forbes family, like Bill's father, were migrants who had arrived in the city a few years before Kate's birth. Kate arrived as the seventh child. Another five children would follow.

When the children were old enough to work, they moved

on and by the time Kate had reached the age of 14 she was employed as a domestic servant – by her sister Helen! Kate's employment at such a tender age was common for the period, but few could have found the circumstances quite as ideal as she did. Helen's life had changed when she met aspiring young photographer Robert Kemp Thomson. Thomson's background was one of reasonable affluence and his family had already made quite a distinguished mark on the Edinburgh landscape – his grandfather, Meikle Kemp, had designed the Scott Monument on Princes Street in 1840.

Robert and Helen married in 1888 and set up their first home at 54 Cockburn Street, near its junction with High Street on Edinburgh's Royal Mile. The address doubled as a studio from which Thomson, who later became a member of the Edinburgh Photographic Society, operated. The studio had been in use previously by several others, including John Annan, who was the brother of the celebrated Glasgow photographer, Thomas Annan. Ironically, many of the Rangers pictures in later years would be taken at the Annan Studios in Glasgow.

The couple had their first child, Robert, in 1889 and two years later they decided to take on a domestic servant. They advertised the position in the 18 February 1891 edition of the *Scotsman* newspaper: 'Girl smart and tidy, about 14, to assist with housework and keep baby; go home at night: 8s monthly. Apply Thomson Photographer 54 Cockburn Street.'

There may have been a few applicants, but just one attracted attention when she showed an interest in the position – Helen's sister Kate. She was an obvious choice, and besides, the baby in her keep (Robert) would be her own nephew. By the end of the year, Helen had another child, Alexander, whom Kate would also tend to.

Photographic studios around the period often struggled to make ends meet, but life for Helen and Kate would have been considerably more comfortable than the one they left in Fountainbridge, where the Forbes family had shared just a single room.

For Helen, the future promised much, and Kate would undoubtedly have seen her elder sister, with a successful husband and children, as an aspirational role model in the new, vibrant Edinburgh. In 1895, Helen gave birth to a third child, William. However, the family's happiness was about to be destroyed. Within a year, Helen was struck down with illness and died of septicaemia in Edinburgh Royal Infirmary. For Robert, it was a devastating blow, and he was left with a family of three children, all aged under eight.

Seeking some family stability for his children, Robert entered into a relationship with another woman, Jane Ross, whom he married within a year. Jane bore Robert two children, but the marriage was a disaster and was short-lived.

Robert continued the business at the Cockburn Street studio for a short time afterwards, but his dreams lay in tatters. Jane left the family home, taking her children, while Robert moved south to the border town of Wigtown, where he opened a new business, operating under the name Photo Tamson. He never returned to Edinburgh. Young Robert and William went with him, but Alexander, or Alex as he would be known, remained in Edinburgh with Kate and her parents – an indication, perhaps, of the close bond that she had built up with the children during her period as both nanny and auntie.

Robert's life went into free fall in the aftermath of Helen's death, and Kate's future also looked uncertain as she cared for young Alex in the cramped conditions of her parents' home.

However, if the days seemed dark and oppressive following the death of her sister, a new bright future was literally just around the corner in the form of a charming and smart young man called Bill Struth.

It is unclear when Kate and Bill first met, but the parallels in their lives at that time were such that it appears almost inevitable that their paths would cross. Perhaps it was through the stonemason profession, which Bill shared with Kate's father. More likely is that they met on the street as they lived just a few hundred yards apart. Whatever the circumstances of their meeting, the young couple found love and for Kate, at least, the relationship offered some solace from the solemnity of her life. The passion that was ignited between the two carried them to the altar and they were married on 4 February 1898 in Glen Street Hall, just a few yards from Bill's home. The circumstances of the marriage were quite unusual in that Bill and Kate had a ready-made family with their adopted son, Alex.

The Hearts connection

The couple looked for a home of their own and discovered new tenemental properties being erected, essentially for the working classes, at Wheatfield Street in the Dalry area of the city. The area had been increasingly urbanised in the latter years of the nineteenth century, with the construction of a number of broadly similar four-storey blocks. Bill's parents were also attracted by the property on Wheatfield Street and they decided to move there, too. Bill, Kate and Alex shared one apartment at Number 8, and Bill's parents, sister Helen and cousin James shared another. Today, the tenement blocks of Wheatfield Street are much the same as they were back then.

The biggest employer locally was the North British Distillery, which, until recently, adjoined the street to the north. However, it was not all work and no play, particularly for Bill. A football ground, Tynecastle Park, backed on to Wheatfield Street to the east. Home of one of the top clubs in the country at that time – Heart of Midlothian Football Club – it was in the throes of reconstruction and, with a decent running track, it also catered for athletics.

Hearts had won the Scottish Cup for the second time in 1896, but by the time the Struths moved to the area, their fortunes had dipped. They did manage to finish second in the Scottish League Championship in 1899, but Struth could not have failed to be impressed by the winners – Rangers. The Glasgow club won the title by 10 points, winning every match in the process, a feat that has never been repeated. It completed a League and Scottish Cup double for the Glasgow side they called 'the Light Blues', as they justified their claim to be the best team in Scotland. The following year, Rangers played hosts to Hearts in the opening of New Ibrox Park.

Living in proximity to Tynecastle, it was natural that Struth would develop an affinity with his local side. However, football was not his first love and there is no record of him ever having played the game at any decent level, other than his dalliance with Orwell Thistle. Struth's primary interest in Tynecastle was in its track, which he regularly used for his own training. His passion was athletics and he had begun to make quite a name for himself as a champion professional, appearing in races throughout the country from at least 1898. As a fine athlete who clearly maintained a high level of fitness,

Struth was dismayed by the training of football players at the time, dedicated as it was to producing or supporting workhorses, not speedy thoroughbreds.

Struth reasoned that footballers could learn a thing or two about fitness from the regime that he and his contemporaries endured. However, it was several years before he got the chance to show the players his training methods.

In 1901, Bill Struth was in the fourth year of his marriage. With a new home and a stable career ahead of him as a stonemason, he and Kate had every reason to look forward to the future, even though their young marriage had not brought them any children of their own. Kate had continued to care for Alex. It was a role she chose, while many other young wives would have looked forward to building their own families. Perhaps the pressures of raising Alex, who by now was 10 years old, discouraged them from adding to their family at that stage. Maybe she delayed her own family, or simply had difficulties in bearing a child. Whatever the circumstances, the otherwise seemingly idyllic life that Bill and Kate shared was about to be shattered. There would be a child for the couple, but it would not be Kate's.

A child is born

The faint cry of a newborn baby boy disturbed the quiet night air at Montgomery Street in Edinburgh on Saint Valentine's Day, 1902. His mother, Margaret Jackson, had travelled from her residence in Shielfield Terrace, Berwick, where she was employed as a 'domestic servant'. Sixty-five years later, Rangers would suffer perhaps their most infamous defeat at Shielfield Park in the Scottish Cup at the hands of the local

'Wee Rangers'. However, as Margaret travelled to Edinburgh to give birth to the baby, any notion of football or, indeed, any sport would have been far from her mind. Instead, she must have been a troubled and anxious girl as she made her way, most likely by train, to Waverley Station in Edinburgh. This was no ordinary journey for a young expectant woman, and we can only imagine her torment. Margaret was travelling to Edinburgh for the birth of her child, but it appears that a decision had already been made that she would pass the baby over for adoption following the birth. Whether through poverty or the shame of bearing an illegitimate child, it seems that she had decided, or agreed, that there was no way in which she could keep the baby.

The father was Bill Struth, but we have no information on how they met or the background to their relationship. Despite hours of laborious research, the trail on Margaret Jackson and what became of her lies cold. All that remains of her is a neat signature in the registration of the birth of the baby. Perhaps she was travelling to the city of her birth, but we can only speculate as her origin is uncertain. Making various assumptions on her age and marital status, we examined several possible candidates for the 'real' Margaret Jackson, but results were inconclusive. However, the circumstantial evidence points to a young girl who resided in Edinburgh.

It is not clear from the historical records why Margaret Jackson relocated to Berwick, although one suggestion may be that it took her to a safe house away from her home. It was quite normal for an unmarried pregnant woman to be spirited away from her home to avoid the ignominy of an obvious bundle beneath her petticoat. Margaret's employers in Berwick were George and Isabella Walker, who originated from

Edinburgh or, more precisely, Leith. It is possible that they were friends of Margaret's, or perhaps even the Struths, since George lived just a short distance away from Bill's parents when they stayed in Balfour Street. Regardless, the fact remains that Margaret was domiciled in Berwick when she was pregnant, but travelled to Edinburgh for the delivery.

Illegitimate birth was not unusual in Victorian times and the rates were particularly high in parts of Scotland. However, the social stigma was such that young women would often turn to 'baby farmers', who traded infants and sometimes disposed of them by killing them. Most, however, were like Margaret and left the family home for a period. Ironically, neither Kate nor Bill's families were strangers to illegitimate birth, although in most circumstances the moral position was restored with the 'erring' couple joining in marriage when they realised a baby was on the way – just as Bill's parents did!

Our researches suggest that Margaret had no family connection at 75 Montgomery Street, where the child was born. The building was occupied by several families and people of various trades and professions, including a private midwife known as 'Nurse (Barbara) Morton'. It was commonplace for women to act as midwives in late Victorian times, in places where the privacy of the mother could be maintained. Indeed, in the 1891 census, Barbara Morton listed her profession as a 'ladies' nurse'.

Nurse Morton was presumably paid to assist the birth and it seems that, for three weeks at least, the baby remained with his mother. It was after this time that Margaret went to the Registry Office in the St Andrews district of Edinburgh. As the child's mother and in the absence of the father, she had the legal right to register and name the child. She named the baby

William Struth Jackson, then signed the register in a neat hand, simply writing Margaret Jackson.

From discussions with family members, it seems that she then disappeared from the lives of both the child and his father. Indeed, the episode appears to have been erased. The birth certificate is the only evidence of Margaret as the mother. Margaret Jackson may have departed from the life of young William, but her legacy was to remain with Struth until his final days. Young William was handed over to Bill's parents, who took temporary custody of the child. Kate already had young Alex to look after and would hardly welcome the idea of looking after a baby that was not her own, so it is perhaps no surprise that guardianship of the child was entrusted to Bill's parents.

If the birth of a baby is cause for sympathy, then none of that would lie with Bill Struth. The two troubled parties were Kate and the child's mother, Margaret Jackson, each of whom would carry their own scars of the child born out of wedlock. Eventually, however, the young William would be absorbed into Bill and Kate's household.

We can only imagine how Kate must have felt as the sanctity of her marriage was destroyed within four years of her wedding. Showing enormous courage and resilience, she remained in the marriage when many others in similar circumstances would have walked away. Young William would be a permanent reminder of a moment of indiscretion by the man she loved. Moreover, he lived in the same building, although not in the same house at first. Kate owed a duty to her sister to rear young Alex and nothing would deflect from her obligation to provide a stable and happy family environment for him.

She would continue her life with Bill, setting aside the anger and the hurt caused by the affair. Eventually, she would look after young William as if he were her own. From recent conversations with young William's daughter Anne, it seems that Kate was a good mother to William. Indeed, the discussions on his true mother arouse a degree of confusion. Kate may not have been young William's blood mother, but by all accounts she was no less of a mother to him. In later years, it would appear to all outsiders that he was *her* child, inflicting a strange irony on a woman who was destined never to bear a child herself.

Margaret Jackson disappeared into the night, never to appear in their lives again, but undoubtedly harbouring her own pain and regrets. That moment of indiscretion would remain with Bill Struth, although he gained redemption by standing by William, and seeing him virtually daily through a spell of over thirty-five years when he employed him at Ibrox. William went on to have a very happy life, far removed from the troubles surrounding his birth. Did Margaret watch him from afar? Given the fame that Bill was to achieve, it seems almost certain that if she was alive, she would have been aware of his movements and would have had more than a passing interest in the development of her son. In the case of the latter, she may have felt some quiet satisfaction with the man that her son was to become. William was popular, earned his living as a motor electrician and raised his own family in a loving environment, becoming a father then a grandfather.

In his time at Ibrox, young William became the face that visitors often met at the front doors, while his father worked upstairs. He travelled regularly with the reserve team, assisting on match days. He also had a responsible role to play on match day at Ibrox, since he was charged with depositing the takings from the day's game in the Clydesdale Bank night safe in the city centre. William carried on serving Rangers long after Bill Struth died. In fact, his picture appeared in the *Rangers News* of 8 February 1978, when he was presented with an award for long service to the club. He worked for Rangers for a remarkable fifty-nine years, longer than his legendary father.

Bill's granddaughter Anne also had a great love of Rangers and when she was old enough, she would spend Saturday afternoons along with her mother in the directors' box. The lineage continued through to her own son Billy, who served as a ballboy at Ibrox during the early eighties.

BILL STRUTH – TRACK STAR

An aspiring young athlete

If Struth's personal life had become more complicated, he could always find solace on the athletics track. He was rather a free bird when it came to sport and that is where his real passion lay, nurtured in the fields around Milnathort. As each day brought hard labour down at the local builder's yard, sport was to become a welcome recreation for the 14-year-old Bill Struth. He found that both Milnathort and Kinross offered a wide variety of pursuits for the sports minded. The cricket club was well established, although we have no information to suggest that Bill showed any real interest in the wicket.

There was also football with Orwell Thistle, and the Loch Leven Rangers club, which had formed a few years earlier, seemed to be especially well organised. Their outfit mirrored their more famous Glasgow equivalents. For those in the area with notable agility, Gymnastic Sports were held in the grounds of Kinross House and in 1881 these were considered to be the foremost in Scotland. However, the pinnacle of the local calendar, involving most of the community, was the Milnathort Highland Games and Fair.

Participation in sports was encouraged at the time as a means to enhance fitness, health and general wellbeing, particularly in Scotland's major cities, where serious concerns were being raised over nutrition, sanitation and, even then, environmental pollution. Swimming, rowing, cycling and gymnastics were popular, as well as the team sports of football, cricket and rugby. The young Gallant Pioneers of Rangers would be found rowing, running and playing football, but Bill's greatest love was for athletics. He was to become a keen enthusiast of the culture surrounding Highland Games, or more particularly their track events. On the track, as a 'pedestrian' or 'ped', as athletes were then known, he had a decent turn of speed and discovered a steely determination to break the tape before any other. Moreover, he also recognised that there was decent money on offer for professional runners.

Times were hard for the majority of young Scots who were employed in any form of manual labour, skilled or unskilled, in the late nineteenth and early twentieth centuries. Money was scarce, but Struth found that he could supplement his meagre income through athletics. He favoured sprinting and middle-distance running and often earned considerably more on the track than his normal weekly wage as an apprentice stonemason.

Athletics was very much a two-tier sport in the Victorian era, in social terms as well as in the conflict of amateurism against professionalism. The upper and middle classes pursued the sport on a gentlemanly basis, firmly motivated by the 'thrill of the chase', so to speak. In contrast, the working classes were drawn to the professional circuit by the prize money on offer. As a working-class man, Struth's interests were financially motivated, but he also had a love for the sport, which was evident throughout his life.

By his teens, Struth was running in local meetings and picking up prizes, although he still found time to do a variety of odd jobs. 'I was glad to get a tanner for a couple of hours' digging,' he once said. When he moved back to Edinburgh in 1895, it is generally believed that he became a member of Edinburgh Northern Harriers athletics club. In listings of events, his name is followed by '(Edinburgh)', indicating his base, or club. Even after he moved to Glasgow, he still carried this annotation, perhaps lending further credence to the notion that he was affiliated to the Edinburgh club.

In one photograph we uncovered, apparently taken at Inverleith in Edinburgh, close to the tracks of both Powderhall and the Gymnasium, home of St Bernard's FC. Struth is shown wearing his track clothes together with some fellow athletes (see Plate). The photograph is particularly interesting because it includes Jimmy Wilson, who was to go on to become Rangers' trainer in 1897. The picture probably pre-dates this and is likely to have been taken in 1895 or 1896. At that time, Wilson was the trainer at St Bernards and Struth's age would have been around 19 or 20. In the picture, Wilson appears to be wearing the rosette of a judge, although he was also a trainer at Powderhall. Jimmy Wilson was to figure more prominently in Bill Struth's future in later years, as will become evident.

The rise of the athletics clubs

The Edinburgh Northern Harriers, formed in 1889, was one of the first organised athletics clubs in Scotland. The membership of such clubs was typically made up of men who had a wide interest in sports, and some clubs developed strong connections in swimming, rowing and cycling, as well as with the rapidly evolving football clubs. One such club, which is generally accepted to be the earliest outside public schools, was

Clydesdale Harriers, formed on 4 May 1885. Struth was clearly affiliated to the Edinburgh scene, but he would have been aware of the Clydesdale club and possibly their training facility – at Ibrox Park.

Clydesdale had strong connections with Rangers and, indeed, two of the Light Blues' Gallant Pioneers – Peter and Moses McNeill – were integral to the club's formation. The connection remained strong for much of their first twenty-five years. The clubs shared the Kinning Park ground and when Rangers took up residence at Ibrox in 1887, the Clydesdale Harriers members decided to join them. Harriers' president, John Mellish, was invited to be president of Rangers, and other notable members of both clubs included William Wilton, Tom Vallance and John R. Gow.

It seems to be around the time when the Harriers followed Rangers to Ibrox that the Harriers Sports were instigated. They date from at least 1889, and it is interesting to note that while all the organising was done by the Harriers, Rangers took all the financial risks. If the event made a loss, the Light Blues would cover the costs. Harriers meetings continued at Ibrox until 1922. Rangers actively promoted the Harriers for a long period and they were to continue this in later years in their relationship with Bellahouston Harriers, allowing members to have access to their own key to Ibrox in order to train on the track.

Clydesdale was typical of many of the athletics clubs, which became increasingly reliant on a connection with football clubs to sustain them as an important and credible force in sport in Scotland. They could share ground facilities and became more and more dependent on the regular crowds that the football clubs could bring. In the case of Rangers, the new track at Ibrox was one of the best in the UK, and the association with

Clydesdale, like many clubs, was somewhat symbiotic. While football was by far the most popular of the sports and attracted decent crowds, the promotion of cycling and pedestrian races earned added revenue. As this revenue diminished, the interest from the football clubs evaporated. Sadly, athletics went into something of a decline, particularly through the twentieth century when many of the football clubs severed their association with the sport.

The murky trade of the professional 'ped'

While he appears to have been affiliated to one of the Edinburgh amateur athletics clubs, Bill Struth was motivated by the rewards on offer on the professional circuit. That was where he learned that there was no room for the Corinthian spirit in the business, and the trade could be a murky one, often abused by handicapping. In a spirit of egalitarianism, both the professional and amateur athletics circuit employed the handicap system for many races, so that every athlete had the opportunity to succeed, unlike today's events, which are strictly 'scratch'. The athletes would provide details of recent performances to the handicappers, who in turn would set their appropriate handicap distance. The impact of the handicaps was such that race distances had to be increased and the 200 yards became the 215 yards race. There was a maximum handicap limit depending on the race distance, with the mile, for example, having a maximum of 130 yards. Struth was invariably heavily handicapped, such was the standing he achieved in the sport.

To maximise their chances in competition, professional athletes had to be prepared to 'work' the handicap system, managing their performances in the lead-up to the most lucrative events. They worked to get the best possible handicap and, in turn, increase the chance of picking up the best prize money. Inevitably, with decent money and prizes at stake, the sport attracted some outside influences, which were not for the faint-hearted. Bribery was commonplace and there were very real concerns among many that the bookmakers had some undue influence with some handicappers. The athletes, too, were often subjected to sharp practice. Favourites would be 'encouraged' to lose while money piled on weaker rivals. For some big races, it was often thought that the 'bookie' and his heavies had as big a say in results as the athletes themselves. Even publicans who offered accommodation for itinerant athletes would distort the betting and the race by asking athletes to slow up. If they told you to lose, you would do it!

There is no evidence that Struth was involved in any of this, but it gives some indication of the tough culture that existed in the sport and the resilience that athletes needed as they toured the circuit.

On one occasion, Struth had to address a flaw in the handicapping to give himself a decent chance in a race he quite simply needed to win. He had invested considerable time and expense travelling by train deep into South Wales, to Porthcawl, 25 miles west of Cardiff, arriving shortly after midnight. He had entered the mile race to be run later in the day, but firstly, he had to find somewhere to stay. He did not have the money for lodgings, so he made his way, in the darkness, to the sports ground, where he bedded down for the evening in the competitors' changing tent. He recalled:

I woke, drenched with the morning dew, but that mattered nothing to me in those days. I was fit, very fit.

Not a penny did I possess. There was only one way to get out of Porthcawl – win that race. The mark they gave me, however, was grossly unfair, and made it impossible for me to win. I decided to do something about it. Professional running wasn't for the weakling. [They were] tough days, but challenging and exciting. I've always thrilled in a challenge. As we lined up, I slipped my number from back to front, eased my way along the avenue of spectators as though chatting to them and I wasn't really a competitor. I stole the 20 yards and as the pistol barked, I was away.

The finishing post was out of sight of the starter. So when I breasted the tape, and was handed a voucher, which, I was informed, could be cashed at the local bank, I dashed to the tent, gathered up my clothes and ran for my life, still in my running strip, for that bank. I knew the protest would be raging behind me. I simply had to get out of Porthcawl without a moment's delay. I was lucky. The bank was open, and though the clerk looked at me in astonishment, he didn't waste any time in handing over the cash when I explained I had a train to catch. Then came another race against the clock, to the station. My luck still held. I jumped on the train as it was steaming out the station. I had no idea where it was going but I was at last clear of the irate officials.

In effect, Struth cheated to win the race, albeit he desperately needed the victory. If this 'win at any cost' attitude does not portray him in a favourable light, he brought closure on the story several years later when he repaid the money and some. The £50 he paid to the Porthcawl Sports meeting was ten times the £5 he won that day. Apparently, the money was returned to the great hilarity of their athletics officials. It is a measure of his principles that he did not leave the debt unpaid.

The story is an important one in giving some insight to Struth's character. It showed a sense of remorse that he had taken the prize unfairly, no matter his desperation to win. Even though the race had taken place years earlier and was long forgotten, Struth was determined to settle his dues with the Porthcawl officials. His repentance was clearly received with some humour by those in Wales, but if they were initially angered by this Scotsman who literally ran away with their money, it is without doubt that he would have emerged with their greatest respect.

Although handicapping was a source of aggravation at times, it was generally popular among athletes. Indeed, the great Olympian Eric Liddell considered that the handicap system was hugely beneficial to his success. His view was that had he raced from scratch, the chances are that he would have won every race with some ease. This was not arrogance but a simple matter of fact. Being handicapped, however, meant that he had to push hard, running at his best to have any chance of winning. He was not always successful in handicap races, but the stern challenge he faced in every race honed his ability and performance levels, such that he ran at his optimum with some regularity, characteristically driving towards the line with his head up.

The athletics circuit

Bill Struth's domain was the professional circuit and there is no evidence that he had any interest in amateur competition, which suggests that his prime motivation was money, although there were prizes to be won on the amateur circuit. As a professional 'ped', he would have found the pro circuit a lonely one, where it was very much a case of every man for himself. However, the events were many and he would undoubtedly have built up a circle of friends, perhaps travelling with them between towns.

The records show that Struth was a regular competitor on the athletics circuit for almost twelve years at least, running mainly in his favoured middle-distance races and some novelty events, such as three-legged and wheelbarrow races. Prize money was prize money after all! The earliest record we have uncovered of Struth's prowess on the track is from 1 January 1898, when he finished second in a one-mile handicap at his local track at Powderhall. Although he was a regular competitor at the track, he rarely achieved the same levels of success that he enjoyed around the Highland Games circuit. He regularly ran in heats for the world famous Powderhall New Year Sprint. The event was one of the most important on the calendar. Substantial prize money attracted a huge field of sometimes more than 150 highly competitive entrants, necessitating several heats. Struth's performances at the event were varied. He never qualified, according to the results we found. Perhaps the competition was just too strong or the handicapping too limiting.

While the New Year fixture was never memorable for Bill Struth, he did have more success in other events at the Powderhall track. In October 1900, he ran in a 300-yard handicap and won his heat. However, despite being priced at 4/1 to win in the final, he finished out of the top four. In 1901, the same thing happened. The following year, Struth achieved his greatest success at Powderhall, winning the half-mile handicap and picking up the £9 prize after coming from behind to beat the favourite. In comparative terms, the prize would be worth just under £800 in today's money. This was more than Rangers players earned per week in the 1940s. Rich pickings, indeed! Sadly, the ground, which had been a venue for athletics since 1870 and then greyhound racing and speed-way, is now closed. It retains, however, an important place in the pantheon of Scottish sport.

Athletes had their favourite events and Struth, like most, seems to have been a regular competitor on the track at several Highland Games meetings. It seems that he ran anywhere he could, travelling up and down the country. Among the meet-ings he attended on a regular basis each year were those at Jedburgh, Kelso and Saughton.

The Highland Games circuit operated from June to September and was immensely popular. It seemed that every town had an event, and some of those that held successful meetings would not be readily considered 'highland'. Indeed, some of the more popular games were held in Border towns. The Jedburgh Games was one of the major meetings of the professional circuit in the early twentieth century, remarkably drawing spectators from as far afield as Canada and Australia. Many exiles used the games as an excuse to return home.

In July 1902, Struth was runner-up in the Jedburgh Prize Handicap 215 yards, behind Native American backmarker Williams, who ran off a handicap of 9½ yards. The following year proved even more successful for Struth, when he collected the princely sum of £3 for winning the half mile Merchant Handicap race. In 1904, despite what may be considered an ungodly early start of 6 a.m., he ran off a 15-yard handicap to win the Jedburgh Prize Handicap comfortably, and its prize of £7. He retained the title in 1905, by which time the Jedburgh

Games meeting was rated the blue-riband event of the summer sporting calendar. The prize money on offer at the games brings the professional events into sharp focus with their amateur counterparts. The amateur Ibrox Sports meeting had a maximum prize value of £10 right up until the event ended in 1962.

At Braemar, Struth ran in front of King Edward VII. Records show that he competed in 1902 and 1904. In 1904 he also won the consolation 100 yards at the Alva Games, when the starter was Jimmy Wilson!

In August 1908, Struth finished second in the 300-yard sprint and won a 300-yard handicap at Strathallan Games. Interestingly, the Ibrox Sports took place on the same day, but since that was an amateur meeting, Struth would have had no more than a passive interest in what was taking place at the stadium. However, he did compete at Ibrox at least twice. His first appearance came in the Highland Games held at the Rangers ground on 27 June 1903.

Interestingly, the records suggest that Struth reduced his attendance at athletics events from 1908 onwards, presumably as a result of his advancing years and his more dedicated interest in football, as will become clear. However, even when he was not listed as a competitor, he attended some events as a judge.

It is not evident when Struth finally left the competitive circuit, but the final reference we uncovered suggests that it may have been in 1909. That July he took part in the Alloa Highland Games and finished second in the 110-yard handicap. By then, his attention had firmly turned towards football and his opportunities to compete would have become increasingly limited – especially during the season. Had he wanted to continue to compete, he could have easily done so. The handicap system would have taken account of his increasing age.

The athletics circuit bred some real characters and perhaps none so colourful as Donald Dinnie, arguably the first sporting superstar. Struth competed alongside him at the Strathallan Highland Games on 7 August 1905 and would not have been disappointed to find himself in the shadow of this great athlete. Dinnie, who was also the son of a stonemason, won a remarkable 10,000 events during his career, including wrestling, hammer throwing, shot putt, caber tossing, running, hurdles and jumping. His fame was global, and he was the second athletics figure selected by Barr's to promote their fizzy drink, Irn Bru. His image adorned the label, proclaiming: 'I can recommend BARR'S IRN BRU to all who wish to aspire to athletic fame, signed Donald Dinnie, All-round Champion Athlete of the World.' Dinnie also had the unique honour of having First World War heavy artillery shells nicknamed 'Donald Dinnies', apparently on account of their power.

That is some measure of the appeal of the top athletes at the time, and Struth would have revelled in some of the adoration in the games he frequented. However, if he was not to achieve Dinnie's fame in athletics, it appears that he did nonetheless gain considerable respect in the sport as an athlete of some repute, particularly over the shorter distances. Many of the events in which he competed were probably unrecorded, but we have been able to identify a number of the meetings that he took part in between 1898 and 1910. We suspect that he had many more events to his credit, most notably in England, but this is mere speculation. Strikingly, he seems to have walked away with prizes in the vast majority of the events for which we have a record.

A compilation of the events in which Bill Struth competed and earned some success appears on page 38. The list does not include competitions where he was not successful or those events for which there is no record. What the record shows is that he was a prolific competitor for over a decade, during which time he appears to have won a number of races and, crucially, a significant amount of prize money. The list of events also highlights the distances that Struth travelled in order to compete and chase the prize money on offer, venturing as far south as Gloucester on occasions. He would have travelled by train, and it can also be assumed that he carefully selected the events that offered the best prize money. As the Porthcawl incident shows, it could be a long, long journey home with no fare in your pocket.

Towards the end of the nineteenth century football had become a predominantly professional sport, and to ensure that the players were at the peak of physical fitness, many clubs, seeking a competitive edge, turned to the peds. Athletes had a different, more rigorous training schedule than that typically meted out to the players. Although his best days as an athlete were behind him, Struth believed that he 'could show [the footballers] a thing or two' about fitness training. He came from a background where conditioning and discipline were paramount and he wanted to pass that knowledge on to his football colleagues. At Tynecastle, Struth got the opportunity to develop his own ideas, which were quite different from those adopted by footballers at the time. His regime had a great impact, improving the physical performance of the team and their results. Athletics had taken Struth into a new sport, which would ultimately become his life. He would never relinquish his interest in athletics – he was a man of the track, but he was about to become a giant of the playing field.

Year	Event	Performance
1 January 1898	Powderhall, Musselburgh	Second in one-mile handicap
4 January 1898	Celtic Professional Sports	Second in mile
14 August 1898	Saughton Highland Games	Second in 500 yards (Obstacle Race)
3 January 1900	Powderhall, Musselburgh	Third in quarter-mile handicap
14 July 1900	Alloa Highland Games	Won 880 yards and 300 yards
16 July 1900	Dunfermline Highland Gathering	Won 120 yards. Second in 400 yards
9 August 1900	Alva Highland Games	Second in 120 yards and 300 yards
22 August 1900	Elie and Earls Ferry Sports	Won half mile
29 August 1900	Abernethy Highland Games	Won half mile and Pitch & Water race
29 December 1900	Powderhall, Musselburgh	Third in half mile
1 January 1901	Powderhall, Musselburgh	Second in heat one for New Year Sprint (130 yards) and failed to qualify
7 January 1901	Victoria Recreation Grounds, Glasgow	Second in heat for 130 yards
21 June 1901	Swinton Games	Won 440 yards
22 June 1901	Clackmannan Highland Games	Won half mile
20 July 1901	Kinross Games	Second in 120 yards. Third in 300 yards

17 August 1901	Crieff Highland Games	Won 220 yards and 440 yards
29 August 1901	Birnam Highland Gathering	Won half mile handicap. Third in Comedy race
30 August 1901	Strathallan Highland Games	Second in hurdles
4 September 1901	Aboyne Highland Games	Third in mile. Second in 200 yards
4 November 1901	Powderhall, Musselburgh	Second in 300-yard handicap
1 January 1902	Powderhall, Musselburgh	Second in heat five for New Year Sprint (130 yards) and failed to qualify
3 January 1902	Edinburgh Gymnasium Handicap	Second in 300 yards
7 April 1902	Powderhall, Musselburgh	Won half-mile handicap
24 July 1902	Dunfermline Highland Gathering	Won 110 yards. Second in 300 yards and 400 yards
11 August 1902	Saughton Games	Won 300 yards open race
3 November 1902	Powderhall, Musselburgh	Lost heat for 300-yard handicap by 6 inches
17 March 1903	Arkindale Highland Games	Won 440 yards. Third in 120 yards
6 June 1903	Hawick Common Standing	Second in half-mile handicap
8 June 1903	Edinburgh Harriers Sports	Third in 500-yard hurdles
27 June 1903	Rangers FC Highland Games	Won half mile
23 July 1903	Leven and Methil Games	Won 440 yards. Fourth in 120 yards

24 July 1903	Thornton Highland Games	Third in half-mile handicap
27 July 1903	Kinross Games	Third in half-mile handicap
31 July 1903	West Calder Highland Games	Second in egg and spoon race
1 August 1903	Strathallan Highland Games	Second in 300 yards
20 August 1903	Crieff Highland Games	Won 440 yards
22 August 1903	Denny Highland Games	Second in 440 yards. Third in 300 yards
1 January 1904	Powderhall, Musselburgh	Won heat 14 for New Year Sprint (130 yards) but not placed in final
11 April 1904	Powderhall, Musselburgh	Won heat three for 300-yard handicap
19 April 1904	Royal Gymnasium Edinburgh	Won heat for 120-yard handicap easily but not placed in final
7 June 1904	Lumphinnans Highland Games	Second in 300 yards
17 June 1904	Swinton Games	Second in half mile and 120 yards. Third in 300 yards and 600 yards
14 July 1904	West Linton Games	Second in 120 yards
16 July 1904	Alloa Highland Games	Won 220 yards
20 July 1904	Dunfermline Highland Gathering	Won 400 yards
25 July 1904	Kinross Games	Won 300 yards. Third in 120 yards

27 July 1904	Airth Highland Games	Won 300 yards
31 July 1904	Coleford Gala	Won half mile. Third in 440 yards
6 August 1904	Strathallan Highland Games	Third in 440-yard hurdles and 110 yards
12 August 1904	Alva Highland Games	Won Consolation 100 yards
18 August 1904	Helensburgh Highland Games	Won half-mile handicap
19 September 1904	Braemar Highland Games	Second in half mile
3 October 1904	Powderhall Autumn Meeting	Won heat for 220 yards
24 October 1904	Powderhall, Musselburgh	Won heat for 300-yard handicap but not placed in final
3 January 1905	Powderhall, Musselburgh	Won heat for New Year Sprint handicap (130 yards). Fourth in semi-final
17 April 1905	Powderhall, Musselburgh	Won heat for 130-yard handicap
15 May 1905	Powderhall, Musselburgh	Won 130-yard handicap (£7)
19 June 1905	Selkirk Common Riding	Second in 440-yard handicap. Won 300-yard flat race
24 June 1905	Dundee FC Sports	Won 100 yards. Second in 300 yards
4 July 1905	Broxburn FC Games	Third in 300-yard handicap

17 July 1905	Kinross Gymnastic Games	Won Obstacle Race. Third in 120 yards
20 July 1905	Methil Games	Won 440 yards. Second in 120 yards. Third in 300 yards.
21 July 1905	Kelso Highland Games	Won 300 yards and hurdles. Second in 100 yards. Third in 440 yards
22 July 1905	Thornton Highland Games	Won 120 yards
26 July 1905	Errol Highland Games	Won 100 yards. Second in 300 yards. Third in quarter mile
31 July 1905	Dunbar West Barns Highland Games	Second in 120-yard open handicap, 300-yard open handicap and 440-yard open handicap
7 August 1905	Strathallan Highland Games	Won 300-yard flat race. Fourth in 440-yard hurdles
18 August 1905	Glenisla Highland Games	Won hurdles and Obstacle Race
8 August 1905	Lydney Rugby Club Sports	Won 120 yards and quarter mile
18 August 1905	Glenisla Highland Games	Won 700-yard hurdles and Obstacle Race
19 August 1905	Crieff Highland Games	Second in 100 yards
23 August 1905	Lochaber Highland Games	Won 600 yards. Second in Consolation Short Race. Third in Sack Race
26 August 1905	Bute Highland Games	Dead heat in 300-yard handicap

7 September 1905	Braemar Highland Games	Second in Obstacle Race and half-mile handicap
18 September 1905	Powderhall, Musselburgh	Second in 220-yard handicap (15 shillings/75p)
5 January 1906	Royal Gymnasium, Edinburgh	Won 600 yards (New Year Handicaps)
18 June 1906	Selkirk Common Riding	Second in 300-yard, 440-yard and 100-yard flat races and hurdles
22 June 1906	Tranent Games	Third in quarter mile
16 July 1906	Kinross Highland Games	Won 300 yards
20 July 1906	Thornton Highland Games	Won hurdles. Second in 300-yard handicap
22 July 1906	Forfar Highland Gathering	Won Living Wheelbarrow Race with McKenzie. Third in 250-yard Consolation
24 July 1906	Blairgowrie Highland Games	Won (equal first) hurdles. Second in 250 yards
6 August 1906	Strathallan Games	Won 440 yards and 110 yards
5 September 1906	Aboyne Games	Won 200 yards and hurdles
6 September 1906	Braemar Highland Games	Second in Obstacle Race. Third in half mile
11 May 1907	Kelty Rangers Sports	Second in 120-yard handicap. Third in 300 yards
18 July 1907	Methil Games	Won Obstacle Race
19 July 1907	Thornton Highland Games	Fourth in 120 yards and 300 yards

24 July 1907	Errol Games	Second in 300 yards
3 August 1907	Strathallan Games	Won hurdles
12 August 1907	Saughton Highland Games	Won 130-yard handicap (£10). Third in 300 yards
17 August 1907	Gullane Annual Sports	Second in 440 yards
1 January 1908	Powderhall, Musselburgh	Won 220 yards (30 shillings/£1.50)
2 June 1908	Lumphinnans Games	Second in 220 yards and 300 yards
11 June 1908	Bowness on Windermere Games	Second in 300 yards and 150-yard hurdles. Noted as a Glasgow runner
18 July 1908	Alloa Highland Games	Second in 300 yards. Fourth in 200 yards
22 July 1908	Dunfermline Highland Games	Won 120-yard handicap and 300 yards
24 July 1908	Thornton Highland Games	Won 300 yards
27 July 1908	Kelso Games	Won hurdles
1 August 1908	Strathallan Games	Won 300 yards
8 August 1908	Dundee Police Sports	Won quarter mile. Second in half mile
25 August 1908	Powderhall, Musselburgh	Second in 300-yard handicap
15 May 1909	Falkirk Highland Games	Won 300 yards. Third in 100 yards

CLYDE AND GLASGOW BECKON

A career in football – with Clyde

The Heart of Midlothian Football Club website provides an interesting account of the history of the club during the period that Struth frequented the track. One extract explains:

> During season 1904–05 the club ran into financial difficulties because the limited company formed in 1903 was unable to continue after debts amounting to £1,400 had accumulated. In March 1905 at a Quarterly General Meeting, a resolution, 'Proposal for Temporary Loans from Present Shareholders', was defeated by 94 votes to 72, but later that month, three resolutions were passed and the company was voluntarily wound up. On 29 April 1905, the present company was incorporated on the Register of Companies and the new concern picked up the debt, which had increased to £1,600. Despite a problem selling all the new shares it cleared this debt within a reasonably short time.

The story is interesting for two reasons. Firstly, it highlights that despite Hearts' success in winning the Scottish Cup just four years earlier, the club's financial position forced them to wind up. Secondly, they cleared the debt with a new share issue and several years later Bill Struth acknowledged that he was a shareholder. It is speculation, but possibly a reasonable suggestion, that he acquired his shares at the time of this issue. He was, after all, making use of the Hearts track and would have possibly felt some moral obligation to support the club in its time of need.

When Struth arrived at Wheatfield Street, his primary interest in Hearts was in the track at Tynecastle. However, by 1906, the club had returned to the top, winning the Scottish Cup at Ibrox, ironically. Interest in the club was reignited with their Scottish Cup win and they were attracting huge crowds. It was around this time that Bill Struth offered his services as a trainer, probably as an assistant to Bob Waugh, operating under manager Willie Waugh. He was also probably well aware of the trend for peds to move into football, exemplified by the role that Jimmy Wilson enjoyed at Rangers.

If season 1905–06 was somewhat historic for the club, the following season was to be a huge disappointment, despite the side reaching the Cup Final once again. Many of the players had left and those who arrived in their place failed to inspire the same level of confidence. Indeed, the Hearts website records that in the trainer's opinion the players were 'in poor physical shape'. It seems that Struth was introduced to try to improve the team's fitness, which besides giving him a role with his local side, also served to introduce him to the Association game at a professional level.

As a trainer at Tynecastle, Struth developed his own ideas and methods of bringing the players' fitness levels up to what he would have expected of athletes. He knew his techniques could make a difference and were innovative in comparison with the more traditional approach adopted by football trainers at the time.

No matter his interest in training at Hearts, the role was low key, informal and unpaid. As a stonemason, he earned 38 shillings (£1.90) a week and this was dwarfed by his prize winnings in athletics. However, Struth wanted more. If he had been paid for the role at Tynecastle, he may well have developed his career in football with Hearts, and his footballing life may well have taken a different turn. He was keen to set aside the mallet and chisel and to continue his interest in training footballers. Whether he let this be known to the wider footballing community is unrecorded, but his interest and ability in training had not gone unnoticed elsewhere.

In 1907, Struth had been one of the trainers at Hearts for just seven months when he was alerted to an opportunity at Clyde Football Club. The club were seeking an assistant for Alex Maley, the manager, whose role was more in the administration of the club than the 'hands-on' team manager position that we recognise today. In that respect, team affairs tended to lie with the assistants and trainers, upon whom there was a great reliance. Struth knew Maley through athletics, but that would be no guarantee of the job. Maley was the brother of the Celtic boss Willie Maley. Struth was encouraged to apply for the position, but he was initially reluctant to consider the prospect of a move. He was settled in Edinburgh, but he recognised that a move to Glasgow offered him an opportunity to work inside the game.

He later admitted that he applied for the job 'as a joke', not believing that he had a realistic chance of securing the position. He even added a few years to his age in order to avoid Clyde thinking he was too young for the role. To his surprise, he was invited to an interview and, keen to impress, the first thing he did was to go out to buy a new suit – not just any suit, but the best in the shop. At his interview at Shawfield, he captivated the Clyde officials, who later admitted that he was so much better dressed than any of them.

Struth later revealed that he had bought the suit not simply to impress the directors, but to give him a feeling of importance. He said, 'I have always placed great emphasis on this point of dressing properly on and off the field. I would not permit any of my teams to be slovenly. The new suit cut a big hole in my savings but it was an investment for the future. I felt I had to sacrifice and take risks to get anywhere. I believe most young men felt like that in those days.'

Struth was clearly ambitious and his athletics career had shown that he was a man driven with a desire to succeed. He did not feel that he was experienced enough for the position, but he was determined to give the interview his best shot. The essence of his character was not that he was willing to 'sacrifice and take risks', but that he had the desire to get somewhere, or indeed 'anywhere' that would be better than the lot he had. The role was a first formal step into football and the managerial ranks, albeit as assistant at Clyde. The experience of his interview highlighted to Struth that while clothes do not make the man, they can certainly be a mighty weapon.

Struth's wage as assistant manager was 35 shillings (£1.75) a week – less than he could earn as a stonemason. However, he had an opportunity to increase his revenue through the regular sports meetings held at Clyde, where he was allowed a share of the gate money. Besides, he was continuing his athletics career, so it seems there was a healthy flow of cash into the Struth household.

The Struths, with young Alex in tow, left Wheatfield Street, Edinburgh to settle into their new home in Glasgow. They took on rented accommodation at 102 Polmadie Road, a short distance from Shawfield, leaving young William with Bill's parents back in Edinburgh. By then, William and Isabella had moved to 18 Ponton Street, Edinburgh, sharing a home with Bill's sister Helen and her new husband, William McCulloch. Young William was registered in the 1911 census as the 'adopted son' of Bill's parents.

Friendship with Mattha Gemmell

The job at Clyde was a fresh start for the Struths, and it also opened up a new circle of friends for both Bill and Kate, who was involved with the Order of the Eastern Star, a recently constituted organisation in Scotland at the time. At Shawfield, Bill met the man who was to become his assistant trainer and best friend in football, Mattha Gemmell. It is fair to say Gemmell is as much of an iconic a figure to Clyde as Struth was to become at Rangers. They cut a peculiar pair, the original 'odd couple', Bill so smartly turned out while Gemmell was more likely to be found in rather modest attire. Nothing at all wrong in that, but it emphasises that they were at opposite ends of the elegance spectrum, even if their origins as working-class men were similar. Perhaps it also reflected their contrasting ambitions.

Although Mattha was born in Lochwinnoch in 1874, the Gemmell family had moved to the Bridgeton area of Glasgow in search of work. His local team was Clyde, who at that time played at nearby Barrowfield, and as a youngster, he would follow their fortunes. His love affair with football began there and developed into a lifelong obsession with the 'Bully Wee'. Indeed, it was Gemmell who was to give Clyde that nickname, inspired by recognition that the players were capable of getting a result against the bigger teams if they were to get stuck in and 'bully' them – hence, the 'Bully Wee'.

Even after he was married in 1898, Gemmell spent all of his spare time at Barrowfield. He became friendly with the trainers and was always willing to help out by doing odd jobs. He was always looking out for opportunities to have hands-on involvement at the club. When Clyde moved to Shawfield in 1898, Mattha followed and he later said, 'They couldn'ae get rid o' me so [they decided] we may as well give him a job.' Mattha was unpaid groundsman and assistant trainer.

Gemmell assumed that Struth's arrival would spell the end of his time at the club and, out of respect, he thought he should leave. He considered that if he were to remain, he would be treading on the new man's toes. Struth was otherwise minded. He recognised that this man was a kindred spirit, who also shared his love of athletics. He realised, too, that Gemmell could be a great assistant, so he offered him the job full time on five shillings (25p) per week. The wage was not enough to compensate Gemmell for giving up his job in the local tube-works. However, there was another strand to the offer, in which Struth showed remarkable benevolence and understanding. He offered to split his share of the gate money from the sports meetings at Shawfield with Gemmell. This allowed Mattha to commit full time to Clyde and, an agreement in place, the duo set about trying to put Clyde back on the map.

In the years that followed, Gemmell had several offers to further his career away from Shawfield, but his heart belonged to Clyde. Queen's Park made an audacious attempt to lure him to Hampden and Gemmell agreed to the move, subject to one very important proviso. He insisted that his contract contain a clause allowing him to go to watch Clyde every Saturday! His talent was recognised at the highest levels and for a time he worked as trainer for Scotland.

The resurgence of Clyde

Morale at Clyde FC was at a low ebb when Struth arrived, and the club was in a state of some disarray, both on and off the park. To say that the players were in poor shape would be an understatement, even allowing for Clyde's part-time status. Off the field they were poorly organised and many a time the players' wages were not paid when due. Struth experienced this himself when he went to secretary John McKnight's office on wages night. He was met with a sign on the door, which read: 'No wages money tonight – goodnight. McKnight.' Struth realised the enormity of the task ahead of him and that any success he could bring on the park would surely improve matters off it. He took on his role at Shawfield with typical enthusiasm, attending to the players and even the condition of the ground. He scrubbed and polished the dressing rooms twice a week in a demonstration of fastidiousness that was eventually to characterise his reign at Ibrox.

Some years later, John McMahon, who was a well-known former chairman/director of Clyde and president of the Scottish Football League from 1946 to 1949, was asked what motivated him to invest in Clyde at a time when they were almost down and out. McMahon said he visited the club premises one day and saw a man – Struth – engrossed in the task of making the dressing room as 'clean as a new pin'. If this club, for all their desperate plight, could have such an enthusiast, Mr McMahon reasoned, then they deserved what help he could give them. He duly invested.

On the field, Clyde seesawed between the top division and second tier of Scottish League football. They normally struggled in the First Division, although in the season before Struth's arrival they had finished eighth. However, in his first full season, 1907–08, there was no evidence of the improvement that he was eventually to bring to the club. The Shawfield side won just five matches and finished second from bottom.

At this time, there was no automatic promotion or relegation, and movement between divisions was done by an election system. In 1904–05 for example, Clyde had won the Second Division by four points but were not promoted. Instead, Aberdeen and Falkirk went up despite finishing second and seventh respectively. If they were hard done to on that occasion, the system was to work in Clyde's favour at the end of Struth's first season. They were saved from the drop along with Port Glasgow Athletic, receiving the highest number of votes in the promotion/relegation poll.

Clyde's fortunes began to turn and it soon became clear that Struth and Gemmell were the driving force behind the resurgence. Struth's influence was in the thoroughness of his training, drawing from his years of conditioning as an athlete. He instilled high standards of fitness, while gaining the respect of the players. If he asked them to work hard, it was no less than the effort he would put in himself. He explained, 'When I got the job at Clyde, I brought to it a few new ideas. I would, though, not ask anyone to do something I would not do myself. When I took the players for a run, I started out in front. When we came back, I was still in front.'

The days when cash and points were in short supply were coming to an end at Shawfield as both Struth and Gemmell worked tirelessly to instil a degree of consistency that the team had not previously attained. Following their close brush with relegation, there was a complete transformation in the 1908–09 season, when the team finished third, just three points behind the winners. To this day, it is the highest position that Clyde has reached in the First Division, emulated just twice more in later years. Arguably, it is unlikely that they will ever achieve such a placing again.

Over the next few seasons, Clyde built a reputation as a solid Cup side and consolidated their position in the top division. Their League record throughout the period of Struth's tenure is remarkable for a club of Clyde's stature. With the exception of that first season when he was settling into the role, the team never finished lower than ninth in the next six seasons under Struth.

SEASON	P	W	D	L	F	A	Pts	Pos
1907–08	34	5	8	21	36	75	18	17
1908–09	34	21	6	7	61	37	48	3
1909–10	34	14	9	11	47	40	37	5
1910–11	34	14	11	9	45	36	39	7
1911–12	34	19	4	11	56	32	42	3
1912–13	34	13	9	12	41	44	35	9

Clyde's solid performances each season were reflected in a good record against Rangers. In season 1909–10, they defeated the Ibrox side 2–0 in the first round of the Scottish Cup at Shawfield in front of 32,000 spectators. The accounts of the match suggest a dour clash played in dreadful conditions, when the stamina of the Clyde players helped make the difference on the day. Conditions were not conducive to top of the pitch players, such as Rangers' Alex Bennett. The Rangers keeper, Herbert Lock, also had a most uncomfortable 90 minutes. Contemporary newspapers commented that although Rangers may have lost by greater margins in the past, they had seldom been so comprehensively outplayed.

The physical fitness of the Clyde players would not have gone unnoticed by those at Ibrox. The board would also have reflected on their decision to take the Rangers players down the coast in preparation for the big game, unlike Clyde, who kept their players at home and gave them extra work.

A first taste of silverware for Clyde – and Struth

In the early part of the twentieth century, the success of any team in Scotland was not measured by victory in the League Championship but by success in the Scottish Cup. By 1910, Clyde had gained huge respect in the game and Struth inspired the side through to their first Scottish Cup Final. Their opponents were Dundee and the expectation was that the Shawfield side would go on to lift the Cup for the first time.

The final was a close-run affair and required three games to settle it, all coincidentally played at Ibrox. The first game was played in front of 60,000 fans, who saw Dundee score two late goals to take the match to a replay. The second encounter was played in heavy rain and ankle deep mud – 'mud plugged', as it was described. Indeed, it was reported that only Ibrox was capable of hosting the tie due to its excellent pitch. Such was the energy-sapping nature of the conditions that the young Clyde player Jackson collapsed with exhaustion. The sight of his mud-splattered body being removed from the field provided the remaining players with sufficient motivation to keep going, but the match finished scoreless after extra time.

In the second replay, a few days later, Clyde took the lead after three minutes, but they eventually lost 2–1 to the Dens Park men. Dundee were worthy winners, employing a methodical, confident, close-passing style. Clyde rued their missed opportunity from the first match when they squandered a two-goal lead. That Scottish Cup disappointment was the first of many for Struth before he finally mastered the tournament. By then, however, it would be in the blue of Rangers, not the red of Clyde.

Immediately after the final, Struth received an approach from Rangers who were looking to replace Jimmy Wilson as trainer. Struth declined the offer, reasoning that he did not want to deny a man already in the job. It wouldn't be the Ibrox Club's last approach.

Struth got the players back on track the following month when they at last lifted their first trophy in the shape of the Glasgow Merchants Charity Cup. Their opponents, Third Lanark, or 'Thirds' as they were known, started the game strongly but Clyde soon took control, forcing numerous corners before taking the lead through Chalmers, and it stayed that way until the interval. In the second half roles reversed and Thirds equalised. The score remained level at full time but Clyde secured the trophy 8–3 on corners. Interestingly, Clyde beat both Rangers (again) and Partick Thistle 1–0 on their way to the final.

The Merchants Charity Cup was clearly of enormous

importance to Clyde and to Struth, since it was the club's first-ever trophy, but it was of some significance to Rangers, too. This was the first competition won by Rangers in May 1879, with a team that included Moses McNeil, Tom Vallance and Peter Campbell. Indeed, Campbell's medal is displayed at Ibrox, loaned to Rangers by a fan. The competition was mainly restricted to Glasgow clubs at first, but others from outlying areas were eventually invited to take part. The Cup was first competed for in 1876 and the concept came from the Scottish Football Association (the SFA), who felt that it would be 'a graceful as well as a rightful act' to close the season with a match for the benefit of some 'charitable institution'. Accordingly, Glasgow played Dunbartonshire in April of that year, raising £100 for the Glasgow Western Infirmary. Around the same time, a group of Glasgow merchants also organised a charity football contest. By 1878, the two competitions had merged into one, which was run by the Glasgow Charity Cup Committee (GCCC), a joint board of merchants and SFA representatives. Often referred to as the Merchants Cup, this Glasgow Charity Cup competition spanned almost ninety years and raised nearly £350,000 (about £11 million in today's terms) for good causes. It was last played as a cup competition in 1961.

Interestingly, the Rangers archives show that when Bill Struth took over, he was well disposed to clubs and associations seeking to use the stadium for charitable purposes, and the team playing benefit games. It was a culture that appeared to prevail within the game and he was clearly in favour.

Not only were Clyde's fortunes on an upward curve on the park, but also off it. Handsome profits were earned and a new main stand was built at Shawfield on the basis of flourishing returns. It included a reading room, recreation room, board-room, modern baths and team room. The stand was a huge undertaking for the time and the bill exceeded £4,000. It was officially opened in August 1911 by the future Rangers chairman Sir John Ure Primrose. To mark the occasion a match was played against the Light Blues. The crowd was 30,000, generating record receipts of £821.

A battle with Rangers

The Charity Cup provided a taste of glory for Clyde but they hankered for the greatest prize of all – the Scottish Cup. Alex Maley's Clyde side, inspired by Bill Struth, reached the final again in 1912. Along the way they met Rangers once more, this time in the third round at Shawfield. A very tousy League match had taken place at Ibrox on 13 January, a few weeks prior to the Cup tie. The Clyde approach was robust and clearly meant to unsettle Rangers – indeed they lived up to their name, the 'Bully Wee'. Rangers' William Hogg, in particular, took great exception to the behaviour of the Clyde players and complained constantly to the referee about his failure to book a single player for 'ungentlemanly conduct'. To compound the agitated mood of the Ibrox contingent, Clyde prevailed by 2–1.

When the Cup tie took place at Shawfield, many felt that not enough time had elapsed since the League match, and bad blood still flowed. The ground was literally full to overflowing as a remarkable 52,000 (Clyde's record attendance) gathered inside Shawfield. The crowd was packed in so tightly that many fans were pushed almost on to the field of play. Similar scenes were played out a few years later at Wembley in the famous 1923 'White Horse' FA Cup Final, when the crowd spilled right out on to the pitch. At Shawfield in 1912, as a measure of the anticipation and interest, 20,000 more spectators crowded into the ground than had attended the same tie two years earlier. The fans expected fireworks and they were not to be disappointed. In fact, the crowd had a significant bearing on subsequent events.

In a hugely controversial match, Clyde ran Rangers ragged and several incidents incited a growing feeling of injustice among the Light Blues players and supporters. In one case, Rangers were denied a goal when the ball appeared to have crossed the line. Then, the Rangers players felt that they should have been awarded a penalty after Clyde defender Gilligan charged the ball down with his hand in the penalty box. The final injustice came when Rangers winger Alex Bennett was fiercely chopped to the ground with just 17 minutes left and Clyde ahead by 3–1.

This was more than some could bear and prompted an incursion on to the field from the south-west corner of the ground. At first just a handful of spectators ran on, then hundreds and then thousands. The police were hopelessly unprepared for this kind of pitch invasion and mayhem ensued. During the disruption, Clyde defender Gilligan, who had perpetrated the foul on Bennett, was among those assaulted by the spectators. In the chaos that followed, supporters attempted to overturn a tea bar, the occupants of which were a certain Mrs Gemmell and Mrs Struth! We can only speculate what Bill made of those actions, but it would not have endeared the Rangers fans to him.

The pitch invasion meant the match was abandoned after 75 minutes. The clubs put up a pretence of wishing to continue, but this was clearly impossible as the police had completely lost control of the situation. The question of a replay did not arise. The Rangers directors concluded that the people who caused the abandonment could not be called 'supporters', and they agreed to retire from the competition.

Actually, after the abandonment was confirmed by the referee, the club directors visited their Clyde counterparts, expressing regret they had not been allowed to gain their due reward on the field of play. In fact, the directors probably precipitated the events. Prior to the match they had instructed the players to behave, mindful of the unsavoury background following the League encounter. The guidance seemed to demotivate the Rangers players, whose performance was described as 'insipid' in the first half. Apparently, at the interval, they were given a stern instruction to improve and this reignited the bad feeling.

In the final, Clyde met Celtic at Ibrox, but they were completely outplayed and succumbed 2–0. The Cup was presented to the Celtic chairman by his Rangers counterpart, Sir John Ure Primrose, in the Ibrox Pavilion. Primrose praised the winners and also had kind words for Clyde for the fight they showed, assuring them that their day would come. Cup presentations in those days were strangely low-key affairs, and did not carry the razzmatazz of the events nowadays, with ticker tape and flares.

Another approach from Rangers

Prior to joining Clyde, Bill Struth was well acquainted with Rangers and Ibrox. He had run there a few years earlier and it is certain that he would have come into regular contact with the Rangers manager, William Wilton, and trainer, James Wilson, whom he had known for some time. The Rangers people could not have failed to be impressed by his impact with Clyde when he took over as assistant manager. The Shawfield players were recognised as strong, fit and at the peak of their powers. If Bill could achieve that with the relatively modest resources at Clyde, just how much success could he help bring to Ibrox? The Rangers directors had made an approach in 1910, but they would not be denied their man.

By 1914 all was not well at Shawfield. While the club recorded a profit, strife arose among board members and moves were afoot to reduce the number of directors. Eventually, five board members resigned. It was hardly the epitome of a stable club and environment for Struth to operate in. The Shawfield club did not have their troubles to seek and their woes were about to be compounded – Bill Struth was already casting his eyes westwards towards Ibrox. A new dawn in his career beckoned.

THE NEW RANGERS TRAINER

The Wilton years

While Bill Struth continued to improve the fortunes of Clyde, building a healthy respect for the club within the game, Celtic were generally regarded as the pre-eminent force in Scottish football. The Parkhead side had won the Scottish Cup and the League Championship in Struth's first two years at Shawfield, a period of success that was to continue for several years afterwards.

In the early years of Struth's first dalliance with football at Tynecastle, Rangers had slipped from being the top side in the country to one with some major structural issues in every sense. With crowds growing steadily, the Rangers committee were being increasingly pressured to extend their existing ground at Ibrox and improve the facilities. The decision was removed from their control when the club's landlords, the Hinshelwood Trust, intimated that they needed the land occupied by Ibrox Park, but while giving notice of the club's need to vacate, they also offered the land immediately adjoining to the west. This would obviously necessitate the construction of a new ground and plans were immediately put in place to come up with a design and a cost to complete the project.

When the landlords forced new construction upon them, the committee approached architect Archibald Leitch to come up with a new ground design concept. Leitch worked to the committee's specification and requirement that the stadium capacity be 80,000. The new ground design was presented to an Extraordinary General Meeting of club members in March 1899. The project would cost £12,000 and the club's balance sheet showed £5,600 on account.

It was clear that the ambitious plans would need a massive injection of funding if the dreams of this 'gigantic ground scheme' were to be realised. Incorporation was the only practical way for the club to raise the money needed for the construction of the 'New Ibrox Park'. As such, and following a momentous Annual General Meeting at Glasgow's Trades Hall in May 1899, the decision was endorsed for the club to issue 12,000 ordinary shares to the value of £1 each.

The final business of the meeting concerned the appointment of a manager and a secretary for the new 'Rangers Football Club Limited'. The minute of the meeting reported that 'only one name was put forward, that of Mr [William] Wilton and amidst round after round of applause, [he] was unanimously elected'. The position of 'Manager' at The Rangers Football Club was born.

'New Ibrox Park' was opened on 30 December 1899 by Heart of Midlothian. It is unlikely that Struth would have travelled to the match since he was not involved with the Tynecastle club at that time. In any case, he was preparing to run at Powderhall a couple of days later. However, if he was in attendance, he would have been impressed by the spectacular arena, which drew many parallels with the Coliseum in Rome, if not in design, certainly in its size and majesty. The field was enclosed within an iron-paling fence and outside was a cinder track. Beyond this rose the terraced stands, each tier reputedly broad enough to hold three deep. At each end of the ground the terraces rose to a height of over 40 feet. On the south side, at the position of the present Main Stand, was a grandstand that could hold 6,000. On the opposite side of the ground, a large covered stand had a 13,000 capacity.

Two years later, in 1902, while Bill and Kate Struth came to terms with the birth of young William, Rangers manager Willie Wilton was about to endure his own trauma. He had seen the average ground attendance reach a healthy 13,000 and crowds for the big games against Celtic and Hibernian range up to 35,000. The new Ibrox was designed for future growth and was clearly capable of sustaining even larger crowds. The club was keen to attract some of the more prestigious fixtures in the calendar and international matches had already been staged at the new ground. International contests did not come much bigger than Scotland v. England and in 1902, the club was proud to host the fixture at what they called 'Greater Ibrox'. News of the club's success in luring the international to the ground was followed by an announcement that the Scottish Cup Final would also be held there a few weeks later. There seemed every reason for Rangers to be proud of the new Ibrox Park, or so it appeared. In fact, what should have been the cradle of Rangers' success into the 1900s became the source of despair and heartache for many.

On the morning of the international fixture, William Wilton walked the ground with Archibald Leitch to check that everything was in order. They were comforted in the knowledge that they also had a safety certificate from the Govan Burgh Surveyor. The gates were opened at 12.30 p.m. on

5 April 1902 and the crowds heeded instructions to arrive early. Marching bands provided pre-match entertainment. At the same time, Bill Struth was running the half-mile handicap and probably some other events at Powderhall.

What should have been a celebration for Wilton and his board turned into a tragedy. The ground was, in fact, reportedly full to capacity an hour before kick-off, but still people continued to pour in. Shortly after the game started, part of the western terrace, a large timber lattice structure, failed, plunging a number of fans 40 to 50 feet to the ground. The game was stopped and the players were led from the field, but play resumed after the fans who spilled on to the pitch had been cleared. By the time rescuers reached the dreadful scene at the base of the mangled structure, a number of people were seen to be dead and many more lay seriously injured. The final tally showed that twenty-six lost their lives and 587 were injured, eventually receiving compensation.

Although the subsequent inquiry recognised that there was no particular design fault, or any real blame that could be attached to Rangers, there was a sense of some culpability at the club, if only by virtue of the tragedy taking place at Ibrox. The disaster signalled the end of the timber and iron lattice style of terracing construction as clubs, including Rangers, radically altered the terraces, forming them on earth banks.

Rangers subsequently went into financial free fall. The club set up a fund for the bereaved. William Wilton was the principal trustee and he launched himself wholeheartedly into fund-raising activities, arranging benefit matches, concerts and a variety of other initiatives, which inflated the fund to over £4,000 – a considerable amount in those days. Of greater impact on the club's finances was the commitment to improve safety in the ground. In order to finance the necessary improvements, the club put all twenty-two professional players up for transfer! Some left, although most did not, as Wilton set about the reconstruction of Rangers on and off the field. By 1906, through resourceful acquisition and use of finances, the club was able to spend £42,000 in stadium improvements, and also attained an unlikely partner in its business dealings, or so it seemed.

The birth of the 'Old Firm'

Rangers continued to rebuild in every sense of the word. The team battled through to the 1909 Scottish Cup Final and an encounter with Celtic on 17 April. The two sides played out a hard-fought 90 minutes when four goals could not separate them. The game went to a replay and a crowd of around 60,000 returned to Hampden, many believing that the match would be played to a conclusion – a confusion born out of flawed reporting by one Glasgow newspaper. In fact, the SFA rules stated quite unequivocally that a third replay would be required in the event of a draw. When the replay ended all square, the uncertainties of the fans were compounded when some players lingered on the field instead of walking straight to the pavilion. For many, it seemed that extra time was imminent.

When it became clear to the fans that this was not the case and there would be another replay, some unrest broke out, which led to payboxes being burned, fences torn down and the police, seeking to restore order, being pelted with stones.

A common belief already existed among the fans that the two Glasgow rivals worked in tandem to their mutual financial benefit, giving rise to the term the 'Old Firm'. Indeed, ten years earlier, the Rangers Minute Books referred to an unambiguous collaboration between the clubs on the retention of the 'full stand drawings', when their respective grounds were let by the SFA, or others, for major fixtures or neutral Cup ties. The 'Celtic Agreement', as it became known in the minutes, established a cartel through which the city's two major clubs could further prosper. The apparent reluctance of the sides to play out extra time, preferring a third replay, seemed to be rooted in that same commerciality, at least in the minds of the unsettled crowd. The tie was eventually abandoned following the unruly scenes, which were referred to as the 'Hampden Riot'. Amid the smoke, however, an unholy alliance had been further consolidated.

Rangers were making considerable progress. Crowds were up to over 16,000 by the end of the decade. Most notably, Old Firm match attendances had risen from around 35,000 to more than double that on some occasions. The ground was now pristine, with the fateful lattice terracings removed and replaced with earth banks, and the club's financial position was secure, but this success was not replicated on the field of play. The club had not won the Scottish Cup for seven years, or indeed reached the final in the last five years. In the Championship, they had watched Celtic win their sixth successive title and barely offered a challenge.

It is unclear how much blame for the team's mediocre performance was laid at the door of trainer Jimmy Wilson, but there was clearly discontentment within the board. Like Struth, Wilson's background lay in athletics. He had been a noted middle-distance runner in his early years and had competed in many of the leading Highland Games, achieving a number of notable successes, including the Carnwath Red Hose, the oldest road race in the world, and the All England Sweepstakes at Moorfield Grounds, Failsworth in Manchester. He was also recognised as a 'personality' at the Thornton Games and the *Glasgow Herald* gave him credit for much of the success of that event.

When Wilson gave up competing, he took to training athletes in both long- and short-distance running, mainly for the Powderhall Handicaps. As mentioned earlier, he knew Struth from the early days of the Edinburgh Harriers and may even have trained him. However, like most athletics trainers at the time, Wilson drifted into football. In 1894, he helped Edinburgh side St Bernards' to the Scottish Cup. Three years later, he joined Rangers and became a popular figure both at Ibrox and more widely within the game in Scotland, also serving as trainer to the national side.

Regardless of Wilson's popularity, there was clearly a feeling inside Ibrox that it was time for a change, and this precipitated the approach to Bill Struth, who had attracted some respectability as a trainer with Clyde at Shawfield. Known for his fastidious attention to cleanliness and discipline, Struth had breezed into Scottish football, gaining immense respect among his peers. It was not Rangers' intention that Wilson be totally dismissed. If Struth was appointed, they hoped he would revert to the role of groundsman. However, the need for a decision on Wilson was virtually removed when Struth declined the approach, saying that he could not possibly take a position when he was aware that it would result in the effective dismissal of James Wilson.

Perhaps, as Struth later suggested, the job was too big for him. In an interview in the *Sunday Express* some years later, he stated that he turned down the job because he did not feel ready for a move to such a huge club. Probably, the truth lies somewhere between the two accounts. If, indeed, he felt overawed by the prospect of being trainer at Rangers, his pragmatism and caution are not consistent with his stated character as a 'risk taker'. More than likely, he would have felt uncomfortable at the removal of Wilson, especially considering their friendship that went back over fifteen years to their times at Powderhall and the Gymnasium.

Rangers' archives of the correspondence record Struth's fulsome gratitude towards the club's board for their consideration, not knowing whether the opportunity to be trainer at the club would ever arise again. This is an extremely important event in understanding the character of Bill Struth. There is little doubt that Rangers were an appreciably more attractive and respected club than Clyde. The financial rewards for the role would have been greater, with the increasing wealth of the Ibrox club enhanced by the glamour of its newly constructed stadium. However, it seems that the discussions did not reach any examination of terms. While we can speculate that Struth's friendship with Wilson was a factor in his decision to turn down Rangers, his reasoning also seems to reflect what he thought was right and proper. A gentleman would not seize a role to the detriment of another, and Struth considered himself a gentleman. Whatever his rationale, Struth turned down one of the biggest clubs in the country when his career in the game was no more than embryonic and his promise was little more than that.

By 1914, Jimmy Wilson's health had taken a turn for the worse and he was ailing, debilitated by pneumonia. The club, mindful of his seventeen years' service, arranged a benefit match against Everton on 28 April 1914. It was to be very much a gala affair, with some glamour athletics events as well. Top of the bill was world champion sprinter, Aussie Jack Donaldson, aptly nicknamed 'the Blue Streak', who was lined up to face the last four winners of the Powderhall Sprint. If Donaldson was the main attraction, added interest was to be found lower down the bill. The programme included a 'half-mile handicap', which featured some star athletes of the day. Included in the field were the Celtic trainer, Willie Quinn, and Clyde trainer – Bill Struth! He did not win the race, in what was possibly only his second appearance as an athlete at the Rangers ground. Struth returned to Ibrox with Clyde a few days later for a Charity Cup match.

The testimonial for Wilson was a huge success, raising over £200 for the beleaguered trainer, although he was never to gain the benefit of the event. Just five days after the Everton match, Wilson died. In a testament to his popularity, his funeral was attended by representatives from all of the Glasgow football clubs as well as from Clydesdale Harriers, Bellahouston Harriers and West of Scotland Harriers. He was well respected among the athletics fraternity and they listened to his advice. Indeed, many athletes made Ibrox their head-quarters and, in Wilson, they had one of their own.

Crowds lined the streets to pay homage to the Rangers trainer as the cortege slowly passed on its journey from his home in Princes Street, Govan to Craigton Cemetery. Everton waived their expenses for the match and William Wilton gave the proceeds to Wilson's widow and four children.

Within a week of Wilson's burial, Struth and Rangers were in touch. Perhaps the possibility had been raised when he attended the athletics event at Ibrox. It is uncertain who initiated the contact, but Struth formalised his interest in the vacant role when he wrote to the Ibrox club, requesting consideration for the same position he had turned down four years earlier. Given the turmoil that was unfolding at Shawfield, the opportunity presented by the death of Jimmy Wilson was certainly timely for Bill Struth.

On Wednesday, 13 May 1914, Rangers announced that they had a new trainer – William Struth. The appointment, which was concluded on 11 May, was well received by the media. The *Evening Times* correspondent wrote that it was '. . . an excellent choice'. He went on to comment that Struth's work at Shawfield was '. . . ample proof of his merits and methods'. There is no doubt that Struth was recognised as a trainer of some talent, and he would form a partnership with the game's top administrator, William Wilton. Rangers had finally got the man they had pursued four years earlier. As well as moving to a new club, Struth moved into a new home at 184 Copland Road, paying a rental of around £2 a month.

The move to Ibrox ended Struth's partnership with Mattha Gemmell, but their friendship continued. Indeed, their bond was such that Mattha named his son William Struth Gemmell. In turn, and as a lasting testimony to their deep friendship, Mattha's son named his son, Mattha's grandson, Matthew Struth Gemmell. Mattha was held in some regard by those at Ibrox as well as by those at Clyde, and Rangers provided the opposition for a benefit match for the popular 'Bully Wee' man in 1924.

Struth must have been excited about his prospects with Rangers, and the club, too, looked forward with some optimism to the future. The trauma of the Ibrox Disaster was long past, if not forgotten. However, any belief that the club was about to enter a bright new era was about to be destroyed. As Scottish football prepared for a new season, the dark clouds of global conflict were looming. On 4 August 1914, Britain entered what was to become known as the Great War.

RANGERS AND THE GREAT WAR

The new trainer's responsibilities

The role that Struth was to assume at Ibrox was the traditional one adopted by football clubs' trainers at the time. The trainer was responsible for maintaining fitness among the players and tending to any injuries sustained during the season. While he could offer an opinion on the capabilities of players, team selection was very much in the domain of the selection committee, ably assisted in Rangers' case by Mr Wilton. Similarly, the acquisition of players was beyond the trainer's remit, and players would arrive and depart at the whim of those in the higher echelons of the club. Struth would not have found frustration in any of this since it was typical for the day and similar to his role at Shawfield. Instead, his occupation was very much full on, managing the professional players who attended the stadium for morning and afternoon sessions, then returning in the evening for those on part-time contracts.

Bill Struth had very clear ideas on how to prepare players and he did not find much at variance with the routines already established at Rangers. However, in the very early days of his work at Ibrox, he rather controversially imposed himself upon an established routine about which he believed he had to put his foot down. It threatened to put him immediately into conflict with William Wilton, but it emphasised to everyone that he would be uncompromising when it came to matters he considered important. He later recalled:

> William Wilton said to me, 'There's a bottle of brandy and port in the travelling hamper.' I asked simply, 'Why?' to be told it was the custom then to give the players a nip before the match and at half-time. 'Well that's one custom that stops right now,' I insisted, and it did. In my opinion, no athlete needed alcohol as a stimulant. It was the first time I put my foot down and it stayed down!

Struth saw it as important to instil some discipline in the team in the early days and to consolidate his position as the new trainer. It was essential that he gained their respect, but also that he set limits and standards for them to achieve. There would be no resistance from the players – Jimmy Wilson had been of a similar mind. On one occasion, he had called all of the players to report to afternoon training at Ibrox, but his motives did not lie so much in the fitness of his charges as in their pockets! Wilson's reasoning was that it would '. . . prevent them going to Ayr races'. Players built up a bond with their trainer rather than with the manager or any of the directors. The trainer was the man with whom they would interface daily and he would learn to manage their idiosyncrasies as well as their health.

Struth resolved that fitness and health would be his priorities with the players. A criticism levelled at many clubs was that their focus was on fitness rather than ball skills. One commentator of the period, talking generally of the game, lamented that 'men get nothing like as much actual work with the ball as they need', suggesting that players should be encouraged to 'practise dribbling'. Since many trainers around the country emerged from an athletics background, including Struth and Wilson, it is perhaps unsurprising that the emphasis in training was more on the track than the field. If the Rangers directors were conscious of this criticism within the game, it clearly had little bearing on their desire to attract Struth to Ibrox. In any case, his methods seemed to have been successful with Clyde.

Struth was very much an athletics man and he believed that the players had to aspire to the highest ideals of fitness if they were to reach decent performance levels as sportsmen. That would be his mantra, but when he took up the position at Ibrox, he did not radically alter the training methods that Jimmy Wilson had used. Wilson was of a similar mentality and background to Struth, so their regimes did not differ greatly. In fact, the routines that Struth adopted continued for a long time at Ibrox, if not in the detail, certainly in the spirit. Ironically, this commitment to fitness training rather than ball work would be a factor in the demise of Struth's eventual successor, Scot Symon, over fifty years later. However, the fact that the system, tried and trusted, survived until then showed the great faith that football clubs placed in men such as Struth to bring their players to a state of readiness for the game.

The weekly routines that Rangers adopted through Wilson's period and into the Struth era are revealed in training records retained within the Ibrox archives. They provide little evidence of any interest in coaching football skills, with the greater reliance being placed on methods of bringing the players up to a good physical condition. They show that after a hard competitive match on the Saturday, Mondays would normally be recuperative, the day beginning with a long walk to loosen the tired and damaged muscles. This would be followed in the afternoon by sprints and exercises to tone every part of the body. Apparatus more often found in a boxing gym, such as dumb-bells and a speedball, were typical for many football clubs and an integral part of the training to improve upper body strength.

Ball work was assigned to Tuesdays and Thursdays, but was largely unsophisticated. Apart from shooting practice, training with a ball tended to revolve around short games of five-a-side, or with the players split into two sides. On Wednesdays training returned to the slog of running, or walking, and Fridays were used for sprinting. The best part of the day for many of the players was the hot soda bath that followed, or the massage for those with weary leg muscles.

A key role for the trainer was attention to injuries and most were reasonably adept at rudimentary treatments for the usual cuts, bumps and strains. The treatment normally administered for strains and bruises was the application of hot fomentations to raise the temperature around the injury, followed by a massage using oils and liniments. The trainer would deal with most injuries, but a doctor would come to the ground regularly to attend to any that were more severe.

Struth was not, and was not expected to be, medically qualified, but through his experience in athletics, he could administer the traditional treatments necessary for routine cuts and strains. Indeed, he was generally considered to be skilled in managing players' injuries. He would not have called himself a 'physiotherapist', or 'physical therapist'. Indeed, the term 'physiotherapy' was very much in its infancy and the only authoritative body that managed the profession was the Incorporated Society of Trained Masseuses. This group, established to regulate the practice of massage by four nurses in London in 1894, was not granted a Royal Charter until 1920, when physiotherapy was more commonly regarded as a profession. Struth did not gain formal qualification, but he undertook some training and was generally respected as a trainer who could manage injuries well. The significance of this, and of the profession, was to be enormous to Struth just a few months after he joined Rangers.

Football in a world of chaos

Just six weeks after Bill Struth entered his commission at Ibrox, an event occurred several thousand miles away that was to prove catastrophic. On 28 June 1914, Archduke Franz Ferdinand, the heir to the Austro-Hungarian throne, was assassinated by Serbian nationalists in Sarajevo. That single action catapulted the world into a month of high diplomacy, later known as the 'July Crisis', as politicians strove to avoid the Armageddon of global conflict. In Britain, the populace knew little of the intensity of efforts being made behind the scenes while the world rapidly spiralled towards war. In Glasgow, the people took their annual 'Fair' holiday, heading 'doon the watter' on paddle steamers to Rothesay, Millport and Arran for some fresh air and relaxation, away from the noise and smog of the city.

With the season over and Ibrox little used, Struth's duties were limited. He had to prepare for the Rangers Sports, which, on this occasion, were to be jointly promoted by Rangers and Celtic. The event was held on Saturday, 1 August and attracted over 20,000 people into the ground. A focus of interest for the crowd was the touring Polytechnic Harriers Club, which had been lauded six years earlier for its performance in organising the opening and closing ceremonies for the 1908 Olympic Games at the newly built White City Stadium in London.

The Polytechnic athletes dominated the main events and as well as the high quality of the field, the spectators enjoyed record performances, rounded off with an obstacle race, which added some light relief and, as reported by the press, a few 'hearty laughs'. At the end of a highly successful day, the prizes were presented by Mrs Catherine Wilton, wife of the Rangers manager.

The event was a pleasant departure from growing anxiety over events in Europe. The tone of newspaper reports had altered and while the mood was still to continue with life as before, there was no doubting the severity of the strife between nations as they wrestled over the Austro-Hungarian problem. Then, just three days after the crowds celebrated a fun day at the Rangers Sports, the news everyone feared broke on billboards the length and breadth of the country –'War With Germany Proclaimed'.

On 4 August 1914, Germany invaded Belgium in contra-vention of a warning from Britain that it would be drawn into the conflict under the 1839 Treaty of London, through its commitment to protect the Belgians in the event of attack. The invasion ignited a patriotic fervour, which was enflamed by the authorities. There was no conscription at that time, but none was needed as many young men responded to the rallying call to arms from the new Secretary for War, Lord Kitchener. A poster campaign proclaiming 'Your Country Needs You' was enough to muster considerable support among men aged

19 to 30, and Glasgow managed to raise three infantry batta-lions, each of around 1,000 men, in the first few weeks. Most joined the city's own Highland Light Infantry, while others joined the Cameronians (Scottish Rifles), the Cameron High-landers, Seaforth Highlanders, the Black Watch, the Gordon Highlanders and the Argyll and Sutherland Highlanders.

For those who took the 'king's shilling', the war was an opportunity for some excitement, camaraderie, a regular wage and a suit of clothes. The reaction in the country in these early months was one of complacency, an assumption that the conflict would be short-lived.

Sporting associations throughout the country gathered to determine whether they could continue to operate at this time of national emergency. In Scotland, the football authorities initially favoured a temporary stoppage of competitive matches. However, following a top level meeting with the War Office, they were advised to continue. The reasoning was that recruit-ment would be enhanced through the football clubs and the Scottish Football Association was asked to canvass support from all of the clubs.

The honorary president of Rangers, Sir John Ure Primrose, was appointed a recruitment officer for the area and he sent a letter to the club, in that capacity, asking that it send two representatives to attend a meeting with other clubs. The meeting was intended to pursue means by which the clubs could lend their support, but particularly asking that the clubs '. . . consider what [they] can do towards raising recruits for the Army at this time of National Danger'. Rangers responded with an endorsement of their support for the cause by issuing a circular to the press notifying that the club would do '. . . everything in its power to make the recruiting movement a success'. Members were asked to canvass eligible young men and persuade them to enlist at Ibrox Park. They were told that they would be part of a 'Football Battalion', which was attached to the Highland Light Infantry. This was a common ploy by the authorities seeking to attract recruits. 'Pals Battalions' were set up locally with the promise that recruits could serve beside their friends or those of a similar interest.

The first recruitment day at Ibrox was on 8 September, when the doors were open from 10 a.m. to 4 p.m., then from 6 p.m. to 9 p.m. The edict from Rangers to its members must have been uncomfortable for Bill Struth. Although his son was just 12 and not yet old enough to be considered by the recruiting agents, Kate's nephew Alex Thomson was 23 and well within the age range of interest to the armed forces. Alex had essentially been Kate's adopted son following the death of her sister and the departure of his father to Wigtown. He lived with the Struths at their home, which was by now at 7 Edmiston Terrace. Being a corner house, it also had the address of 193 Copland Road. Alex did not answer the call to Ibrox or any other recruiting station at this time, like the majority. However, his time would come. While many young men *did* rally to the call and Glasgow compared favourably with Edinburgh in its recruitment levels, Kitchener's campaign needed more and more recruits to compensate for the losses sustained on the front line.

A couple of days after Rangers actively engaged in the recruitment campaign, Sir John Ure Primrose attended a rally in the city's St Andrews Hall along with the Lord Provost, the Secretary for Scotland and a number of other dignitaries. There were long lines of people waiting to enter that hall and the *Scotsman* newspaper commented that it was gratifying to see so many young men 'to whom the meeting might prove a fortunate and fruitful inspiration'. The audience listened attentively to the national anthems of the four allied nations before calling for, and standing to, the Belgian anthem. The Provost reported that there had been 27,000 recruits from Glasgow, highlighting that they had enlisted to fight for principles. At the end of the evening, the crowd could not have denied the justification for Britain's entry into the conflict. With passions ignited, many more would join the rallying call.

A few weeks after Rangers opened the doors of Ibrox to the recruiting sergeants, newspapers carried information on the establishment of a 'Sportsmen's Battalion', affiliated to the Royal Fusiliers, with recruitment at the Central Hotel in Glasgow. They were looking for '. . . men of good character and physique, who were used to outdoor sport'. Three young Rangers were among the first to join up, listed as Dr Thomas Gilchrist, George Dickson and J. Dunlop. Several more left to serve, 'on government work'.

Apart from opening Ibrox and contributing money for recruitment costs, Rangers curiously extended their assistance by sending dozens of footballs to the soldiers at Aldershot. There was no doubting that the soldiers welcomed the initiative. One, Gunner J. Thomson of the 27th Battery, wrote to the *Evening Times* early in the war, thanking Rangers 'very much for the ball sent – [we] hope to have many good games with it'.

The club itself also received numerous letters of gratitude for the many balls sent to the troops in France. One of these letters was signed by thirty of the infantrymen. However, the most poignant, which captured the circumstances that the servicemen faced, was reported in the newspapers from an officer of the Argyll and Sutherland Highlanders.

The first football you sent me I found waiting for me when we came down for the trenches last night. You can hardly realise at home how much good football does our men. They are in the trenches for four days, where movement is limited to a few yards. Consequently, when we get down for four days' rest, route marching is out of the question, but somehow or other the men always summon up enough energy to play football. This . . . the best medicine in the world for them . . . just gives relaxation and excitement as the men cannot leave billets without a pass and no places of amusement are open here, so they must find their own amusement.

If football was important to many of the Tommies on the front line, they could scarcely have imagined the role it would play in their encounter with the enemy on Christmas Day 1914. The diaries of some of the British troops recount an exchange during an agreed ceasefire between the forces, when the Germans called out across no-man's land, 'You come halfway and we will come halfway and bring you some cigars.' The troops from both sides met, exchanged greetings, sang carols and then played football, using steel helmets as goal posts. By one account, the Germans won 3–2 before the truce ended and the soldiers returned to their trenches. Some reports suggest that similar games were played at other positions along the lines. We can only speculate that the ball involved came from Rangers, but there is no doubt that this small gesture of sending balls to the front line was well received by the troops.

As the national fervour led more and more to the recruitment offices, Rangers readied their players for a potential intro-duction to the conflict by establishing a rifle club, and paying for ammunition. The players embarked on firearms training at the Parkhead Forge Rifle Club, which assembled each Tuesday and Thursday. Both William Wilton and Bill Struth joined the party.

While the players showed commendable enthusiasm in learning how to handle firearms, they could not enlist initially due to contractual liabilities, which tied them to the club for a year. Eventually, the authorities gave the clubs permission to allow players to break their contracts if they wished to volun-teer. However, the response generally from the professional players in Britain was poor and there was a growing disquiet in the country that professional footballers had not rallied to the cause as well as the amateurs. As one critic highlighted, 'The response [from the professionals] could not be described as enthusiastic.' Even the enemy taunted the apparent lack of conviction from young footballers. One German newspaper, the *Frankfurter Zeitung*, reported that 'The young Britons prefer to exercise their long limbs on the football ground, rather than expose them to any sort of risk in the service of their country.'

Desperate to play their part, however, Rangers announced that any of their players who felt they wanted to enlist would continue to be paid by the club, receiving half wages. The clubs had already been asked by the authorities to reduce the wages of their higher paid players and to levy their gate money to help support some weaker clubs.

The ability of players elsewhere to opt out of the national service through their contractual obligations to their clubs was not universally accepted or welcomed. In England, just a few weeks after the country entered the war, Arthur Conan Doyle, who had tried unsuccessfully to enlist at the age of 55, appealed for footballers to join the armed forces. Impassioned, he wrote:

> There was a time for all things in the world. There was a time for games, there was a time for business, and there was a time for domestic life. There was a time for everything, but there is only time for one thing now, and that thing is war. If the cricketer had a straight eye let him look along the barrel of a rifle. If a footballer had strength of limb, let them serve and march in the field of battle.

As 1914 drew to a close, it was becoming increasingly apparent that the conflict would not be ended quickly. Kitchener intimated as much, as the jolly adventure on mainland Europe sank deeper into a mire of frustration and despair. The mood in the newspapers altered as the compositors assembled reports of heavy fighting on different fronts, around an increasing number of thumbnail pictures showing the fallen.

If the Rangers players were slow to join up initially, a number did eventually rally to the cause. For Wilton, who was almost 50 years of age, and Struth, 38 when war broke out, their assistance in the war effort in that first year of the conflict was restricted to maintaining some degree of normality as football continued. Some on the Rangers board were unhappy for the club to continue to play through the turmoil. Wilton confided to a friend that 'there [was] big agitation in here just now to have the game stopped until the war is over'. These views were replicated in the Scottish game, causing a major division between the two authorities of the Scottish League and the Scottish Football Association. The League continued their competition, while the SFA postponed the Scottish Cup. For many, it seemed illogical that one competition should continue while the other did not.

The press suggested that the disagreement between football's two authorities would be the catalyst for a new dawn and the emergence of a single controlling body. Ironically, almost a hundred years later, the structure of the game remained as complicated as it was then.

The disagreement between the two Scottish bodies extended to the English FA, who had intimated that they would cease to play the FA Cup after the 1915 final. As the dispute between the associations continued, the English FA withdrew from the annual Scotland v. England fixture. While the cessation of football seemed a natural consequence of the changing focus of the populace brought about by the war, closing down the game was not as simple as it may have appeared. Rangers needed an income and, as for other clubs, attendances dropped markedly as the young men went to war. In the first season of the conflict, the average crowd at Ibrox fell by over 25 per cent and the club faced economic hardship. In England, Chelsea's average attendance fell even more, from 43,000 to 18,300, and Tottenham Hotspur's crowds halved from 30,000.

In Scotland, professional players were informed that they could no longer be paid through the four months of the close season. At Ibrox, the assistant trainer and assistant secretary had to be dismissed as the club strove to cut costs, but both

Wilton and Struth were retained. The cuts fed their way through to the players and, at the instigation of the Scottish Football League, clubs were asked to seek a reduction in players' wages in response to their financial plight. Rangers resolved to refund any shortfall at the end of the war, but the attention of many of the players had already turned to army service. Wilton responded by supplying them with the terms of service and many left to join the increasing numbers required on the front line. For those who remained, jobs were found in the yards and factories near to the stadium.

If the clubs in Scotland were toiling, Struth's former employers at Clyde had more than their fair share of troubles. The grandstand at Shawfield, which had been erected at a cost of £4,000 just three years earlier, burned to the ground in September 1914.

The war visits the Struth household

Struth continued to work at Ibrox Park, trying to maintain some degree of normality in the face of increasing anxiety surrounding events in Belgium. His first meeting with Clyde players and officials since leaving Shawfield came in a league match at Ibrox on 9 January 1915. Kate Struth joined Bill at the match and despite the Light Blues losing narrowly, the day finished nicely for the Struths. At the end, the Clyde contingent presented a barometer to Bill and a clock to Kate. The gesture highlighted the esteem in which he was held by his former charges and employers.

Both Bill and Kate heard of the sorrow and anxiety of other families caught up in the conflict, and must have realised that eventually the war would impact closer to home. Three days after enjoying their reunion with the Clyde party, the news that they had undoubtedly dreaded arrived. Alex announced that he had enlisted in the Royal Naval Reserve (RNR), whose headquarters were in Whitefield Street, just a few hundred yards from the Struths' home. He most likely joined up at the recruiting centre at the Gladstone Institute in Govan.

Alex was assigned the rank of able bodied seaman, initially as a merchant seaman. Perhaps the family had discussed the possibility and the options, but the RNR seemed to be less likely to be drawn onto the mire of the Somme and would have seemed eminently more attractive to many parents than the Highland Light Infantry. However, the recruiting agents promised that those enlisting would see active service.

When the RNR was set up in August 1914, more men enlisted in the division than could be carried on available ships, and so the men were more widely deployed, particularly in North Africa as part of the Mediterranean Expeditionary Force. Alex left home to head south on the adventure, leaving Bill and Kate at home in Glasgow. Not long after joining up, Alex was struck down with dysentery in the latter half of 1915. He recovered and rejoined his battalion in Mudros, on the island of Limnos (Lemnos) in the Aegean in 1916.

Since it was evident that the war was not going to end soon, the country's demands to maintain the war effort continued. In October 1915, a wartime hospital was set up at Bellahouston Park to deal with the increasing number of casualties flooding back to Britain from the front. The facility, which was built by the Scottish branch of the Red Cross Society, originally provided 500 beds, but as the war took its toll, the hospital's capacity was raised to 1,200. The hospital contained special orthopaedic and physical therapy departments and when it opened, both Wilton and Struth applied to assist. They each received a letter from the Red Cross accepting them in part-time positions. Struth was recruited as a masseur and Wilton as an assistant administrator in the general running of the hospital.

That was the start of the close affinity that developed between Rangers and Bellahouston. Many fundraisers were arranged at Ibrox Park and some accommodation was reserved at the ground for wounded soldiers. Besides helping Bellahouston Hospital, the club also helped the nearby Merryflats Hospital in Govan, now known as the Southern General Hospital. The club donated a piano and an organ to both Bellahouston and Merryflats, which Wilton apparently used to full benefit, arranging concerts to keep up the spirits of those who had endured the ravages of the war.

Mindful that he was not formally qualified to practise as a masseur or physiotherapist, Struth requested, and was granted, special leave to train in London in order to enhance his Red Cross work. Regardless of formal training, Struth had considerable experience in tending to injuries, gained through the exertions of sport. While war injuries were quite different in many instances, his experience proved to be invaluable in the rehabilitation process as part of the physical therapy clinic. The contribution provided to the war effort by both Struth and Wilton was recognised by the Rangers board, who voted a 'war bonus' to each man.

Rangers, like most clubs, found it difficult to maintain consistency in selection as more and more players left to join up. They still relied on those in service to come and play when they were stationed in Britain. However, that in itself presented problems, on one occasion aggravated by fog. Three players were delayed in transit to a match against Falkirk in the latter part of 1915. Rangers took to the field with just nine men and included forward Alex Bennett in goal. When winger Scott Duncan was injured in the first half, the team was left with just eight players. In these circumstances, their 2–0 defeat was perhaps more creditable than disappointing.

In 1916, with no end to the war in sight, demands for recruits increased as casualties rose sharply and voluntary recruitment fell. The government were obliged to introduce conscription and the Military Service Act came into force in March 1916. The act specified that men from the ages of 18 to 41 were available for conscription unless they were married, or served in one of a number of reserved professions. By May, this was extended to include married men. Struth, who had been considered too old for enlistment, was now in the age band that would render him available for call-up. Although he worked at Bellahouston Hospital in what would have been considered a reserved occupation, this exclusion applied only to those in full-time employment. Struth's role was very much part-time.

Meanwhile, Alex was being drawn deeper into the conflict in Europe. By the middle of 1916, his Anson Battalion had been assigned to the War Office from the Admiralty and was sent to France. They disembarked at Marseilles and were transferred to the fields of Belgium, far removed from the sea. Alex found himself on the Somme in the front line. In November 1916, a telegram arrived at the Struth home in Edmiston Terrace, informing them that Alex had been wounded. Each day that Bill Struth walked the short distance to Bellahouston Hospital, he must have wondered if he would see Alex among the scores of casualties who regularly arrived.

The Struths waited anxiously for more news and, just after Christmas, another telegram arrived from the War Office, notifying the family that Alex was 'wounded and missing'. To add to their anguish, they were informed a few weeks later that the case may have been confused with the plight of another serviceman. In April, the Struths contacted the War Office for information and were told that there was still no news about Alex. Weeks turned into months with no further news until a final telegram arrived at their home in July 1917. It notified them that Alex had 'died from wounds' seven months earlier, in the Battle of the Somme.

It must have been a devastating blow for Bill, but more so for Kate. Alex was virtually her son and her sole tangible connection with her long-deceased sister, Helen. Kate had a special relationship with her young nephew that went all the way back to those happy days in Cockburn Street, Edinburgh, where she nursed him as a newborn baby. When Helen died, Kate had been Alex's guardian, and he was very much part of the Struths' family. Now he was gone, only young William, who had since joined the Struths in Glasgow, remained. Bill was very aware that unless the war ended soon, he too would be called to arms.

The king's visit and the heroes at Ibrox

In 1917, the conscripting officers reached Struth. In a letter from the authorities, he was instructed either to commit himself to full-time service for the Red Cross or join the services. Although at 39 within the age range for conscription, Struth would hardly have had an appetite for going to war. With Kate grieving for Alex and young William remaining at home, it was neither the best time nor circumstance for Bill to leave. He decided that he would remain at Bellahouston Hospital, committing to full-time duties, as required.

He continued to devote some time to Ibrox in the evening, but his absence during regular hours proved to be problematic for Rangers. The players could no longer rely on his constant, attentive care, but more importantly, the loss of Struth placed enormous pressure on William Wilton, who found himself running the club virtually single-handed.

Wilton was a tower of strength through this period, leading fundraising efforts at Ibrox while continuing his dual roles of managing the club and working at Bellahouston. The task at Ibrox was all the more hectic since the ground was frequently in use by other groups, all playing their part in the war effort. The culmination of Rangers' and Wilton's efforts in assisting the cause came when the ground was selected for the first investitures by George V in Scotland, on 18 September 1917.

The ground was opened at 1.30 p.m. to allow in almost 10,000 uniformed women from the National Projectiles factory in Cardonald. As the king entered the ground and was driven around the track in an open car, flags of the allied nations fluttered under blue skies on poles especially erected at the back of the terracings, while the crowd ecstatically waved Union flags. They were among the 70,000 who had assembled to see the king present awards to many servicemen and civilians. One of the women received an MBE for her unstinted service to the factory, but the greatest cheers were reserved for three soldiers, each of whom was awarded the Victoria Cross. It was a very proud occasion for both Rangers and Wilton, who was presented to the king at the end of the occasion. Struth stood on the sidelines, but must have felt immense pride as the monarch travelled around the track to the cheers of the crowd.

On the field, the war years were unremarkable for the club. A number of players who would become the heart of successful teams in the future were introduced, including Bob Manderson, Andy Cunningham, Sandy Archibald, Tommy Muirhead and Arthur Dixon. As football struggled through the war years, Rangers finally got some reward for their efforts on and off the field by winning the League Championship. The title victory was celebrated on 13 April 1918, the last day of the season, when Rangers defeated Clyde while their nearest rivals, Celtic, could only draw against Motherwell.

The war seemed to be nearing an end, but the strain was beginning to tell on William Wilton. Drained by his efforts at Bellahouston and Ibrox, he wrote in private correspondence to a friend that his 'time had been taken up with Red Cross work and football for the past three years'. He had arranged countless benefit matches for a variety of war-relief funds in addition to competitive games, as well as diligently attending to his duties at Bellahouston. He organised games between Rangers and Glasgow Highlanders, Ayr United, the British Army and a Renfrewshire Select all in aid of the Red Cross. He had also sent parcels to Rangers 'players on foreign service' as well as 'greetings and cigarettes' to those players on home service. The club continued to send footballs overseas – 175 were despatched between March and July 1918.

We have no record of Struth's thoughts or condition at this time, but he must have been similarly drained by his efforts in the hospital and long hours spent at Ibrox after his Red Cross uniform had been hung away.

As 1918 drew to a close, Rangers were notified that Harold Vallance, elder son of Thomas, one of the early pioneers of the club, had been killed in action. He was the final notable casualty connected with the club as the Great War finally ended on the eleventh hour of the eleventh day of the eleventh month 1918. Rangers had played its part and many young men who were connected with the club had seen active service in the worst conditions. Records show that at least twenty Rangers players left Ibrox to enlist and a further fourteen or more joined up either before or after they became players at the club. Among those who were famous for football exploits and served admirably through the conflict were Dr Jimmy Paterson, Andy Cunningham, Jimmy Gordon, Willie Reid, Jimmy Speirs, Jimmy Galt, Tommy Muirhead, Finlay Speedie, Alex Bennett, George Livingstone and Sandy Archibald. Others, mostly lesser known, were equally brave in discharging their duties to the country.

A number of players were wounded in the conflict and, sadly, four made the ultimate sacrifice – David Murray, James Speirs, John Fleming and Walter Tull, the first black player to sign for the club. Aside from the playing staff, the sons of three directors – William Craig, Walter Crichton and William Danskin – were killed in action. It seemed that scarcely a family had not been scarred by the terrible conflict and the Struths were no different, but life would go on for Bill and Kate Struth, as well as for William Wilton – or so it seemed.

THE NEW MANAGER OF RANGERS

The tragedy of William Wilton

When the war ended, Bill Struth returned to his full-time duties at Ibrox. The beleaguered William Wilton was rewarded for his efforts on two fronts with a benefit match in April 1919, organised by the directors at Rangers. Wilton wrote to the intended opponents, Everton, and asked them to keep the arrangements quite private: '. . . the proceeds go as complimentary to the writer after thirty years' service. I do not wish, however, to advertise it as a "Benefit", so it will just be billed as an Ordinary Match.'

It seems he was almost apologetic about the gesture, but the match was well deserved. Wilton had laboured hard for Rangers for years and almost single-handedly held the club together through the latter half of the war. Around 20,000 attended the match, which the Light Blues won 4–0, ensuring a decent payday for Wilton.

As the country emerged from the dark days of wartime, there was a resurgence of interest in football. Crowds returned to the grounds and children struggled to find available space to play the game in public parks. Youths set about organising their own teams and it was claimed that there was a football team formed on every street corner. As attendances rose across the country, the Old Firm seemingly attracted record crowds every time they played. In the New Year's Day fixture of 1920, almost 80,000 crammed into Celtic Park to see the sides share the honours with one goal each. In March 1920, the Old Firm were drawn together in the quarter-final of the resurrected Scottish Cup and the crowd rose to 85,000 – a record for a match between two club sides in Britain at that time.

Rangers won that encounter and continued to challenge on all fronts. The side was settled and included many of the great names who were to be the backbone of the team through the next decade and beyond. Among them was a newcomer to the club – a young Davie Meiklejohn.

The pressures on both Wilton and Struth increased in the closing weeks of the season and although they slipped out of the Scottish Cup in the semi-final, the league challenge was strong. Many clubs were gearing up for testimonials for favoured players, but Rangers had to turn down some requests to provide opposition because the calendar was becoming congested. In April, William Wilton wrote to one club that Rangers had three games per week up to the end of the season, quite apart from other testimonial commitments, including a benefit match for the club's own Jimmy Gordon. Indeed, Rangers ultimately played ten matches in April, plus several Alliance matches and second eleven Cup games.

It was an exhausting period for both manager and trainer. Struth diligently carried out his coaching role during the day and in the evenings, also tending to the tired bodies of his players. Wilton attended to his day-to-day work in administering the business of the club, and spent the evenings talking to his agents and other clubs about players. Although team selection involved the directors, Wilton had been charged with acquiring new players and he relied on his agents to source those who had become available.

Their efforts were rewarded on 28 April, when a draw at Dumbarton's Boghead Park provided Rangers with a tenth league title, won with an impressive record points total.

It had been a successful season for Rangers, but now the attention of the sporting media turned from football to sailing and the great yacht challenge for the America's Cup, which had been postponed during the war. The United States boat *Resolute*, the defender, was fancied to beat the challenger, *Shamrock IV*, owned by Thomas Lipton. Lipton had been born in Glasgow and opened his first shop in Anderston, so there was considerable local interest in this race of the fast yachts, to be staged in New York City harbour. A former Rangers Director and good friend, James Marr, owned a 19-tonne two-masted yacht, or yawl, named *Caltha*, which was anchored in Cardwell Bay, Gourock. He invited William Wilton and fellow director Joseph Buchanan to join him on board for the long May weekend. Perhaps the invitation was stimulated by the media interest in sailing through the America's Cup race, but it was a very welcome opportunity for Wilton to relax.

In his last letter before the break, Wilton wrote to one of his agents enclosing a money order in settlement of 'outlays' incurred in the acquisition of players, which he said would 'close their little arrangement'. The next day he turned up at Ibrox for the last league match of the season, against Morton. It was a meaningless tie, but gave the supporters the opportunity to shower plaudits on the new champions. Rangers closed the season with a 3–1 win and as the crowds left Ibrox, William Wilton and Joseph Buchanan also left to head west along the Clyde to Gourock. As he left Ibrox, Wilton remarked to Sir John Ure Primrose that he was 'fatigued with the heavy season's work'.

They reached Gourock in the evening and were welcomed aboard by James Marr, the skipper of the little yawl, and his mate. As they bunked down for the evening, the wind howled and the boat hauled on its anchor. During the night the storm intensified. Wilton realised that the vessel was drifting and he alerted the others sometime between 2.00 a.m. and 3.00 a.m. The boat was being driven by the easterly wind and the tide towards the Caledonian Pier, but the men were helpless and unable to signal their distress to other vessels in the vicinity or to the shore. The boat smashed into the pier and the beleaguered crew and passengers realised that their only hope was to climb the mast, then jump from the boat to the jetty.

Wilton was the last to leave the boat and although the others tossed him a rope, he failed to grasp a safe hold on the pier as the mast rolled away. He lost his footing and plunged into the sea between the boat and the pier. We can conjecture that he was crushed as the boat continued to smash against the structure, although reports tell only of a faint cry as he disappeared from sight.

Newspaper headlines relayed the shock news of the death of the Rangers boss. The Glasgow *Evening Citizen* called him the 'Prince Among Football Managers'. More than seven weeks later his body was found, floating in Cardwell Bay, and recovered for a proper burial at Cathcart Cemetery on 29 June 1920.

The depth of Wilton's appeal was apparent from the countless tributes paid to him. A good tenor, he sang with the Glasgow Select Choir and was associated with the Choral Union. He also enjoyed golf and bowls, but it was through football that he had earned plaudits, as the Rangers manager and a key administrator in the Scottish League. Generally recognised to be a courteous man with a reserved nature, he was also firm and had achieved enormous respect in the game. In particular, newspaper accounts told of the love he had for his 'boys', whether director, trainer or player. He left behind a widow and three daughters and, at Ibrox, a gaping hole that could not readily be filled.

In the immediate aftermath of Wilton's death on 2 May 1920, Rangers considered postponing the Jimmy Gordon benefit match against a select side of international players, scheduled for the following evening. Chairman Sir John Ure Primrose was vociferous in his reluctance to call off the match. A number of tickets had been sold and no alternative date was available, so the board decided that the match should continue, to celebrate the contribution of a player who had given them twelve good seasons.

Bill Struth appointed manager of Rangers

As the Rangers board grappled with the problem of replacing William Wilton, one candidate began to emerge as the man who would have the capability to take on the job – Bill Struth. Struth related the story of an encounter with one of the directors to a newspaper reporter some years later. He recalled:

On a Sunday soon after the accident, Bailie Buchanan stopped me in the street and took me aside telling me they wanted me as manager. 'No, no, no,' I replied. 'Get yourself another manager – leave me in a job I know.'

A heated discussion ensued and Struth insisted that he was not up to the task. The prospect excited him but, he was to later confess, it also filled him with trepidation. If the seed was already sown, the conversation with Bailie Buchanan probably consolidated the idea that he *could* take over from Wilton.

Two weeks later, the club headed to the Isle of Arran for the weekend, at the invitation of the Marchioness of Graham. At Lamlash, they played a match against a local select to raise money for the Isle of Arran War Memorial Fund. Struth was probably in attendance, although his mind would have been preoccupied, in all likelihood, by the notion of taking the reins at Ibrox.

Once Struth had been convinced that the board was unanimous in their conviction that he was the man to take up the mantle and lead the club forward, he set aside his concerns. Formalities concluded, on 15 June 1920 Bill Struth was confirmed as the second manager of The Rangers Football Club. Logically, he was the right choice since he knew the players and they knew him. Perhaps more importantly, they also respected his methods. He may have been a hard task master, but the players had high regard for him. After the tragic loss of Wilton, the club were simply glad to see the season over and to have time to regroup. The new season would soon be upon them, with new challenges and a new manager.

During his time with Wilton, Struth had been learning his trade, increasing his contacts and improving his knowledge of football. He had built up respect within the game, through his influence at Clyde and Rangers, but also with Scotland, whom he served as trainer. His work with the national side culminated in a trip to Wembley, so his star was most certainly on the rise.

Struth was particularly affected by the loss of Willie Wilton. The two men had developed a close working relationship, especially during the chaos of the war years. Wilton probably had no thought of mentoring his trainer. He would not have expected to relinquish the manager's chair quite so suddenly. He was, after all, just 54 when fate conspired to rob him of life. In 1920, stepping into Wilton's shoes would have been the furthest thing from Struth's mind, but he had undoubtedly gained immense experience from watching his manager attend to the day-to-day affairs of the club. Unplanned as it was, the events were actually timely for Struth. He was just a month short of his 45th birthday and as ready as he would ever be to step into the manager's chair. Bill Struth's moment had arrived.

Ready he may have been, but it is interesting that Struth was apparently reluctant to contemplate the position in the immediate aftermath of Wilton's tragic death. This was quite peculiar since he was obviously a man driven by desire and ambition, committed to making the most out of life and of any opportunities that came his way. It was not the first time that he had shown some hesitancy about taking a step forward in his career. Ten years earlier he had declined an approach from the club when they offered him the opportunity to be trainer. On that occasion, he offered the moral line that he would not want to take another man's job. Perhaps on that occasion the morality issue was overriding, but when he was offered the job of manager, his initial reluctance was an indication that, for all that he had an aura of confidence about him, some self-doubts remained. He had been at Ibrox just six years, after all, and now he was being propelled into the biggest job in football.

The *Daily Record* applauded the board's new appointment and the depth of his knowledge. 'What "Bill" does not know about football or sport in general is not worth bothering about . . .' they wrote, adding that the decision to award the position to Struth was unanimous among the board. The *Evening Times* called the appointment 'popular and sensible'.

The board had realised that it would be difficult to find a man who could fulfil all of the duties that Wilton had adopted through his years as both manager and secretary. Recognising that Struth had no particular experience, or knowledge, of administration, they decided to split the role, and appoint him manager with responsibility for regular team matters. Wider secretarial duties would be another role, which they would themselves address in the short term. They eventually turned to William Rogers Simpson, who was appointed club secretary.

The close season afforded Struth an opportunity to adapt to the new role, but he had to find a replacement for the position of trainer. The job was advertised and on 10 July the club announced that George Livingstone, who was manager and secretary at Dumbarton, would move to Ibrox. Struth would have favoured the appointment of 'Geordie'. They went back some way. Livingstone was Dumbarton born, but he had played for Hearts around the time Struth began training at Tynecastle. He had joined Rangers as a player in 1906 and stayed at Ibrox for three seasons before heading south to join Manchester United, where he won a Championship medal. He retired at the outbreak of war and returned to Dumbarton after the conflict to take charge of the 'Sons'. As a former player and with experience as a trainer, Livingstone seemed ideal and a good fit for Struth.

It was the dawn of a new era for Rangers.

THE STANDARDS OF RANGERS

The new manager sets his ideals

The death of William Wilton was greeted with widespread dismay, particularly among the Rangers fraternity, who recognised how important he had been to the development of the club. It was Wilton, the administrator, who had managed the club into its incorporated status, raising the capital for the new ground. As the first manager, he had enjoyed tremendous success on the field, culminating in victory in the Championship in his final fateful season. That the club had grown to be a respected institution was as much down to Wilton as it was to anyone else in its history at that time. He set high principles for the players, not just on the field, but off it, too. He established the dress code and enforced standards of discipline that would be embraced wholeheartedly by Bill Struth. Wilton was an ideal role model for the new manager, and a hard act to follow.

If Bill Struth had any real uncertainties about taking up the position of manager, they do not appear to have been shared by those around him. In the light of that, Struth swept aside any lingering lack of self-belief and, backed by the confidence of the board, threw himself into the position with some vigour. The day after his appointment, he called the *Weekly News* offices with a quite unambiguous request – 'This is Struth, Rangers. I will be available for photos this morning.' The *News*, eager to get the first pictures of the new incumbent in the Ibrox hot seat, obliged and a cameraman was promptly dispatched to the ground. Inside, Struth was dressed in what he was to refer to as 'his number ones' – a stylish blue serge suit, bowler hat, rolled umbrella and gloves. 'Take any pictures you want of me,' he declared, as he strolled around the edge of the Ibrox pitch. The sun shone and Struth radiated pride, basking in his new role. Once the cameraman's job was completed, Struth told him, 'Now you have up-to-date pictures of me as Rangers manager. Please destroy all those you have of me as trainer. When you now want to use a picture of me, use one of these taken today. Good morning.'

To some, this may appear vain, but his motives were rooted in what he believed was right for the club and befitting the role. He did not want a picture from the past to obscure the fact that he held one of the most coveted jobs in football, manager of the Rangers. As manager, he could not be seen wearing training attire and from then on he would wear clothing befitting his status.

By that simple exhibition of importance, Struth laid down a mark to the media, the players and the fans. He was keen to reinforce his position by setting standards that would start with his own appearance. Dress was always of immense importance to Struth in highlighting status, and directors aside, there was no station higher than that of the manager at Ibrox. He was keen to widen his influence, instilling his ideas in those around him, particularly the players. It was a reflection of his interview with Clyde some years earlier. For Struth, being smartly dressed was one of the most important standards that a player, or gentleman, should adhere to.

Struth set high standards with his own wardrobe and his suits were always made-to-measure. The manager looked the part and was always an impressive character in his fine clothes. He frequently changed more than once in a day and his natty clothing would eventually earn him the title of the 'Beau Brummel of Football'. By setting these exceptional standards, he believed that he was helping to set the club apart from others, and giving it an aura of dignity. He may have been of working-class stock, but the working togs were well behind him now. No one could doubt from his finery that he was a man of some standing. As manager of Rangers, Struth had become what he longed to be – a man held in some respect.

The seasoned professionals at Ibrox very quickly knew what Struth demanded of them, but new players had to undergo some scrutiny by the manager in their first few weeks. When they arrived at Ibrox, he would tell them, 'You're a Rangers player now. I want you to act like one.' For those who turned up at the ground wearing an open-necked shirt, or a suit that was the worse for wear, Struth would wait his chance to take them aside for a few words of advice. Invariably, those who fell foul of his standards on their very first day were chastened and sent off to rig themselves out in a new outfit, more often than not at the club's expense. A favourite trick was to slip a business card into the youngster's hand, saying, 'There you are, my boy – that's the name of my tailor. Tell him I sent you – he'll put you right.'

The twenties was the era of the bowler hat, and, even today, the Ibrox dressing room has coat pegs with long extensions for such hats. Under strict orders from 'upstairs', every first-team player had to provide himself with a bowler. It made for quite a spectacle when the players arrived at the station to travel to an away fixture. One anecdote from the period concerns a match against Celtic, due to be played at Ibrox. Looking down Edmiston Drive, one of the Rangers directors could see two players making their way to the ground, each wearing a cloth cap. They were so far away that their identity could not be confirmed, but the director knew that they were not Rangers players – neither of the two was wearing a bowler!

When the team travelled, Struth insisted that the players walked to the ground from the station, allowing them to stretch their legs before the match. This gave the side a lift but there was another crucial and clever aspect to the routine, which gave them a psychological edge over their opponents. Despite signing the diminutive Alan Morton, Rangers players, such as Andy Cunningham, Tom Hamilton and Davie Meiklejohn, were invariably tall and strongly built. Seeing them arrive at an away ground in bowler hats and heavy dress coats must have been an imposing sight for any opponent. The walk itself had to be orderly and disciplined. Players were forbidden to put their hands in their pockets and were told to swing their arms. They must have looked like the advance party of an invading army rather than a football team.

It was not just off the park that everyone had to look their best. Struth also had strong ideas about his team's appearance *on* the park, demanding equally impeccable standards. Jerseys and pants were always freshly laundered, stockings were in top condition, and the players' boots, provided by the club, had to be freshly polished. Not all the players would wear the boots supplied and so the Boss's desire for regulation and tidiness could have been compromised were it not for his regular pre-match inspection of uniform. Walking around the dressing room, he would conduct the examination with the air of a sergeant major inspecting his troops. 'Now come along,' he would say, 'look at these stocking tops – all different depths. Get them even!'

Goalkeeper Jerry Dawson, who arrived at the end of the decade, recalled Struth's apparent infatuation with fine apparel in an interview for the *Rangers News* in 1971:

The Boss was very strict when it came to dress, both on and off the field. For example, in the dressing room before a game you didn't put on your pants until the last minute in case you got a crease in your shorts. Your sleeves, if they were rolled up, had to be even, and the same with your stockings. Off the field you certainly had to conform. The style at one time during my time at Ibrox was the short jacket with wide trousers. They were out at Ibrox, though, as they were not considered at all suitable, much too casual. Bill Struth was known to send players to his own tailor so that they could be kitted out properly.

He was very particular about shoes, too. Pointed shoes were out. You had to wear a nice pair of black, box toe-capped ones. Such were the rules and if they were maybe a bit irksome, nobody stepped out of line, and everybody had the greatest respect for the manager. In many ways Bill Struth was ahead of his time. He was possibly the first to apply psychology in football. Like his ruling about pants. He felt that if they were immaculate, then the other team would respect you all the more.

When Rangers played in their change strip of white shirts with black shorts, Struth insisted that the shirt sleeves be neatly rolled in above the elbow. Sandy Archibald, always the jester, liked to leave his sleeves buttoned over the wrist. This always precipitated a beckoning finger from the Boss. 'Come here, Archibald,' he would say, and then he would proceed to unbutton the sleeve and roll it up himself. It almost became a pre-match ritual. The white shirts were not at all popular among the players. They seemed to be very cold to the skin and seemed to be of a looser fit than the traditional royal blue shirts. This was long before Underarmour bodywear, of course, but Struth had his own unique solution to the player's complaints – he would rub methylated spirits into their bodies, proclaiming, 'That will keep the cold out.'

As well as demanding the highest standards of dress, Struth also established a code of behaviour, which included many 'do nots', all designed to protect the reputation of Rangers. He did not like to see any of them drink or smoke, although he accepted that this was part of everyday life. He had a particular distaste for smoking, probably through his failure to understand how any professional sportsman could bring himself to abuse his body in that manner. At the time, the majority of players smoked, but they made sure that they drew on their cigarettes in places where they would not be caught by his eagle eye. It was quite normal for a pall of smoke to hang around the dressing room, which he would accept – so long as there were no cigarettes in his presence.

He was fiercely protective of the club, although he did recognise that there needed to be some degree of flexibility with the players. He said, 'I do not believe in inflexible rules. There was never a complete ban on players smoking or taking a drink except the day before a game. I have always left things to their own good sense.' That may well have been the case, but often he would show them what good sense meant! He went on, 'If any did go overboard, I stepped in.'

Gambling was also a part of the working-man's routine and he accepted that his players would play cards and be tempted to have a flutter at the bookmakers. He was not averse to either when his 'boys' travelled to away fixtures, although it wasn't really his thing. He always kept a close eye on what was going on and if the stakes rose above the standard penny or ha'penny, he would come down on the perpetrators like a ton of bricks. 'Cut that out!' would be the curt instruction. 'I don't want to see any of you losing to any extent and then maybe harbouring a grievance. It spoils harmony.' These words would be all that was required and in an instant the stakes were lowered, or the game stopped, with no questions asked. Struth's word was final – it was always that way, because he was, quite simply, the Boss.

The use of what is now termed 'industrial language' is commonplace in modern football and, some would say, in everyday life. Struth abhorred swearing, and the players did not dare let loose any cuss in his proximity. He did not feel that swearing conformed to the standard expected of a Rangers player, insisting that no foul language should be uttered in public, to protect the reputation of the club. It was freely used on the field by some players and Tommy Cairns highlighted one incident, which indicated Struth's tolerance:

I recall a day when a young player [who was] not long with us and who had been given his first run in the team, complained to Mr Struth that I had used a swear word.

I later learned that Mr Struth rose from his desk, patted the laddie on the back [and] as he led him to the office door with the advice to return to the dressing room, said, 'You know, laddie, you'd have had me more worried if you were to come and tell me that Tommy never used a swear word during a game; then there would be something wrong with him.

Timekeeping was something else that Struth was strict with the players about. Jerry Dawson recalled that the Boss would not allow players to take the underground on their way to a match. The Glasgow District Subway had opened in 1896 and provided a good service to the local station on Copland Road. Dawson explained, 'The Old Man was of the mind that the tube could break down and that anybody on it would be stranded.' The players had to find other means of getting to the ground, but they dared not be late. The manager was a stickler for timekeeping and never accepted any excuse for being late.

Struth exercised many strict controls on the players, which in this modern day may be referred to as 'professionalism'. Dawson recalled in the *Rangers News*:

If we wanted to go to the pictures the night before a match, we had to go to the first house, then straight home by a respectable hour. Another rule was that if we went swimming, we could only do so in salt water. We couldn't go to fresh-water baths because Mr Struth figured they were not so healthy. Then in the close season we were not allowed to play tennis because it tightened up the muscles. He was a strong man and when he wanted a private talk, he would take a vice-like grip on your elbow, then lower his voice as if he was going to tell you the best-kept secret at Ibrox; however, as like as not he would just say, 'I've seen you look better. M'boy, you must get to bed earlier.'

When the club built its new grandstand in 1928, the players were to learn that their place at the club was firmly below the manager's. While he retained an office upstairs, they languished in the dressing room, prohibited from climbing the stairs except on business directly with the Boss. He would have found it quite strange to see players walk freely up and down the stairs at Ibrox today.

If Struth's standards were rigid, it was simply because he wanted the club and its players to be the best. From this, he coined his mantra that 'only the best was good enough for Rangers'. He carried his philosophy through to every aspect of life for the players, seeing that they travelled first class on the trains and stayed at the best hotels. He aspired to be a gentleman and he expected his players – as Rangers players – to seek these same ideals. They would be the best dressed and well behaved, because to him, they represented the club at every turn.

Bill was very canny in his dealings with his boys. As described already, he used a variety of different approaches from the curt dismissal to gentle encouragement. He could be the persuader or the listener, who would act upon justified grievances. Players summoned to his room could tell his mood by how they were addressed. He would call them by their first name if they were to be gently rebuked. On the other hand, if matters were of a more serious nature, the call would be a stern, 'McPhail!'

We use McPhail as an example because he was no stranger to such a summons. He recalled:

My problem was one of early retaliation. If someone kicked me, then I kicked them back. I believed in an eye for an eye, and opponents soon learned to their discomfort that if they kicked McPhail, they'd get a bloody hard one in return. Bill Struth did not like my philosophy. He would have me upstairs, give me that piercing look and be telling me, 'What you are doing is not good for Rangers. All eyes are on you when you are wearing the jersey. If you are playing the player, then you are not getting the ball, and this is what we are paying you to do. If you are fouled, leave things to the referee. You must not retaliate.'

It is an interesting story because therein lies one of the legacies of Struth. In one of his first games for the club, Sandy Jardine made a rash challenge, but otherwise had a good game. He was approached afterwards in the dressing room by director George Brown, who said, 'We don't do that as Rangers players.' Jardine was surprised. He expected praise for his performance, but the story reflects the words of Struth. Perhaps he would call it 'the Rangers way'.

If Struth knew the players he could come down on, he also knew those who needed the softer approach of an 'arm round the shoulder'. Alex Venters was one such player and after an ineffective start with the club, he made his way up the marble staircase to express serious doubts about his ability to make it with Rangers. Struth sat him down and simply said, 'Young man, you carry on. We'll tell you if we are not pleased.' Venters left the room lifted and feeling ten feet tall, comforted that the manager had such confidence in his ability. Struth was not to be disappointed in Venters, who went on to score 155 league goals, managing to find the net eighteen times against Celtic. Struth did not play the game at any significant level, but he knew a decent player when he saw one.

In truth, while many of the standards that remain today may be traced back to the preachings of Struth, most were already well established at Ibrox under William Wilton. However, Bill Struth was obsessed with maintaining his ideals for the club and many are engrained in the very fabric of what is considered the best of Rangers.

A NEW TEAM FOR THE NEW MANAGER

Rebuilding for the twenties

Several of the players who had been instrumental in the success of the club under Willie Wilton left prior to the commencement of season 1920–21. One who moved on was Jimmy Gordon, whose benefit match was played in rather sombre circumstances immediately following the death of Wilton. Having been trainer for six years, Struth was well aware of the capabilities of the many players he had at his disposal and he considered Jimmy Gordon to be above them all.

In an interview he gave some time later, Struth said that he considered Gordon, who played from 1906 until 1920, making 449 appearances and scoring 95 goals, to be the best he had seen in his time at the club. Gordon had won every honour except the elusive Scottish Cup, but this was somewhat compensated for by his five Championship wins. He had also captained Scotland to victory over England in 1914. Struth commented:

> Best of all for sheer all-round ability was Jimmy Gordon – brilliant versatility and pure genius. He was capped by Scotland at full-back, half-back and forward. His finest game was at Parkhead, New Year's Day. The pitch was rolled smooth, but frozen solid – players were slipping

all over the place, all except Jimmy. He was perfectly poised and didn't stumble once, never once losing his footing. [It was] a display of artistry.

Gordon's benefit match had taken place in the shadow of Wilton's death and his career ended in quite bizarre circumstances a week later in an Old Firm encounter, the Glasgow Charity Cup semi-final. Rangers lost the match by two goals to one, but the main talking point surrounded Gordon's dramatic exit from the field. When he lined up at the start of the game, he was conscious that he was not facing his usual opponent, Jimmy McMenemy. Gordon had a fierce rivalry with McMenemy, but he had also a great respect for the Celt. Instead, he faced the pairing of Charlie Watson and Johnnie McKay, neither of whom he held in the same esteem. Gordon made a mistake that let McKay in for the opening goal. Fierce and angry words were exchanged on several occasions during the continuing 'battle' until things came to a boil in the closing stages.

Celtic were awarded a soft penalty with less than 15 minutes to go, from which they scored what turned out to be the winning goal. Gordon lightly slapped Watson on the back of the head as he ran back to the centre circle, prompting quick retaliation from the Celtic man. Realising his folly, Gordon headed straight off the field to the dressing room without waiting for the referee to make the decision for him. As he took the long lonely walk to the Ibrox Pavilion, located in the extreme corner of the ground, Watson was sent to join him, although it took considerable persuasion to get the Celt to leave the field. The two spent the final 12 minutes inside the dressing room and while Watson would live to fight another day, Gordon's career had ended, rather sadly.

Another important player whom Bill Struth had to replace was outside-left, Dr James 'Jimmy' Paterson, who returned to London to share a medical practice in Clapton with his brother-in-law. Paterson was a hero in every sense of the word. He had served in the London Scottish Regiment during the war and won the Military Cross for his bravery in action in France. Struth had no ready replacement, but if he wanted to demonstrate that he could identify a decent player, he could have done no better than he did with his first-ever step into the transfer market. In what would be considered today a 'marquee signing', he acquired the highly rated Queen's Park winger, Alan Morton.

Morton was already an established Scottish international and a big name in the game when he joined up at Ibrox. At the end of the 1919–20 season, speculation had been rife that he would relinquish his amateur status and move south, like many stars of the period. Struth had identified Morton as a player of the quality that he wanted at Rangers. He stepped in to convince the player that his future lay west and still in Scotland, not south in England.

Morton was born in the Jordanhill area of Glasgow, but he had moved to Airdrie, where he was guided into the mining industry by his father, a coal master. Rather than labouring at the coal face, he followed the scholarly route to the mines, training as a mining engineer. He was keen to complete his studies and this was the key to his decision to remain in Scotland. Struth convinced him to come to Ibrox, where he already knew many of the players, explaining that by playing for Rangers, Morton could continue his studies and enjoy playing with the premier team in the country. The winger committed himself to Rangers in what was perhaps one of the most important transfers in the club's history.

Morton went on to complete his studies successfully, qualifying as a mining engineer. He continued his profession throughout his football career, but also worked hard at his playing skills. As a man who preached hard work and diligence, Struth could not have failed to be impressed by Morton's commitment to the game. He was naturally right-footed but, as a boy, Morton constantly practised to improve his left foot, chipping a ball through a hole in the cellar door. By the time he came to play in organised matches, he had developed tremendous skill and accuracy, with a pivot from the hips that kept him behind the ball and gave him extraordinary balance, and he believed that a curious adjustment to his boots – using three studs instead of the usual four – gave him added mobility. He also had a trademark lob, undercutting the ball to leave it hanging in the air. Employed to stunning effect in crosses, it played havoc with defenders.

The move to Rangers was a huge transition for Morton, who had to get used to being 'just one of many, from being the big star at Queen's', as Struth remarked. He adapted with ease and enhanced both his performances and career under the Rangers boss. Teammate and fellow Rangers legend Bob McPhail recalled:

> He was always going in a straight line for goal. He could take the ball into an opponent's penalty area quicker than anybody I ever saw. He never pulled his tricks until a game was won and then he gave the crowd the entertainment they wanted.

Morton was an artiste supreme who had the rarest of endorsements – from England, where he would regularly wreak terror in international clashes. English journalist Ivan Sharpe baptised him with his famous nickname, 'the Wee Blue Devil', following a devastating 5–1 victory for the Scots over the Auld Enemy at Wembley in 1928. He served Rangers for thirteen good seasons, carving out a place for himself in Scottish football folklore. Aside from his skills, Morton had impeccable standards and was vehemently opposed to anything even slightly ungentlemanly. Struth would have regarded him as the archetypal Rangers player.

Even today, Morton's portrait hangs above the marble staircase inside the Ibrox grandstand, a testament to his contribution to the club. The portrait was gifted to the club by Morton's sister, Peggy, in a ceremony in the Blue Room, inside the main stand, on 1 January 1976. The portrait had dominated the dining room of the Morton family home in Airdrie for forty-two years.

Another player whom Struth lost was Willie Reid. He left to join Albion Rovers as player-manager just a few weeks before Wilton's death. Reid, a centre-forward, was a huge player for Rangers and, like Jimmy Paterson, he had served admirably in the war. Reid was a gunner in the Royal Field Artillery 52nd Lowland Division, but despite the interruptions of war, he scored 279 goals in 297 games, including friendlies and competitive fixtures.

It seems that Struth wanted to replace the ageing goal-keeper, Herbert Lock, and put his faith in Willie Robb, whom the club had signed, from Armadale, just a few weeks before Wilton's death. It was perhaps a surprising move since Lock had excelled in Wilton's last season, maintaining a clean sheet in 20 of the 35 league games he played, including a run of 10 matches without losing a goal. Struth's reliance on Robb was to prove well founded. He went on to play a remarkable 217 league games in succession, including the last seven in Wilton's final campaign. Lock remained for one more season and then returned to England, having served the club for 12 seasons.

Later in the season, Struth acquired Linfield left-back Billy McCandless, from Northern Ireland. The player had come to Struth's attention some time earlier, and, indeed, Struth had recommended him to Willie Wilton. The suggestion was rebuffed, Wilton proclaiming, 'Oh now, he's too old; why, he's bald!' which was quite ironic since Wilton himself shed his hair at an early age. When Struth became manager, he remembered McCandless, and paid £2,500 to secure his signature, a record transfer fee for a player from the Irish League at the time. Despite Wilton's reservations, Struth knew he was signing a talented player. He later commented in an interview for the *Sunday Express*:

> I knew Billy was still a youngster. He was a slight little player who seldom put the ball into touch. He was always poised and could take the ball as it came. Occasionally he cost us a goal by taking risks in clearing his lines, and I recall Bailie Buchanan was not too keen on him.

However, McCandless was to serve Rangers well and his signing emphasised that Struth had an eye for a player. He played with distinction for ten years during which time the side won the League no less than eight times.

The story possibly highlights an important transition for Struth in his role as the manager. Where the team selection was once exclusively in the domain of the board, or in the early years, the committee, Struth's statement shows that at the very least he had some influence in the selection. It suggests that no matter the reservations of a highly influential board member, such as Buchanan, Struth held sway over at least some of the selections. He may not have been wholly in charge of selection, but to all intents and purposes, his opinion was decisive. It would make sense for Struth to have greater influence over team selection since he had greatest knowledge of the players. That was one area in which he had an advantage over Wilton. Whereas Wilton would rely on Struth's feedback on the players, the new boss knew them thoroughly. In Struth, the board had the best of both worlds – a manager and a man who knew the men available to him.

Although he clearly lost some experienced players, Bill Struth inherited a great side from Wilton – one that had secured the Championship. He was aware, however, that football was ever changing and that new young players were always needed to boost the squad. Rangers would not stand still and Struth continued to review talent around the game. He had never been charged with securing players prior to Wilton's death, but it was now integral to his position. Struth built a network of scouts around the country, who would make recommendations on players, which he would then follow up. When some of the younger or less well-known players came to the club's attention, they would be assessed by one of the older, retired players, or an injured first-team player.

It was rare for Struth himself to run the rule over any player other than a professional. In the case of Alan Morton, he took his place in the crowd to watch the winger's artistry. Bobby Moffat spent fifty years working for Rangers, initially as a driver and then as doorman. In an interview he provided for the *Rangers News* in 1971, he gave a fascinating insight into how Struth operated in the acquisition of players. Moffat's father, who had a taxi business, used large Daimlers and Argyles, of which five or six were in service to Rangers. One of Moffat's first jobs was to take Struth to watch 'a wee chappie playing for Queen's Park'. The player was Alan Morton.

Moffat was involved in many of the major signings during Struth's tenure and he related the way the Boss approached scouting:

> Mr Struth would call me in and away we would go to a match, but not into the stand or anything. Everything was done in secret then, so we would pay our way onto the terracing. Mr Struth was never recognised because, of course, there wasn't the publicity surrounding football [that] there is now.

Bobby Moffat recalled Struth's rather surprising Saturday afternoon routine:

> He would see the players out on to the field at three o'clock then, at five past, he would nab me and off we would go to watch some player. Maybe it would be at Shawfield. We would stay there for the first half then race over to Cathkin, for example, for the second half. After he had seen what he wanted, Mr Struth would give me the nod and back to Ibrox we would drive,

arriving just before full time so nobody would know we had been away.

The story highlights the trust that Struth had in his team and also his recognition that once the eleven had been selected, there was little he could do to alter things as they got on with it on the pitch.

Although Bill Struth had a remarkable eye for a player and signed some of the best to have represented the club, despite not playing the game at any significant level, he maintained that there was no exact formula for judging a man's ability. Just as it can take a one-minute conversation to sum up a man's character, he contended that very little longer should be required to decide if someone was a player or not. 'If you can't size up a player in one game, you shouldn't be a football manager,' he would say. 'We never signed a player just because he could play football. So many other qualifications are considered, such as character. That can't be defined but you knew it when you saw it.'

In a contemporary interview, Struth went on to explain the process of acquisition of youngsters:

Young players of promise are watched several times and when they are passed as of suitable ability, they would be asked to go to Ibrox. I always encouraged them to bring someone, such as father, mother, uncle, etc., in order to feel comfortable. I would ask a few questions to see if their heart was committed to Rangers. Finally, I would ask about his ideas for the future – did he have a mind of his own? Then I would make the offer. That was that – simply yes or no. It was up to him, there was no compulsion, no false representation required.

I never could stand hesitation. If a boy wanted to be a Ranger, that was that. If he was doubtful, he was not the type I needed. I recently had one lad up with his mother and father. They hesitated and I asked if they wanted to go into another room to think about things. They returned to say they wanted to talk it over with the boy's grandfather. It seemed to me they had another club in view; if so, I would let them go. The following morning I had a call from the mother to say he was no longer interested. A couple of days later it was confirmed that he was negotiating with another club. I don't blame the boy. The point I am trying to emphasise is the youngster has to be Rangers minded, and not just in it for the money.

Struth realised the importance of transition in the team and he seems to have had some very firm ideas on the evolution of the club and how to secure its future. He said:

Rangers have always tried for continuity. We believe that the past is part of our present. Our older players hand on their knowledge and tactics to the younger men. If any youngster cannot fit into that picture, he doesn't stay with us for long. Rangers do not have a cut and dried policy for recruiting players. We like to take as many youngsters as possible to train on our own lines. It is equally true we are always willing to buy an experienced player.

When some promising players began to emerge, Struth relied on his experienced players to develop them. He explained:

> When I saw a youngster who needed help to train, to head, trap etc., I saw to it that he was taught by one of the old heads. That is as far as I would go. I don't believe you can make a great footballer unless he already has that spark of ability.

The players needed more than ability – they also had to show some responsibility and Struth had a very simple yet hugely effective message for every player, drawing on his own life experience. He told them, 'I am not the architect of your future career, you are. When I took this job, I told myself I had to make my own way. You must do the same. Take all the advice and help you can get. In the end, though, it will be you who will have to make the decisions.' He insisted that the players be accountable for their actions and that they recognised that they were masters of their own destiny. He would present them with the opportunity to do well in their careers, but it was up to them, individually, to seize the chance. In essence, he was adopting an almost paternal role, seeking to guide his boys under his managership and, in effect, following his own roadmap to success.

The squad he assembled was a good mix of young apprentices and a few seasoned players. They operated within a hierarchy, although Struth did not believe in 'star' players. In keeping with the times, there was a very real sense of everyone 'knowing their place'. That was true in all walks of life, and football was no different. For example, when established players got out of the bath, they had their back towel-dried by the trainers. Only when these men were tended to did the younger players get any attention. It was almost a feudal system within the club. Despite this, it was very much a 'family' club and if a reserve broke into the first team, invariably they could expect a 'good luck' telegram from their reserve-teammates on the morning of the match.

The team that Struth took into his first season was a solid one, which blended experience with talented acquisitions, such as Morton and McCandless, while having some youngsters waiting in the wings. In essence, however, it remained largely the same team that had taken Rangers to the Championship in William Wilton's last season. No less than the same level of success would be tolerated by Struth.

TACTICIAN OR MAN MANAGER?

A glorious first season

Bill Struth kicked off his first full season on 17 August 1920 with a home match against Airdrie in front of a sparse crowd of 12,000. In wet and windy conditions, Airdrie had the benefit of the conditions in the first half and opened the scoring after 20 minutes. Cairns equalised for Rangers a minute later to take the teams in level at the interval. After the break, Rangers took control and two goals from Andy Cunningham followed by another from Sandy Archibald gave them victory in Struth's first competitive match as manager.

It was a perfect start for the new boss, inspiring an undefeated run in the Championship, which continued into the New Year. Through the run, Struth also won his first league encounter with Celtic. The Celts gained some revenge by winning the 1921 New Year fixture at Ibrox, but remarkably that was an experience they were never to enjoy again while Struth was boss. It was the last Ne'erday match he would lose to his Old Firm rivals at the stadium in thirty-four years of management!

The setback of that Celtic defeat was Rangers' sole reverse in the Championship and it did not prevent the Light Blues from retaining the title in Struth's maiden season. Indeed, the season ended up something of a procession as the side finished 10 points clear of the runners-up, Celtic. Ironically, Rangers clinched it with a 3–1 win against Struth's former employers, Clyde, in April 1921, in front of 19,000 spectators. The Championship was won with a record 76 points over 42 games. The side failed to win just seven matches. That points haul remained unequalled until the three points for a win system was introduced in season 1994–95. If the points system had not been changed, keeping two points for a victory, Rangers' record from season 1920–21 would remain unchallenged to the present day. While winning the League was not exactly unusual for the Ibrox side, the standard of the play was quite simply awesome.

That title win in Struth's first season as manager was the beginning of the Light Blues' stranglehold on the Championship, which they maintained for much of Struth's tenure as boss. They won eight out of ten league titles over the decade, and both the Glasgow Cup and Charity Cup made frequent visits to the Ibrox boardroom's cabinet. The one disappointment for Rangers in 1920–21 was their performance in the Scottish Cup. Acknowledged and coveted as the premier competition in Scotland at the time, it remained strangely elusive to Rangers, despite the side being unquestionably the best in the country.

Struth's management style

Bill Struth's transition to the role of manager was seamless as far as the club was concerned. To many, he was simply extending his responsibilities over a team with which he was already well acquainted. For the players, too, there would be no significant change, because he was, in effect, continuing where he left off – Wilton may have been manager, but Struth was closest to them. He got them fit, he got them ready and he made them proud to play for Rangers. After that, it was all down to them. He would send them out as a unit and it was up to them to organise themselves and ensure that they played as they could. In that respect, his role as manager changed little from his role as trainer.

There would be no tactical or formation changes, because Struth wasn't a man of tactics. The important decisions affecting the result were made on the field. The players even had to regulate themselves and ensure that they all pulled together. They were encouraged to 'get the whip out' if anyone was slacking, or otherwise not up with the play. Struth believed that if players were swiftly reprimanded by a teammate, the resulting peer pressure would be far more effective than any hollering that he might give them. In any case, he was not the kind of man who was prone to 'hollering'.

Struth carefully selected certain members of the team to influence and direct play on the field. There is no question that he had an eye for the on-field 'gaffers'. He picked men who had some stature and who could be respected by the other players. He also looked for men who could size up the game and identify any weaknesses in the opposition. The only guidance they would normally receive from Struth before they took to the field was a word or two about the state of the pitch.

These leaders on the field had the responsibility of making any changes they felt were needed to win the game. Some of the players would later comment that the great Davie Meiklejohn had the greatest flair for summing up the capabilities and style of the other team. Apparently, he would shout to Rangers keeper, Jerry Dawson, 'You can keep kicking up that right wing because yon left-back couldn't kick his granny.'

The men Struth selected to carry that responsibility would learn from their predecessor on the field, so one generation of Ibrox players helped another. In fact, there were generally a few players within the team who would perform the role, but the prime responsibility to manage the play on the field lay with the captain. The men commissioned to undertake the captain's role through Struth's reign reads almost like the Ibrox Hall of Fame. A procession of legendary figures, they included Muirhead, Cairns, Meiklejohn, McPhail, Gillick, Woodburn, Shaw and Young. However, Struth's sides generally had more than one leader in the team.

Reflecting on his first-ever team, which included Jimmy Bowie, Tommy Cairns and Tommy Muirhead, Struth recalled:

> It was not my place to tell such men how to play. It was my job to discipline them, get them fit, and to make them conform to the Rangers pattern. I let them under-stand that I wanted 100 per cent team spirit and club loyalty. They knew I expected to win. The actual performance on the field was their job and I have always stuck with that principle.

One player of this early period in Struth's tenure, Andy Cunningham, who played for the club from 1914 until 1927 before taking up a career in journalism, claimed that he never saw his manager kick a football. That comment begged the suggestion that Struth was not a football man, reinforcing a popular misconception that he never played the game. We know that he *had* played for local Milnathort side, Orwell Thistle, as a youngster, possibly on the right wing, as one local suggested. Be that as it may, knowing how to play the game was not what Struth was about. He would bring more to Rangers than anyone with a thousand games under his belt could ever offer.

Cunningham, writing in the *Sunday Express*, commented that the manager only ever attempted to give one talk on tactics in his entire career:

We were weekending in Turnberry before a big game. Folk thought we should be drawing up plans, so Mr Struth called a meeting and took the chair. He called for opinions. Within a few minutes arguments were raging. He stood it for a while then suddenly rapped the table 'meeting abandoned'. That was the end of tactic talks at Rangers.

Bob McPhail, who joined Rangers in 1927, noted similar recollections in his life story:

He never talked about the tactics of football or never told you how you should play. You were the professional footballer so shouldn't need to be told. His job was to get you fit and motivate you and make you realise the importance of playing for Rangers.

These reflections from some of the most important players in the club's history provide a valuable insight into how Struth went about his business. Consideration of managerial style is the debate of the modern game and not one that is particularly relevant here. In the early days of football, and probably up to the sixties, managers offered little guidance on playing the game. Their influence extended to selecting the eleven best players they had available to them. Even then, the selection was often made by the committee. Struth had influence on the selection in the early years, but in modern parlance, he would be marked out as a man manager rather than a tactician.

Cunningham described Struth's impact and influence on the side in these words:

> He was a master of psychology. He could always persuade us, even when we thought we were crippled, [that] we were fit. Many a man declared himself unfit, but found himself playing all the same. He was the greatest practical psychologist I have ever known.

Struth also had great rapport with the players and often displayed his acute sense of humour. One incident in which Cunningham and Alan Morton were involved was related by biographer Harry Andrew. The two players faced off at half-time in the Celtic Park dressing room after a first half in which Morton was repeatedly caught offside. Cunningham shouted to the winger, 'Can you not stay onside, you wee devil?' Morton was rarely frustrated or ruffled, but on this occasion he rose up to his full five feet four inches and told his six-foot teammate that he took exception to his remark. 'I'm not standing for that,' he said. 'Who di' you think you are?'

A raw nerve had been touched and things threatened to get out of hand until the manager intervened. Struth remarked, 'Why don't you two pick on someone your own size?' In a moment, the tension was eased as both players laughed, apologising profusely to each other. The gift of peace-making needs little fuss and Struth was a smart exponent. Inwardly, however, he welcomed the passion for the game that the two had shown.

Bill Struth – a man's man

As the players went through their training routine each day under George Livingstone or Jimmy Kerr, Struth watched closely from the main stand. He watched every player and their gait, identifying those who were perhaps limited by injury and understanding the root cause of their debilitation. In that way, he could use his vast experience to assist the trainers in getting the players into good shape. Sometimes, he watched through interest in their conditioning, but when he was aware of injuries, he would put his medical training and experience in Bellahouston Hospital to good use.

Often when a player was injured and unable to come to Ibrox the next day, Struth would call at the player's house. One recalled in the *Weekly News* of 1954:

I'll never forget being helped home by my brother, hardly being able to walk after getting a bad knock on the Saturday. On Sunday Mr Struth arrived in a taxi. He talked to me for a long time and told me what treatment I was to get, convinced me I wasn't as bad as I thought, and had me walking bravely around the bedroom before he left. What's more, his thoughtfulness impressed my wife, telling her he would be sending the trainer round the next day and to be sure to draw back those crisp clean cotton sheets as the trainers were not always so careful with their embrocation.

There are countless instances of players declaring themselves unfit, only for Struth to persuade them otherwise. He would often say, 'What's this I hear about an injury, m'boy? You're a big strong chap and when you go out there with a blue jersey on your back, you're not going to bother about a twinge.' The message was always delivered in such a convincing matter-of-fact way that players were won over and aches and pains would no longer seem so serious or debilitating. While it may sound as though Struth was reckless in his care or attention to injuries, it was not quite as it seemed. His intervention generally followed a word from trainers Livingstone or Dixon on the nature and extent of the injury. Only then did Struth consider whether it was actually realistic for the player to take to the field. When the injury was debilitating, Struth ensured that his boys received the best of medical treatment and that the most up-to-date medical equipment was available at Ibrox.

Despite his insistence that players receive the best of medical care, Struth was not averse to trying his own remedies. Throughout his career, he was always on the lookout for more effective ways to treat that bugbear for all footballers, the pulled muscle. One of the many cures he tried created an uncomfortable situation for Bob McPhail. After sustaining an injury, McPhail was treated at Ibrox, by Struth, before going home. The treatment involved the application of a new type of poultice containing a particularly pungent preparation. 'Maybe they were kidding me,' said Bob, 'but they told me it was certain intestines of a sheep.'

Anyway, poultice and all, McPhail was in church the following morning. It was a very warm day. The sun streamed through the stained-glass windows and directly on to the McPhail family pew, where the young Ranger was soon aware that the man next to him was becoming restive. The lady in front looked over her shoulder twice, a very troubled expression on her face. All around him, something seemed to be troubling the entire congregation. The stench from the 'pioneering poultice' was absolutely putrid and McPhail had to leave swiftly. Not everything Mr Struth tried was a success.

Despite occasional failures, Struth had mastered the gentle art of persuasion with his players, and they firmly believed that he knew more about their fitness than they did. After all, he could draw on his experience as a trainer and his time at Bellahouston, so they saw him as something of a guru in medicine. He would even send them out on to the pitch with a packet of glucose energy tablets in their pocket, telling them to pop one in their mouth if they felt weary, and this would reinvigorate them. In reality, the effect was probably negligible, but having an energy supplement in their pocket gave the players a psychological boost, helping them to get a second wind when necessary.

Struth always tried to ensure that he had a good bond with the players. Indeed, his bond with the team in the twenties was greater than at any other period. He knew many of the players from his time as trainer, of course, and, although they were aware that he had to distance himself from that day-to-day interface, they shared some harmony with the Boss – quite literally. In these times, the Rangers players were a pretty intimidating bunch, with many six footers, but they enjoyed music sessions with Struth after training. Often this rugged group would waltz with each other to tunes played on a gramophone, under the command of their manager.

Struth loved to play the piano, which was located in the Blue Room in the new grandstand. He used it as a way of relaxing after a match or a hard day's work. Self-taught, he was not what could be considered a good pianist, but he had quite a repertoire of Scottish songs, ballads, hymns and psalms.

Tommy Cairns, interviewed by the *Sunday Express*, told the story of a remarkable scene around the piano when Bob McPhail sat beside Struth at the keys. Unlike the Boss, McPhail was an accomplished pianist, and Cairns recalled:

> Bob embarked on the fine old hymn 'There is a Green Hill Far Away' with Mr Struth listening intently. 'Now, Bob,' said Mr Struth at the finish, 'play my favourite, "By Cool Siloam's Shady Rill", and I'll sing it for you.' And there in the quiet of the Blue Room, Mr Struth, apparently dour, aloof, steel-minded manager of the mighty Rangers, sang a hymn to the accompaniment of one of his players.

It was not the first time that Struth was to be heard singing within the stadium. Each Friday afternoon he would do a check of the main stand to ensure it was clean, and he would take the opportunity to test the microphones, but that was really an excuse to indulge himself. He clearly fancied himself as a bit of a singer and it was not unusual to hear his voice booming out from the PA system, crooning his way through some contemporary ballad.

He was never heard to give a team a dressing-down, no matter how bad they had been. He would have considered it a breach of his personal code to show too much disappointment in defeat or too much elation in victory. His philosophy was that, if the players had done badly, they knew and didn't need him to point out the obvious.

Struth developed a close connection with most of his players and much of what we can ascertain about his character arises from the numerous anecdotes coming out of the dressing room, each invariably glowing with sentiment towards the Boss. He may well have exercised control over his players, but that control was not dictatorial. He carried the respect of his players, and rather than telling them what to do with their lives and careers, he steered them in a direction that he thought was best, not just for Rangers, but for them, too.

On one occasion, Andy Cunningham came to see him, to say he wanted to earn some extra money by taking a job as a travelling salesman, selling biscuits. Cunningham was earning £8 a week, which was a big wage at the time compared to the man in the street. Struth pointed out to Cunningham that he could not expect to walk around Glasgow during the week selling biscuits, and then turn up at Ibrox on a Saturday ready to play a strenuous match.

Struth recalled, 'I had to tell him I expected my players to be fresh and fit for the job.' Cunningham's respect was such that he did not even attempt to argue or debate the point. 'You are perfectly right, Mr Struth,' he replied, and that was the last that was ever heard on the subject. Of course, Cunningham's decision was not simply motivated by Struth's guidance on what was good for his fitness. It is doubtful if he would have figured in the team if he had followed through with his original plans. Struth could influence, but he would have had his way, too.

Struth also had an uncanny knack of knowing what the players were up to when they were away from Ibrox – and an unerring way of letting the players know that he knew. He would say, 'I'm surprised you were seen drinking in that pub,' the subliminal message being don't be seen in that pub again!

He was always able to let Bob McPhail know that he knew he had been to church on Sunday. McPhail could never understand how he knew until it emerged that he was friendly with one of the elders at the McPhail family church in Barrhead.

The caring compassionate side of Struth's nature was never far from the surface. When Bob McPhail's father passed away, a private family funeral in Barrhead was arranged. Unannounced and with no fuss, Struth arrived at the graveside to pay his respects. He had gone out of his way to establish where the service was being held and wanted to show his support to his player at a difficult time. Such acts of kindness and thoughtfulness were truly appreciated by the players, and while some of the rules might not have met with universal approval, they recognised to a man what Struth was doing for them. He wanted them to have the same aspirations as himself – to be the very best.

Struth made it his business to know as much as possible about his players' private lives and encouraged them to confide in him if they had a problem. It was not unusual for him to ask someone who had been off form to come to his office. Going up the marble staircase, they had time to prepare themselves for the criticism that they felt was surely on the way. Instead, Struth would look up from his desk and say, 'What you need, m'boy, is a tonic.' Seconds later a bewildered Ranger would be on his way back to the dressing room, self-consciously carrying a bottle of Sanatogen.

Despite the strict regime and code of conduct that Struth applied, the club had a real sense of togetherness. After his retirement, the manager commented to the *Weekly News*:

Spur of the moment singsongs have always been popular at Ibrox, but it does seem to me that players in general have the same light-hearted approach to things these days on the field. The work plus play policy means players do not mingle enough as a complete outfit. Nothing is worse for a team than meeting just once a week, an hour before the match.

Struth went on to give an insight into his managerial ethos:

I made up my mind from the start [that] I would regard the players as part of my family. That meant keeping an eye on their private and football lives. Such things, for instance, as seeing that they put the winter woollies on at the right time. Of course, this made me sentimental about my players, especially when I had to part with an old friend or change his contract. I remember having to reduce Bertie Manderson's terms, as he dropped out of the side to make way for Dougie Gray. Bert came into my room and said, 'Howly smoke, I cannae live on that.' I transferred Bert to Bradford shortly afterwards, making it as easy as possible for him. That is another point that is often overlooked. It is not good business to squeeze the last out of a good servant. We have had many a good player, but we did not put them out of the game with a huge price on their head. I am proud of the phrase 'Once a Ranger, always a Ranger'. That is proof [that] I succeeded in what I set out to do.

THE TWENTIES – A PERIOD OF DOMINANCE

A taste of Europe – the Danish tours

While the League had been won in some style in 1921, the Scottish Cup brought continued heartache. William Wilton had presided as match secretary when the club won the trophy for the first time back in 1894, and his only success as manager came in 1903. Try as they might, Rangers could not recapture the trophy despite their undoubted dominance of the Scottish game. In the pre-war years under Wilton's tenure, Rangers succumbed to sides such as Falkirk, Dundee, Clyde (twice with Struth as trainer) and Hibernian. These were clubs that would not profess superiority over Rangers, but it did not inhibit their drive to succeed as, one by one, they ended the Ibrox side's hopes. Even the change of manager, with the arrival of Struth, did little to alter Rangers' fortunes in the competition. Under Struth, Rangers lost to Partick Thistle, Morton, Falkirk, Clyde and St Mirren. It was little wonder that there was talk of a 'Scottish Cup hoodoo' that dogged Rangers at every turn in the competition, or that they became the butt of the old music-hall jokes.

For the 1921 final against Partick Thistle, a pitifully low crowd of 28,294 turned out to watch. Numbers were reduced due to a boycott in protest at the doubling of admission costs and the switching of the venue from Hampden to Celtic Park. Rangers played in white shirts to accommodate Thistle's dark blue, their registered colour at the time. There was, apparently, no sign of pre-match nerves in the Partick dressing room. In fact, the players were treating it as a bit of a joke that they were playing the mighty Rangers – the team they trailed by 30 points in the League. The relaxed approach of the Jags' team paid dividends and, in a tight match, they grasped the only goal of the game, scoring when Rangers' Jimmy Bowie was off the field changing his shorts. It is the only time that Thistle have ever won the Scottish Cup, which provides some measure of the level of upset.

To help overcome yet another disappointment in the Cup, Rangers headed off on a three-match tour of Denmark, playing against Akademisk, B1903 and a Copenhagen Select. Their traumas began with the boat journey! Struth explained:

We were on our way to Copenhagen in 1921. We had just won the League with a record points haul. We had started a small celebration on the ship outside Leith. Before long things were heating up, but then the ship started to get in trouble. I won't forget that trip. All through, we did not get above four and a half knots. There was a strike on and we ran out of coal. Anything that would raise steam was burned, including the deck-chairs. Sandy Archibald, Tommy Cairns and myself borrowed candles from a steward and went to visit Andy Cunningham, Morton and Bucky McCandless. We held a wake over all three as they looked more dead than alive. I must admit that even the tough lads did not last much longer. One by one they slipped out to the side of the ship. Andy Cunningham was ill for days afterwards.

Over-indulgence plus choppy seas put a stop to the shenanigans.

Despite their journey, Rangers won all three matches on the tour, although none were emphatic victories. However, the tour was to be of some value, particularly in the final match when a skilful, tricky little forward called Carl Hansen caught the eye. Hansen made such an impression that Struth wanted him to return to Glasgow with Rangers the following day. Despite Struth's pleadings, Hansen was unable to accede to this sudden request, with matters of the heart playing a part, but he did agree to follow as soon as a work permit had been secured, and he duly made his way to Scotland.

Hansen's recollections of his arrival in Glasgow are fascinating:

The Rangers manager, Mr Struth, met me at the boat. I had been given a work permit as a student of modern languages, specifically English. I was going to study English all right – I had to as the only words I was fluent in were 'yes' and 'no'. It can be imagined what an interesting conversation Mr Struth and I carried on in the train back to Glasgow. He talked and talked, probably in an attempt to put me at my ease, and used sign language and descriptive gestures, while I nodded or shook my head according to what I hoped was the right answer. We could probably have made a fortune from that conversation had we put it on the stage.

Struth recalled his signing of Hansen just as fondly. He said, 'We went on our first foreign trip to Denmark in 1921 and brought back Carl Hansen.' In fact, it was Struth's first foreign trip, not Rangers' first one. The club had gone to Scandinavia in 1911. Struth continued, 'Hansen played so brilliantly I just could not resist. Seldom had I seen a player who could turn so quickly on the ball, and he was two footed. Worst luck, he got the fractured leg in his second [full] season. Any time he returned to Scotland he visited us.' Indeed, Hansen was to remain closely acquainted with Struth and the two men spent a lot of time together on these visits.

Hansen remained at Ibrox for three seasons between 1921–22 and 1923–24, when he returned to Denmark following the broken leg. He made a total of 23 competitive appearances plus 10 in friendly matches, scoring a remarkable 31 goals in the process. Only his slight build prevented him making an even bigger impact.

In 1921–22, Rangers finished as runners-up to Celtic in the League and their wretched luck in the Scottish Cup continued. Morton, who finished twelfth in the League, a distant 24 points behind the Ibrox men, were the opponents in the final this time. Confusion in the Rangers ranks over whether a free-kick on the edge of the box was direct or indirect did not distract Morton's Jamie Gourlay. His once in a lifetime shot, direct from the free-kick, gave the Cappielow men the lead in 12 minutes and they held out despite incessant and sometimes desperate attacking from the Light Blues. In fact, it was a 10-man Rangers, who lost Andy Cunningham midway through the first half. He had sustained a broken jaw and such was the severity of the injury that a concerned Struth left for Victoria Infirmary in an ambulance with the player, and did not return to Hampden.

The incident was typical of the compassion Struth showed for his players. He was a winner and the Cup was important to him, but Cunningham's welfare was of greater significance. Rangers lost the Cup, but the events marked Struth as a man of some dignity and benevolence. These actions did not go unnoticed by his players and his attention to Cunningham was just one example of many little things that built up the players' admiration for the Boss.

Rangers returned to Denmark at the end of the season, playing their first two matches against the same Copenhagen Select that had produced Carl Hansen a year earlier. The Ibrox side won both matches (1–0 and 3–0), and Hansen netted twice in the second match. The final match of the tour was against the Danish national side and what a tousy affair this ended up being, in stark contrast to the previous trip to Scandinavia. For Rangers, it afforded a very early glimpse into the perils of European football. The match ended 2–2 in front of 20,000 fans but the scoreline was incidental to the events on and off the park. The story was carried by one newspaper, the *Post*:

Willie Struth declared the Danish newspapers made the most of the scenes in Copenhagen. The chief Copenhagen newspaper considered that a complaint should be made to the Scottish Football Association about the ungentlemanly conduct and rough play of the Rangers players. Dear me! Are Rangers to be blamed for all the bother? According to the Danish critic, 'Paul Nicken, the Danish centre-forward, scored the second goal and the whole Rangers defence claimed offside. The referee was, and rightly so, of a different opinion.'

According to the same scribe, Rangers players would not allow any Danes to enter their dressing room at the interval and a few journalists and a cartoonist who tried to get admittance came out quicker than they went in. Later in the match, when Cairns had a goal disallowed for an infringement, the Rangers became crazy with the referee and yelled and bawled so that the game had almost to be abandoned.

During an attack on Rangers' goal, the Danish inside right was knocked down and got two smacks in the face from a 'Ger', but the referee only gave a free-kick and not a penalty. Even that, however, did not satisfy Rangers. They impeded the referee and would not retire the required distance to allow the kick to be taken. In exasperation he blew for full time.

Afterwards the Rangers players lined up and tried to get the Danish amateur team to do the same in order to say goodbye. This was too much for the Danes, who departed immediately. Suddenly, a spectator belonging to the worst slums in Copenhagen broke onto the field and struck a Rangers player. Meiklejohn ran to the rescue and at the same time the spectators from the cheap side of the enclosure dashed over the railings. Several Rangers got black eyes and bruises before they were escorted from the field by the Police and the now returned Danish players. The rough who started the row should have been jailed, but he was not caught. However, the 'Gers were the sole cause of the thrashing they got. Still, they are fine players and their fine technique and beautiful touches were greatly admired.

It is interesting that the Danes thought they could simply march into the Rangers dressing room at half-time, which may betray the amateur culture that existed in Denmark at the time. For all Struth's concern to maintain high standards at the club, there was a line that could not be crossed and it seems that if he did not unleash his players, he did not exactly haul them back to the dressing room. There can be little doubt that these Rangers players could look after themselves and displayed the team spirit and togetherness that Struth fostered. He may have been dismayed at the press coverage, but he would have had a deep sense of satisfaction with the unity of his charges.

Celebrations in the Jubilee year

In 1922–23, Airdrie were Rangers' closest challengers, and Carl Hansen wrote his own little piece in the history books. He became the first foreign player to score in an Old Firm match in the 2–0 New Year's Day win over Celtic. The win helped Rangers to the title, which they clinched with a 1–0 win against Kilmarnock in the penultimate game of the season. Once again, the Scottish Cup remained out of reach. The club's interest ended before January was out, at the hands of lowly Ayr United.

One of the highlights of the season was when the club celebrated its Jubilee on 9 April 1923 at Ferguson and Foresters Restaurant, hosted by Chairman Sir John Ure Primrose. It is generally acknowledged that the club was formed in 1872, but the timing of this event may well have been inspired by the date of the season. If the board considered that the club was formed in the 1872–73 season, a fifty years celebration would be quite acceptable in the 1922–23 season, albeit the actual date of formation was a year out. In any case, the dinner was a huge success with the club's honorary president, Sir John T. Cargill, providing the toast for the evening.

Bill Struth was naturally in attendance along with his players and a few other notaries, such as Jock Drummond, Alex Smith, Willie Reid and Alec Bennett. Possibly the most celebrated guest was Tom Vallance, who, while not one of the original four founders of the club, was to all intents and purposes one of its Gallant Pioneers. There were guests from rival clubs, too – Clyde, Celtic, Raith Rovers, Airdrie, Albion Rovers, Partick Thistle, Hearts, Alloa, St Mirren, Dundee and Hamilton were all represented.

The Celtic manager, Willie Maley, who was to become a great friend of Bill Struth's, proposed a toast to the Rangers chairman on behalf of the Scottish League. Struth was well acquainted with the Maley family, of course, having served under Willie's brother Alex at Clyde. Maley's words were well received, and he said that as an old friendly enemy of Rangers, they rejoiced that they had one of nature's gentlemen to give them wise counsel, and that his friendship with Sir John was one of his most cherished memories. There is no doubt that fierce rivalry existed between the sides back then, but the boundaries of respect were high and there was considerable friendship between the senior officers.

In the summer of 1923, Rangers travelled to Switzerland where they played, and won, six games in ten days, scoring 32 times and conceding just two goals. The tour brought more of the trials and tribulations that seemed to dog encounters on foreign fields. Struth recalled:

We played in a small country town called Les Cheaux des Fundes. The previous games were played in places such as Geneva, Basle and Berne and had been sporting affairs. The day started well. We had been met at the train station by a reception committee, complete with band. We lined up and marched down the street. The Italian band was smartly dressed with long feathers in their caps. We had no idea where we were going and we were marched straight into a pub. I asked the interpreter what was going on and he said they were trying to entertain us.

I had to point out we were there to play football and we'd better get ready for it. Off we then went to the ground, the game got under way and it was clear the Swiss were out for blood. One actually played in glasses – I thought he needed stronger ones, the number of times he barged into our players. The team got fed up with this approach and went looking for retribution. Jock Jameson was left-back, Jock Nicholson left-half, Hector Lawson wing, Tommy Cairns inside. They had a plan. First I heard, 'Let him come on, Hector, and I'll fix him.' There was a succession of such remarks. 'Give me a short pass, Jock, and I'll take the tackle. We've got to teach them not to be so rough.' Perhaps not put as politely as that, but you get the gist. I can only report that Cairns left his boots behind as they were hacked to bits.

We won 3–0 but were more concerned with getting the team away with their shins intact. Before the match we were told we were going to be presented with watches, but when the time came they said they did not have enough money. I gave them £10 to pay for them and clear their feet again. There was no band to play us off when we were leaving, though.

After their traumas in previous tours, it is perhaps not surprising there was no foreign close-season tour in 1924! The autumn of 1923 brought an event that probably had as great an impact as the signing of Maurice Johnston in July 1989. Struth had looked carefully at his attack and how it could be improved and his eye was drawn to Parkhead, and more particularly, to Celtic's centre-forward Tom 'Tully' Craig. Astonishingly, Celtic had no objections to the approach and the transfer was duly completed. It was a move that Celtic would ultimately regret. Tully was a craftsman, equally at home as an attacker or in the half-back line, and he was to make as significant a contribution as any other player. The title was clinched in comfortable fashion again, Airdrie trailing in the runners-up spot, nine points behind. Once more, there was no such joy in the Scottish Cup as Hibernian ended Rangers' interest.

Dominance, but no Scottish Cup

The twenties were fast becoming a period of total domination by Rangers. The *Weekly Record* of January 1924 reflected as much when they reported:

It has been instructive to watch Rangers this season. They have entered on every game, with a vim and forcing power, maintained for a long period, which was almost new to Scottish football. They pursued the ball with relentless speed; they tackled with great dash and vigour, and smashed the ball goalwards with amazing directness and strength. They were ahead of the referee's whistle often at taking free-kicks. They gave the observer the impression that no one but themselves had the right to kick the ball.

It was obvious that Struth's influence was indomitable as the team took the field each week with huge belief that they were, quite simply, the best team in Scotland. During the next season, 1924–25, Rangers battled it out with Airdrie for a third time in succession, and the drama played out right up to the final day. Once again, Rangers prevailed with a 1–0 win over Ayr United. That goal from Billy McCandless was enough to take the Championship to Ibrox for the fifth time in six seasons. The Scottish Cup, however, proved hugely disappointing again. Rangers went down to a dreadful 5–0 defeat by Celtic in the semi-final. Cognisant of the importance of the fixture, the crowd turned up at Hampden in their droves – the 101,714 attendance registered as a record for a club fixture at the time. It also highlighted the massive and growing interest in Old Firm games.

Rangers' disappointment was compounded by their knowledge that they were clearly better than the men from Parkhead. They had already beaten Celtic home and away in the League, by margins of 4–1 and 1–0, and they triumphed by 4–1 in the final of the Glasgow Cup. The Celts had trailed Rangers by 16 points in the League, so it was a shock that they managed to defeat Rangers at all, never mind by such a huge margin. It seemed the Cup hoodoo was destined never to end.

One bright spot in the season was the return of Tommy Muirhead. He had been one of Rangers' stalwarts from the day he arrived from Hibs in 1916. He had turned out for an Army Select against Scotland, following which he was introduced to the Scotland trainer – a certain Bill Struth. A year later, Muirhead was transferred to Rangers, but after playing just a few games, he left to take a commission at Trinity College, Oxford. He was then posted to France, as a lieutenant, which almost cost him his life. During one battle, his helmet was pierced by shrapnel and, although he survived, some pieces remained in his skull until the day he died.

Muirhead was invalided out of the army and began his career at Ibrox, in earnest, in season 1919–20. Then in the middle of season 1923–24, he dropped a bombshell. An old army friend had contacted him, asking if he could recommend anyone to help start a team in Boston, USA. After much deliberation, Muirhead decided he fancied the opportunity himself. He had been at Ibrox a while and felt he needed a new challenge. When he told Struth that he wouldn't be re-signing at the end of the season because he was going to America, Muirhead said that Struth looked him up and down and replied, 'Get out. Away with you.'

Struth did not believe that Muirhead would leave, or would even contemplate leaving, but sure enough, come the season's end, he was Boston bound. He quickly began his duties in the States and established a reasonable side, which did well in his first season. At the season's end, Muirhead decided to come over to Scotland for a holiday. Naturally, one of his first ports of call was Ibrox to visit his old teammates. Muirhead said, 'During one of my visits, Bill called me in one day and asked me if I would come back as a player, and I said I could hardly do that. I had an obligation to the folk in America who had treated me so well. Bill, though, made the point that I had done what I was asked to do (set up a team) and eventually I was persuaded to return.'

Muirhead played for the first team from the end of December 1924 and never regretted his decision. The team went from strength to strength and Muirhead played his part. He later said of Struth, 'He was a wonderful man. He had such a great personality that enabled him to control people so well.'

1925–26 – a season of disappointment

If the frustration of the Cup was to cloud the 1924–25 season, the following year was lost in a haze of disenchantment. The club finished the season trophyless and failed to reach the final in any of the Cup competitions. The Championship turned out something of a disaster as the side lost thirteen league matches and plunged to sixth position – its lowest league placing – while Celtic took the title. In mitigation, it was an horrendous season for injuries. Almost every first-team player succumbed at some point. First-team regulars were regularly posted absent, two and three at a time.

Both Struth and trainer George Livingstone battled to get men on to the field, but no matter the strength of the manager's psychology, players were quite simply unable to play. It is important to recognise that, in this period, clubs relied on their favoured eleven players. Others were given a run from time to time, but the eleven generally picked themselves each week. For that reason, generations of fans always remembered their favourite team, whether ending Miller, Brand and Wilson in the sixties, or Henderson, Cairns and Morton as it did in the twenties. However, in that fateful season of 1925–26, there was no settled side. Whereas 10 players had each played over

36 games in the previous season, just six players played more than 30 matches in the campaign of 1925–26.

Of all those who suffered injury that year, the biggest loss was Davie Meiklejohn. 'The General', as he was known, was irreplaceable, earning this tribute from former player and director, George Brown. 'Meiklejohn was the best of them all. In attack he could spread the most delicate passes, yet if he had to fall back to defence, he was as hard as nails. More than that, he could read a game brilliantly.'

However, the performance of the side that year could not be laid entirely at the door of injuries and bad luck. Struth had to deal with a side in transition when he took up the manager's reins, and he would have to do so again. The team was ageing and new players would be needed in order for the club to regain control in Scottish football. Those who arrived that season included Dougie Gray, Jimmy Marshall and Jimmy Fleming. They would make their own mark on Rangers' fortunes in the future. In his authoritative club history, *Eleven Great Years*, John Allan describes the signing of Marshall. The account gives some insight into Struth's astuteness:

When Manager Struth called on the Marshall household and suggested that boy James would look well in Rangers rig, his father said, 'Yes, very good but we plan to make James a doctor and that comes first.' Struth replied, 'Right, let's see how we can make it work for both of us.' Before that powwow had ended, the life plan for the boy Marshall had been mapped out. The scheme went through without a flaw. James Marshall came into the team, carried on his medical studies, and won everything that could be won on the playing fields, and now it's Doctor James Marshall at your service!

Then there was the signing of the man who would go on to play a record 948 games for the club – Dougie Gray. The acquisition of Gray was not straightforward and Struth had to go to some length to sign the talented full-back from Muggiemoss. Bobby Moffat explained:

Dougie had been playing for a Scottish Junior Select, if I remember rightly, in England, and was due back in Glasgow this particular evening. Many clubs were desperate to sign Dougie and when we got to the station, they were all represented on the platform. But Mr Struth dodged in front of them all, pulled Dougie aside when he stepped off the train and fixed him up with Rangers.

One of the few bright spots in the season came in August, when 30,000 fans watched the unfurling of the 1924–25 league flag at the Rangers Sports. The wife of ex-bailie Joseph Buchanan performed the ceremony, and Bill Struth duly presented her with an ornate manicure set. By then, the sports day was a popular fixture in the calendar, attracting athletes from far and wide. *The Post*, referring to the meeting, noted, 'The brightest sports of the athletic season are associated with The Rangers FC. Ibrox Park is the home of records.'

The crowd was attracted by the prospect of records and Struth encouraged some of the best athletes in the country to attend. However, the attendance can be only partially accounted for by the athletics. For many, the main attraction was the traditional five-a-side tournament, which Rangers, in particular, would use to introduce new signings. This gave supporters an early chance to weigh up the new recruits, and also gave the players themselves an introduction into life at Ibrox. The 'fives' were a huge draw, and Rangers, Celtic, Third Lanark, Partick Thistle and Queen's Park usually took part.

William Wilton had helped establish the Sports at Ibrox back in 1895; Bill Struth raised the event to another dimension. Crowds of 6,000 eventually became 60,000 and the most famous athletes in the world flocked to Ibrox. Struth had experience of what was involved in organising these meetings, albeit on a much smaller scale at Shawfield. Now he had the scope to cultivate something quite special in a setting fit for the very best that the world of athletics had to offer.

New signings and fresh impetus

Normal service was resumed in 1926–27 when Rangers regained the flag with 5 points to spare from Motherwell. New signings Fleming and 'Doc' Marshall proved pivotal to the success. Fleming netted 21 times in League and Cup. The Scottish Cup remained out of their grasp, and in the close season of 1927, Rangers acquired a player who had, at least, held the Cup with his club. Perhaps he would be their inspiration and turn the Light Blues' fortunes in that competition. Bob McPhail was acquired from Airdrie for a fee of £5,000 – a record signing at the time. Struth, proud of his new acquisition, commented that there was, 'Never a better player signed'. Indeed, McPhail went on to collect nine League Championships and six Scottish Cup winner's medals with Rangers, reaching third in the club's all-time top scorers list with 320 goals from 505 appearances.

In his final season for Airdrie, McPhail had scored 33 goals in 31 games and was hot property, attracting interest from Everton as well as Rangers. He was very happy at Broomfield, but Airdrie decided to cash in on the player, putting him on the transfer list, much to McPhail's bemusement. The move generated additional interest from Aston Villa, Leyton Orient, Fulham and Derby. The transfer was, in McPhail's own words, 'turning into a circus'. Sealed bids were invited from all interested parties, but on the day they were due to be opened, McPhail made himself unavailable. He had his eye on a move somewhere closer to home – Rangers. The following week he met Struth in the Kenilworth Hotel and the matter was concluded in a matter of minutes. McPhail was a Rangers player and after the deal was signed, Bill Struth revealed that the Light Blues would never have been able to sign the player if it had not been for the assistance of the Airdrie manager, Davie Martin. Although Everton were enthusiastic to land him, Martin was very keen for McPhail to join up at Ibrox, even if it meant a financial loss. Everyone was satisfied – especially Bill Struth!

Struth welcomed McPhail with a firm handshake and advised, 'Young man, you are with a big club now. I wish you the best of luck.' After a meal in a city centre restaurant, he was driven to Ibrox by the manager. Never famed for his driving ability, the journey prompted McPhail to comment that '. . . he had remembered better drivers'.

Struth, ironically, believed he may have made a huge mistake when he signed McPhail. When he watched him play a Scotland international – his first as a Rangers player – the inside-forward had a proverbial nightmare in the first half and seemed not quite the player Struth had expected. The manager later revealed to the *Sunday Express* what had happened:

> I could not believe my judgement could be so wrong. I decided there must be something up and went down to the dressing room at half-time. 'Look here, what's the matter with you, McPhail? I know you can play better than this.' 'Yes, Mr Struth,' he replied. 'I feel awful.' Then, the story came out. Apparently, just before the team were due to leave the dressing room, the trainer gave every man half a glass of port and brandy. Bob was a teetotaller and all the 'pepping-up' did was to upset him. 'Right,' I said, 'put your finger down your throat and get rid of all that.' He did it and in the second half the difference was unbelievable and McPhail ended as just about the best man on the field.

The match was a Scotland v. Wales Home International and was played at Ibrox on 27 October 1928. The game had some significance for Rangers, because the club used it as an opportunity to open their new grandstand and their reconstructed ground, although the official opening would not take place until 1 January 1929.

Struth's intervention was probably facilitated by the game being played at Rangers' ground. Not many managers would have taken the trouble to go downstairs, or perhaps even been permitted to go to the dressing room to establish what was going wrong with their man. Although McPhail was representing Scotland, Struth was still concerned about the welfare of his player. Given his distaste for any player drinking before a match, it's likely that Struth had a few choice words for the Scotland trainer, too.

Work hard for good rewards

Bill Struth expected a lot of his players – Rangers had to be the top team in the country – but he liked to ensure that it was not all one way. He was nothing if not a pragmatist when it came to work and reward, which he later explained thus: 'Don't imagine, though, I expected everything with nothing in return. That did not breed loyalty.' In comparison to the modern era, when wages have risen to quite obscene levels, the money that Rangers players received seems quite paltry. Their initial wage was £8 per week with a £2 win bonus, and £1 for a draw. In the close season, the wage dropped to £6. When Bob McPhail hung up his boots after thirteen years, his wages remained unchanged. Struth regarded it as an honour to play for Rangers, and the wage structure concept never altered until Graeme Souness came to the club in 1986, although the basic wage had changed somewhat since these early days.

Players who were transferred to Rangers could expect to receive a share of the kitty, fixed at £650 when transfer fees were typically around the £5,000 or £6,000 level. This share increased marginally in the latter years of Struth's reign when it rose to a maximum of £750.

Struth's attitude to recompense for his players was quite simple. He believed that they were well rewarded and they were, in his mind, fortunate to receive the adulation and fine treatment that Rangers players were accustomed to. He also considered that each one was part of a team and no single player was greater than any other. In particular, he did not believe in star players, or that any of his charges should be on special wages. As he saw it, 'The best player in the world is only as good as his other teammates. Nobody is better than anyone else at Ibrox and the players are not slow to let you know.'

He went on to describe his rationale around players' wages:

> If half the members of the team were on top money and the other half paid less, can you persuade me the lesser paid players would be satisfied? I am certain they would not be. Football is a team game. Every member is dependent more or less on his colleagues for his success. A player with a lower rate of pay would not be disposed to go all out to help the fellow receiving more money than himself. In such circumstances, team spirit is impossible, success very improbable. Rangers do not keep their men by paying fancy wages. Not a single player receives more than a first-class player across the border – £8 a week plus bonuses.

If wages in the twenties cannot be compared to the rewards on offer for the modern player, the professionals at Ibrox were still regarded as well paid by most. However, in the close season of 1927, one dissenter was quite disdainful of the professional football player. Curiously, it was Robert Cumming 'RC' Hamilton, who was a major figure in Rangers' pre-war history. He captained the Invincibles team of 1898–99 and to this day remains the club's top goal-scorer against Celtic. In a speech in the Elgin Town Hall, he savaged footballers with comments that seemed to hang heavy with the bitter taste of resentment:

> Football is one of the rottenest professions anyone could take up. A boy must be one of the top dogs before he

Bill Struth at around 10

Bill Struth's son, William,
possibly at Shawfield around 1909

(Back Row, L to R): William McCulloch (Brother-in-Law), Helen (Struth) McCulloch (Sister), Bill Struth, Kate Struth (Wife)

(Front Row, L to R): William Struth (Father), William Struth (Son), Isabella Struth (Mother)

Bill Struth (Back Right) with Jimmy Wilson (Left Middle with cap)
at Inverleith, Edinburgh, around 1895

Kate Struth in Order of the
Eastern Star regalia

Left: Bill Struth at Orwell
Parish Church, Milnathort

Studio portrait of Bill Struth
in Red Cross uniform

Left: Bill Struth in Red Cross uniform around
1916, possibly taken at Bellahouston Hospital

Mattha Gemmell – Struth's great
companion at Clyde Football Club

Right: Alan Morton, Bill Struth and
Davie Meiklejohn (Left to Right)

Bill Struth relaxed on holiday
(location unknown)

Happy times for Bill and Kate Struth

Bill's son, William – A proper gent

Right: Bill Struth, Alison Dallas and
Alice Dallas on holiday in Elgin

Bill Struth (middle far right) and Rangers party receive the gold key (on table) from the Mayor of Pittsburgh, Pennsylvania – 1928 Tour

Back Row: J Buchanan, J Simpson, T Hamilton, J Smith, J Marshall (insert); *Middle Row:* J Kerr, R McDonald, D Meiklejohn, T Craig, D Gray, T Muirhead, R Hamilton; *Front Row:* A Archibald, G Brown, J Fleming, Baillie Duncan Graham, Bill Struth, R McPhail, W Nicholson, A Morton

Snow ball fight in North America – 1928

On board the *Berengaria* –
1930 American Tour

Above: End of
a hard day on
board the *RMS
Andania* – 1928

Left to Right:
D Meiklejohn,
J Bowie, B Struth,
T Muirhead, and
A Cunningham on
RMS Andania – 19
American Tour

Bill Struth – The Gentleman

Left: Mr Struth – A Highland Gent

Billy Williamson, Joe Craven, Johnny Hubbard, Willie Woodburn, Jimmy Smith and
Willie Thornton survey the blueprint as Bill Struth outlines his plans for Ibrox

Captive audience of players and partners at the Rangers Ball,
with Mrs Alice Dallas seated to the left of Mr Struth

Bill Struth and his 1930's saloon

At home in Dalkeith Avenue,
Dumbreck, Glasgow

could make anything out of it, and the game did him more harm than good. At least 75 per cent of players I have come into contact with are men who were previously used to getting 30 shillings a week but who in pre-war days were making up to £4 a week. That meant that of the £4, the wife got the usual 25 shillings a week and the pub got the rest. The man got into the method of living that was absolutely false.

Although RC's words were not specifically directed at the Rangers players, Bill Struth was stirred to respond in defence of professional players:

I certainly think he [RC] is greatly exaggerating. I don't need to elaborate. You know Doctor James Paterson very well, don't you? Well, you remember he was enabled to take his classes in medicine at the university. The lad Marshall who is doing so well for us is also studying medicine and is greatly assisted by his football salary. I assure you that Alan Morton regrets he did not turn professional sooner. Surely Alan, who is a mining engineer and would probably always have a good position, would not have joined the professional ranks if he had thought he was to associate with men such as described by ex-bailie Hamilton. I would say that 99 per cent of players greatly improve their position by taking the salary of a professional. It was quite ridiculous to suggest that they are addicted to neglecting their wives and spending their wages in public houses.

Struth had, of course, entered the arena of sport as a

professional, so he was well aware of the rewards and how these could be abused. However, with his philosophies well based in the fitness and welfare of his players, he would have found it difficult to reconcile the experiences of Hamilton with those around him at Ibrox. The story highlighted the changes that had taken place at Ibrox since Hamilton had departed. Perhaps the Rangers players of an earlier period were not quite the professionals whom Struth modelled. Perhaps, also, the story highlights that Struth had higher principles and standards for his players than Willie Wilton had. The Rangers manager's response was sharp and supportive to his boys, and, in the twenties, carried much more respect than the ramblings of a player who had long since departed the game. This was Struth's era and, by now, his methods were without question.

1928 AND A NEW DAWN OVER IBROX

The end of the hoodoo

Rangers entered the 1927–28 season with every confidence. They were champions and they commenced the campaign with virtually the same side that had secured the title the previous year. They got the race off to the best of starts with a win at Pittodrie and by April 1928, they looked to be on course to retain the league flag, although Celtic were in close attendance. However, the month was dominated by a fixture of immense importance to Rangers and Struth. The Light Blues had fought their way to the final of the Scottish Cup for the second time in as many years. Their opponents at Hampden Park would be old rivals Celtic, who had ended Rangers' hopes of lifting the trophy two seasons earlier in embarrassing fashion.

Bob McPhail, in an interview for the *Rangers News* in May 1980, recalled:

We didn't have any special preparations for the match. Bill Struth took us to Hampden, having told us the team days before. Our captain, Tommy Muirhead, was injured and David Meiklejohn was captain in his place. We didn't even have special tactics for the game. Bill Struth said football was our profession and we should use our common sense. We used our own brains and there were no complaints afterwards.

This was to be the first Old Firm final since the infamous 1909 game, when the Cup was withheld after rioting. Again, a record crowd for the time, of 118,115, gathered inside Hampden. Match reports capture the emotion and the tension as Celtic played with a stiff wind behind them in the first half. They nearly took the lead early in the match with a shot from outside-right Connolly, but it was deflected by Rangers goalkeeper Tom Hamilton. The ball fell into the path of Celtic outside-left Adam McLean, who sent it blazing high over the bar. It is often said that the outcome of matches can turn on a moment of brilliance or bad luck, or, as in this case, a failure to take a gilt-edged opportunity. Had Celtic scored, anxiety could well have influenced the outcome. Rangers were well minded that the Cup had not been inside Ibrox for twenty-five years. On such moments are the destinations of trophies decided. The teams went in at the interval with the scoresheet blank and the tension building.

With just 10 minutes played in the second half, Rangers were awarded a penalty when Celtic full-back Willie McStay punched out a shot from Light Blue's centre Jimmy Fleming that had left the keeper, John Thomson, scrambling. Those closest to the action, including Davie Meiklejohn and Bob McPhail, claimed that the ball had actually crossed the line before McStay got his hands to it, but the referee ignored their appeals and pointed to the spot.

Rangers' captain for the day, Davie Meiklejohn, grasped the ball, and took responsibility for possibly the most important spot-kick in the club's history at that time. It called for enormous character from Meiklejohn, since he was not the regular penalty taker. Normally, either McPhail or Cunningham would take the kicks, but both stood aside on this occasion. In fact, the routine had been for a penalty taker to continue to take the spot-kicks until he missed. Just prior to the match, Bob McPhail had scored three in a row, but then missed one, so he would not have been expected to take the kick, but he did not fancy it anyway. Years later he admitted that his timing in missing that penalty had been impeccable because he would have 'hated' to have taken the kick in the final.

Who knows what must have gone through Struth's mind as he watched Meiklejohn pause before beginning his run-up to take the penalty? He had never savoured victory in the blue riband of Scottish football, having lost the finals of 1910 and 1912 with Clyde, then endured similar wretched fortune with Rangers. His own personal hoodoo had lasted almost as long as the Ibrox club's jinx. 'Cometh the hour, cometh the man', he would frequently say to his players. In that critical moment, the strength and fortitude of his captain was put to the test.

Later, Meiklejohn related his own thoughts at the time, and they showed a man whose mind was spinning, but who retained enough conviction to do what he had to do:

I saw, in a flash, the whole picture of our striving to win the Cup. I saw all the dire flicks of fortune which had beaten us when we should have won. That ball should have been in the net. It was on the penalty spot instead. If I scored, we would win; if I failed, we could be beaten. It was a moment of agony.

Indeed, if he had missed, the trophy could well have gone east, because that had been the way of things for Rangers in the Scottish Cup. To all intents, Meiklejohn had conceded that the team may not have recovered from the disappointment of being denied a goal that they believed they had scored, only to see the penalty missed.

Meiklejohn hit the ball well and true, and it blasted into the net behind Celtic's young keeper. His assessment of the importance of the kick was correct. Confidence went surging through the ranks and Rangers went on from there to score three more times with further goals from Bob McPhail and a Sandy Archibald double, smashing all remnants of the 'hoodoo'. It had taken the club twenty-five years to win the Cup for the fifth time. For Struth, it was a first and he showed some emotion at the end as he saluted his heroes with a tear in his eye.

After the victory, Struth walked into the dressing room and shook hands with every player, never uttered a word, then walked out again. He feared that if he dared to speak, he would be completely overcome with the sentiment of the moment. To the players, his emotions were confined to the twitching of a little nerve in his jaw, but his heart must have been bursting with pride. It was a huge moment for Rangers, but particularly for Bill Struth. The players got an £8 bonus for winning the Cup, equivalent to a week's wages. It was a nice reward for the times, and a jeweller presented each of the players with a watch to commemorate the victory.

Meiklejohn relayed his delight to the supporters through a message published in the *Daily Record*:

I am proud and happy to be the captain of the Rangers team that won the Scottish Cup after twenty-five years striving. In our victory we think of our old teammates Arthur Dixon, Tommy Cairns and Bertie Manderson who helped to keep the colours of the old club flying, and who with the welfare of their former teammates at heart, sent us messages of good cheer just before the great tussle began.

Never again would there be talk of a hoodoo. In fact, Rangers went on to become as familiar with the trophy as they were with the Championship. In the next eight years they won the Cup a further five times.

The following week, Rangers made more history by clinching the league title against Kilmarnock, securing their first-ever League and Cup double. The *Daily Record* described the day as follows:

It was a day for which there was no replica, for to their week-old Scottish Cup success they were engaged in adding a Scottish League Championship. Upon their first double achievement, Chairman James Buchanan and manager William Struth warmly congratulated the team in the dressing room. All the players were quietly delighted at the tribute thus spontaneously bestowed, but I doubt if there were two happier players than the two old warriors, Andrew Cunningham and Alan Morton. They had been through many hard-fought battles together, and now the greatest ambition of their football lives had been realised.

It was such a display as ought to be given by a team attempting to justify its title of champions. I doubt if I have seen Rangers more compact, more self-assured, or more suggestive of power in defence and attack than this match. In conditions that were favourable to fast, correct football, the champions seemed capable of doing pretty nearly anything they aimed at. The wings worked out some ornate designs, which were executed with a crispness that was delightful to see.

Before the game began in front of 27,000 enthusiasts, the Cup was carried round the track by Archie Swann, now in civvies, with the band swinging behind, playing a rousing march. The trophy now with red, white and blue ribbons and a natty silk Union Jack brought from Denmark by manager Struth, who had kept it for such an occasion – ever the optimist.

For the record, Rangers were comfortable 5–1 winners on the day with two goals from Andy Cunningham and a Jimmy Fleming hat trick. It was a perfect end to an historically triumphant season.

One player whom Struth tried unsuccessfully to sign in May 1928 was Jack Harkness, the legendary Wembley Wizards and Queen's Park goalkeeper. Unfortunately, Harkness had to decline Struth's approach because he had committed himself to Hearts just two days previously. 'Keep your promise,' implored Struth, before sending him off with good wishes. Unbowed, the Light Blues boss said, ' . . . I am a Hearts shareholder myself and I'm sure if I hadn't been at Rangers, I'd have been one of Hearts' most enthusiastic supporters.' It was an interesting admission of support for the Edinburgh side. Struth was not a huge Hearts shareholder, possessing just two £1 shares, but he was raised in Edinburgh and, having served them as a trainer, it is unsurprising that

Heart of Midlothian was his first love. However, if he was disappointed that Harkness did not join Rangers, he could savour the side he had, and both the Scottish Cup and League Championship trophy, which were proudly displayed at Ibrox.

The American tour of 1928

At the end of the season, in something of a celebration, Struth took his players on an American tour, their first abroad since 1923. Wherever they travelled, they were greeted by thousands of exiled Scots, all delighted to see their heroes from the old land. Struth insisted, though, that it was to be no holiday trip and Rangers were to play to win every match. They did not win every match, but in the ten games they played, they emerged without defeat (winning seven and drawing three). There was to be no dropping of standards – the club's reputation was at stake and he wanted it to be enhanced further.

There were many memorable moments during their stay in the States for a variety of reasons. The trip brought an interesting dilemma for the recently signed Bob McPhail, who was a strict church goer. Before Bob had left with his team-mates, his father, who was a church elder in Barrhead, had asked him to respect his Christian values and not to play on a Sunday. Unfortunately for McPhail, Rangers were due to play Fall River on Sunday, 3 June. After taking several days to pluck up the courage to face up to the Boss, McPhail approached Struth to tell him, 'I'm sorry but I cannot play on Sunday.' When pressed by the manager, McPhail explained the background, and Struth simply replied, 'Well, young man, if that's what your father told you to do and that's the way you feel about it, then I'll leave you out. I understand.' Struth would have been unreasonable to deny McPhail his request to be left out, but the manager handled the situation in a compassionate way.

Perhaps McPhail had a premonition about how this match might unfold. In any case, his timing was impeccable. The day started off well. The team received a tremendous reception with bands on parade and flags waving. They marched from the train station, into the ground and on to the track to the cheers of the 15,000 crowd. It was a beautiful afternoon and all seemed right with the world – then the match started! The pleasantries ceased the minute the referee blew his whistle for kick-off. Struth later recounted the story to the *Sunday Express*:

Jimmy Fleming was bustling around in his usual style, and the Americans didn't like it. At one point he was stamped on and went flying into the crowd, though he did return wearing a straw boater, which some wag had stuck on his head. Keeper Tom Hamilton spent most of his time in the net, as every time a cross came in he was barged into the goal. There were so many Scots and English in the Fall River side they were hugely motivated to be playing against us, and were determined to show us a thing or two.

After the game I could not get into the dressing room. There was no directors' box – just seats around the trackside – and when I headed to the dressing room, the place was mobbed by spectators. We kept a bottle of whisky in the dressing room to entertain Scottish visitors but that had been quickly emptied. It was absolute chaos. We only stayed in Fall River a day and went back to New York on an evening sail on one of the old river steamers. I have never seen such a well-appointed boat, and we had some interesting fellow passengers, including an antique dealer who made his own gin.

On the tour, Struth encountered substitutes for the first time. He was not at all happy about the idea and was aghast at the thought of Rangers having players on the bench. He said, 'Substitutes cannot find a place in our game, not even for an injury. Players could feign injury in order to be replaced. This should not be allowed. Football's a man's game and each team should take the chance of losing a player or two.' This was the old pro runner coming out in him – the kind who knew the wiles of the track and how to manipulate a handicap to its best advantage. He did not want football to end up down that road, where the rules could be abused in substitutions. It seems a bizarre outlook now over ninety years later, but we must not forget that these were very different times. Struth was simply eager to retain the tradition of the sport.

The American trip was considered to be a huge success. As well as the matches, there had been several other, non-footballing, highlights. Struth was presented with a gold key to Pittsburgh by the Clan Grant, which is now framed and hangs in the Ibrox Trophy Room. There was also a constant flow of visits to every type of ex-pats club or society imaginable. The team attended a baseball match to watch the legendary Babe Ruth playing for the New York Yankees, and they were invited by the great boxing heavyweight Jack Dempsey to dine at his restaurant. Several of the players commented that Dempsey's handshake had not been as firm as they may have expected, but they never tested his clenched fist, thankfully.

Struth the bigot?

It has long been accepted that Rangers had a policy of signing non-Catholics only, and it has to be recognised that no notable players of that religious persuasion played for the club in Struth's tenure as manager. The policy had been established before Struth took up his position, but by continuing the practice, he could be described by some as 'bigoted'. However, this would be a crude misrepresentation of the man. In fact, Struth *did* try to introduce a Catholic player to Rangers in 1928 – one whose father had played for Celtic.

Barney Battles was just 22 when he played for Boston Soccer Club against Rangers in the club's 1928 tour of America. The youngster had emigrated to Massachusetts with his mother when he was a teenager and quickly impressed with his football skills. An outside-right, he joined Boston Celtics, and then was recruited by Boston Soccer Club. His influence in the American Soccer League was such that he was capped for the United States. Details of Boston's match with Rangers are sketchy, but the game finished all square at 2–2 and it seems that Battles impressed Bill Struth. He was invited to Scotland by the Rangers boss and signs were that he was on his way to Ibrox. However, Battles' mother was concerned that the signing of her son, as a Catholic, might prove controversial and she denied the youngster the opportunity.

Struth was understanding of the position and resolved to get Barney fixed up with another club in Scotland. Through his close ties with Hearts, he endorsed Battles' transfer to Tynecastle, where he was to become a huge success. In his first season he scored a record 31 goals in 28 league games and went on to become Hearts' record goal-scorer in a single season. Battles' career was disrupted by injury but he spent six seasons at Tynecastle and his performances were rewarded with international recognition by Scotland. In 200 games for Hearts, he scored 218 goals.

The story, which was related to one of the authors by football journalist Jim Rodgers who knew both Battles and Struth in later life, is of enormous significance to the understanding of the manager's position on religion. He would have had no problem in signing a Roman Catholic player for Rangers, but clearly felt bound by the tradition that had built up around Ibrox. Perhaps he saw the move as an opportunity to break with the tradition, but any hopes that the signing would signal a new era were dashed by the concerns of Battles' mother.

It was not the first time that the Rangers boss had attempted to break with the tradition. In the early twenties he had countenanced the idea of signing Celtic's Tommy McInally, who was a source of grief for Willie Maley, but the move never materialised.

Perhaps chastened by these abortive attempts, Struth reverted to the old tradition and there is no evidence that he tried to bring any other Catholic player of note to the club. He could be accused of failing to break the tradition, but he was not a bigot. Indeed, he frequently permitted Catholic charities to use Ibrox for fundraising events, or collect from around the ground on match days. Those who benefited, at least, would subscribe to this view, if it does not always sit well with others.

The new grandstand

The American trip served to bond Struth and his players even more than before, and they returned to see the new Ibrox growing in stature. The club was booming, success followed success on the park and the directors had decided to capitalise and provide a ground befitting the team. An ambitious new stand would also be a statement of the utmost intent that things were going to get even better. In advance of the rebuilding an advert had appeared in the national press: Grandstand for sale. Stand capable of seating 5,000. Available to view daily from 10.00–12.00. Demolition and removal to be mutually agreed. Further information from William Struth to whom offers should be made by 16.4.28 at 12.00.

Kilmarnock FC were interested in taking the stand, although the Ibrox archives do not confirm that the deal was concluded. However, by the time the players returned from America, work on the new grandstand was well under way. It would provide nineteen rows of tip-up seating for 10,500 people. Struth, having been a stonemason, felt competent to assess the construction. 'It's all good Welsh brick and it cost £95,000 to build. Moreover, it will be here long after the others have gone,' he said, in defiance of those who suggested that the new building was too ostentatious and grandiose for a football club. Prophetic words indeed, considering that the Category B Listed building remains while many of its contemporaries have long since been demolished. A total of 1,018,000 bricks were used in the scheme, along with two miles of electric cable and 11,600 square feet of windows. The magnificent entrance hall included the famous marble staircase and oak panelling.

The new grandstand was in operation as early as October 1928, when Scotland faced Wales, but it was officially opened by the Lord Provost, Sir David Mason OBE, on 1 January 1929, before the New Year's Day match against Celtic. *Daily Record* reporter Waverley described it thus: 'Everything that mere man can think of has been brought in by the Ibrox people to make their administrative and training block the most sumptuous thing extant.' The facilities surpassed anything else available in Scotland at the time. The players found an ample dressing room with a plunge bath measuring 12½ by 6½ feet and three feet deep. The water was heated by a special boiler in the basement. Facilities for the directors and guests were ample, and a room was provided for the manager. Struth treated that room like home for much of the remainder of his life. The new building also made the required statement that Rangers were the top team in Scotland and were fully intent on staying there. As if to emphasise the point, Celtic were thumped 3–0, with goals from Sandy Archibald and a Jimmy Fleming double.

Afterwards, all of the directors were presented with a timepiece and Struth was given a diamond ring to mark the occasion. Director Jimmy Bowie acknowledged the huge role that Struth had played in the development, by saying, 'His work has been unceasing.' The manager stated, 'Everything at Ibrox is done by example. We try to lead, not be driven. We may not always succeed, but it is our method, our road to greatness to whatever we have earned.'

By then, the grandstand had become Struth's castle, and the manager's office at the top of the marble staircase was his throne room. The club was run by the directors, but the administration of Rangers lay firmly at the door of Mr Struth, assisted by William Rogers Simpson, the secretary. Struth spent much of his time in the manager's office and his meetings with the players were generally held there. Perhaps the word 'meetings' conveys the wrong impression of the nature of these encounters. Players did not often precipitate a 'meeting' – they were summoned. As a consequence, this office in the newly constructed grandstand often threw players into some trepidation. Even today, the room, which has remained largely unchanged, has a cold air of authority.

Jerry Dawson recalled the terror of going up the staircase to see Struth in his room:

> In those days he had two lights on his door – orange if he was engaged and blue when you could go in. I remember on a few occasions, when I was steamed up about something, plucking up the courage to go to his office. I would march up the stairs ready to tell him how strongly I felt about this issue. Then the orange light would be on, and the angrier I was, the longer the light seemed to stay on. So, by the time I got in, all the steam had gone out of me and I found myself standing in front of the desk saying, 'Yes Boss, no Boss, thanks very much.'

Struth used his new office very much to his advantage, but it was intimidating to the younger players. Peter Black, writing in the *Weekly News* in 1954, said:

> I sometimes think Ibrox was designed to hypnotise young fellows entering its doors. That awesome marble hall, that wide stairway leading to the door with the frosted glass inscribed 'Manager'. A bit of a surprise

here when you knock, a panel lights up at the side of the door. 'Engaged' it says if you are out of luck, or 'Enter' if you have timed it right. You can't help but notice the quotation framed: 'Brief, I pray you, for you see it is a busy time with me.' You can imagine the effect of all this on a young player. Most are so overwhelmed they'd be glad to do anything to be allowed to sign.

The blue light may well have simply signalled Struth's availability, but it was also a means of controlling the players and any other visitors. Essentially, he would see them when he was ready to see them. He was the manager and he kept them very much in line and dancing to his tune. For those who were honoured to have the opportunity of joining Rangers, the message was clear – behind this door lies the Boss. There was no doubt that here was a man of substance and one to be respected. It is what he always aspired to.

While Rangers were at the pinnacle and pushing the limits higher, Struth was mindful of the importance of the lesser teams. It is ironic that in season 2012–13, when the club was obliged to play in the lowest division in Scotland, they brought a windfall to every club in their league. Struth's words all those years ago could have been easily applied to the circumstances the club was to find itself in, nine decades on. He said:

A cheque from Ibrox has often meant sudden wealth to many small clubs. We are pleased that this should be so. It is not just little clubs who count on Rangers and Celtic to help them out. A number of league clubs would have a very thin time otherwise. We always help the

173

smaller clubs whenever possible for friendlies including paying our own expenses.

In light of the club's experience in the summer of 2012, he would have been heartily disappointed that the goodwill the club showed then to others was not reciprocated. Struth recognised that while he wanted Rangers to be dominant, the club needed competition to make the game meaningful, and it was essential that the smaller clubs thrived and prospered. After all, they provided players who would only help to improve Rangers' fortunes.

In the penultimate season of the decade, Rangers won the title again after setting the pace in the opening games, then leaving every other challenger trailing in their wake. The Light Blues won the title by 16 points from Celtic, having surged into a virtually unassailable lead in the first seventeen matches, of which they won sixteen. Indeed, they did not taste defeat until 27 March when they lost 3–1 to Hamilton at Douglas Park – their only league defeat of the season. In the following season, Rangers won the title again, this time leaving Motherwell in the runners-up position. Importantly, with the 'hoodoo' despatched to the history books, the Cup was also won, to secure the double.

As the passage of time caught up with the magnificent team of the twenties, Struth set about rebuilding and reinventing his side with shrewd acquisitions, including Alex Venters from Cowdenbeath and 19-year-old Jimmy Smith from lowly East Stirling. Smith was brought in to replace Jimmy Fleming eventually, and was an outstanding success, going on to fill the role of club trainer. He was a battering-ram type centre-forward, over six feet tall, weighing 14 stone and possessed of a ferociously competitive spirit. Bobby Moffat later recounted what happened when Jimmy Smith committed himself to Rangers:

> It was about ten o'clock this night [when] we drove out to Jimmy's house. Mr Struth went into the house and I stayed in the car. It seemed like hours he was away and I was starting to get hungry. I slipped out of the car and got myself a fish supper. No sooner had I finished it when Mr Struth, with the signing completed, came to the door of Jimmy's house and called me in for a slap-up feast that was laid out on the table. Needless to say, after my fish and chips I could hardly do justice to the feast.

Jimmy Smith went on to score 418 goals in 443 games and was one of Rangers' greatest players.

America again after a remarkable season

Season 1929–30 was a triumph of epic proportions. Rangers won every competition at first-team and reserve level. Celtic were defeated at Celtic Park in the New Year fixture for the first time since 1902. Rangers went on to clinch the title from Motherwell by 5 points, Partick Thistle were beaten 2–1 after a replay in the Scottish Cup Final and Celtic were beaten in the finals of the Glasgow and Charity Cups. For good measure, the reserves won the Alliance League and Second XI Cup.

When Rangers sealed the League with a 3–0 win against Clyde, they had several youngsters in their line-up. Many of the first-team regulars had international commitments and Struth could have requested a postponement, but he considered Rangers' strength in depth was sufficient and well up to the task. It was not the first occasion that season that international commitments could have derailed the Rangers challenge, but such was his confidence and faith in the reserves, Struth had no hesitation in including them – even for an Old Firm clash. When Celtic came to Ibrox on 26 October, Rangers were missing seven first-team regulars – four were away with Scotland and three were injured. The club would have been within its rights to have requested a postponement, but they played and triumphed, 1–0. The victory was greeted by the Rangers players in the Scotland party in Cardiff with both delight and surprise. A fortnight previously they had defeated Celtic 4–0 in a one-sided Glasgow Cup Final with a goal from Sandy Archibald and a Jimmy Fleming hat trick. The league victory was all the more significant as everyone assumed Celtic would have been itching for revenge.

The Scottish Cup Final and replay against Partick Thistle were played before an aggregate of over 211,000 spectators. The first match was a turgid affair. Barely a chance was created in an uninspiring 0–0 draw. The replay had a six o'clock start the following Wednesday – no floodlights in those days – and both clubs were banned from playing in their first-choice blue shirts. The Light Blues made two changes to their line-up with McDonald and, most significantly, Alan Morton returning to the team. The match was played in a fashion that was in stark contrast to the first tie, and both teams went at each other hammer and tongs. The Light Blues also had the small matter of revenge for the 1921 final defeat in mind.

Despite just returning to the side, Morton retired injured after 15 minutes and Rangers had to play out the remaining 75 minutes with ten men. Rangers eventually clinched the trophy with a narrow 2–1 victory through goals from Marshall and Craig. The winner came from Craig's speculative lob, after Jags keeper Jackson was blinded by the setting sun in his eyes. Commenting after victory, Bill Struth said, 'Both games were strenuously contested but had been fought out in a sportsman-like manner. I think we were just the better side and deserved to win. I must congratulate the losers on their gallant fight.'

Bumper crowds watched the reserves, too, that season. Aberdeen recorded a record attendance of 12,000 at Pittodrie for the visit of the Rangers second string, for the second leg of the Second XI Cup semi-final. The first leg of the final against Kilmarnock at Ibrox on 19 April attracted a massive 21,000 spectators. It is worth noting this was a higher attendance than 13 of Rangers' 19 first-team home league matches that season. Rangers won the first leg 2–1 with Jimmy Smith netting a double. In the second leg a few days later at Rugby Park, the Light Blues clinched the trophy with another 2–1 win in front of 10,000 spectators.

The world was experiencing some harsh economic challenges at the outset of the Great Depression, which originated in America in 1929 and gradually spread to Britain. World trade collapsed and unemployment shot up, eventually reaching a peak in the summer of 1932 – 3.5 million Britons were out of work. Industrial and mining areas in Scotland were hit hard by the downturn, and in some places unemployment hit 70 per cent. Before then, huge numbers of workers from the shipyards of Govan would regularly make their way to Ibrox on 'their half-day off', so it is little wonder Rangers experienced a decline in crowds. The high attendance at the reserve fixtures was probably as a result of the reduced admission costs, which made the matches all the more attractive.

The final trophy up for grabs that season was the Charity

Cup and this was clinched on 10 May against Celtic in dramatic circumstances. A crowd of 35,000 watched as the teams fought out a 2–2 draw. Extra time and corners (at 4–4) could not separate them. This final match of the season was to be settled by the toss of the coin. The odds must have been heavily stacked against the Ibrox men since they had already won both the toss at the beginning of the match and the one before extra time. Davie Meiklejohn stepped up with a sense of foreboding. Celtic's Jimmy McStay must have been confident that the footballing gods surely would smile on him this time, wouldn't they? McStay tossed the coin into the evening air and, incredibly, Meiklejohn called correctly for the third time. So it was Rangers who clinched the season's final silverware. Struth had presided over the perfect season. All the hard work had paid off and one wondered how Rangers could top this.

After the match, the team made their way by coach to St Enoch station where they were due to head off for Greenock. There they would board the Cunard liner *Andania* and literally sail off into the sunset, Canada bound. Around 500 people were at the station to wave the team off, and all along the route crowds gathered in the small stations to wave the team on their way. In Greenock, significantly more people had assembled than had gathered in Glasgow, and were in buoyant spirits. Newspaper reports of the time estimated them to number several thousand. The players were in high spirits after their victory, and were excitedly looking forward to the trip ahead. On board, they made their way to the rails of the upper deck and serenaded the crowd with a rousing chorus of 'Follow, Follow'. All was right with the world and Rangers were right on top of it.

This follow-up tour was arranged due to the huge success of the 1928 trip, and the clamour from the North Americans to have Rangers back. The hospitality had been so warm and welcoming that the directors felt a moral obligation to return. The ex-pats came in their thousands to catch a glimpse of their heroes from far off Caledonia. For ninety minutes they could imagine they had been transported thousands of miles back across the Atlantic to Govan. It must have been a pleasure, but tinged with a yearning for their homeland. Bill Struth was incredibly proud that the club could provide this service to fellow countrymen, and in a lot of respects the results gained on the trip were incidental, although his competitive instinct always took over.

The tour proved every bit as successful as the one to America two years previously. Struth summarised the whole tour nicely, in these words:

> When one considers that of the 51 days of the tour we had only 35 days in which to play 14 games and at the same time travel 8,000 miles, it can readily be recognised the value of such an unbroken record. The reception throughout Canada was really magnificent and one only has to go there to feel how most Canadians appreciate a visit from a club such as Rangers. America has, on the other hand, not yet recovered from its upheaval and will take some time to do so according to the present state of affairs. I am naturally proud of the boys and I consider this to be the best performance in the history of the team.

These comments have to be taken in the context of the punishing schedule and the players displaying the fortitude, stamina and motivation to maintain their momentum right to the end of the last tour game, which incidentally they won 6–1. After the history-making domestic season just completed, it would have been understandable perhaps had the team slackened off a little. Struth would not countenance that, though. The club's reputation was always at stake. For the record, 14 matches were played and Rangers were victors in every one, scoring 68 goals in the process.

Struth's *ad hoc* treatments came to feature once again on the squad's return trip to Scotland. The arduous season and subsequent exhausting tour appeared to have taken their toll, understandably enough, and the players were looking more than a little 'battle weary'. Struth decided that they needed a wee tonic to have them in rude health by the time they arrived back on Scottish shores. Soup had been the staple pick-me-up, twice a day on the journey home, but this was now to be replaced with bottles of stout. Even among those who liked a tipple, this was not exactly popular. However, Struth insisted it was for their own good, and stood over his boys to ensure that the bottles were downed. Despite their reservations, the tincture appeared to do the trick and the players returned to Scotland the picture of health.

As well as the usual tourist-related gifts, Rangers returned from the summer tour with a new left-back in the shape of Bob McAuley. Originally from Wishaw, McAuley was brought up in Canada after his family emigrated. He was an overconfident young man and prone to backchat, so his stay with the Light Blues was brief. With Struth, players had to conform and to follow the club code or they did not last long. McAuley was swiftly transferred to Chelsea in 1932, but he returned to Rangers in later years as chief scout and had the distinction of bringing some great players to the club, including John Greig, Sandy Jardine and Ralph Brand.

At the end of the season, two stalwarts departed. Tommy Muirhead, who had been with the club since 1917, retired and went into sports journalism. Later he managed St Johnstone and Preston North End. The other notable departure was Billy McCandless, who returned to Belfast.

In the twenties, Rangers won the title eight out of ten times, scoring over 100 league goals on three occasions. Truly, Bill Struth had taken the club to an unprecedented level of dominance. This, though, was simply a prelude to the most complete season in the club's history as they entered the 1930s.

THE THRILLS OF THE THIRTIES

Great strides

Bill Struth was 54 at the start of the thirties, but if the years were marching on, they were certainly not taking their toll on the Rangers boss. Infatuated with health and fitness, he could easily have earned the title of 'fittest manager in football', if such an honour had existed. It is little surprise that the Rangers players, too, were considered to be in the finest condition of all of the teams. They had to work hard on the rigorous routines set down by new trainer, 'Little Arthur' Dixon, and they had Struth right beside them when they started their sessions.

The morning training sessions started at 10.00 a.m. sharp and before the players had even changed out of their clothes, the Boss would present himself, point to one of his boys and say, 'You will be my partner today. Come along. Let's get going.' He would pick his walking companion with great care. For many years his preference was Bob McPhail, since their stride patterns matched, but Struth always took the inside (ever the cunning ped – it never left him).

Out they would go on to the track. Struth, wearing his usual immaculate suit, would set a mighty brisk pace in walking around the track and the others followed behind. The players walked in little groups, each with his special pals. After a lap the Boss would fall back to join the group behind, and so on for never less than four laps. The distance was at least a mile, based on the size of the Ibrox track. The walk was his way of keeping in touch with the players, getting to know about the trials and tribulations of their life outside of football. It was also his opportunity to pick the brains of his most trusted players about future opponents and how the upcoming matches should be approached. He was able to judge the mood on the 'shop floor'. When Struth had completed his laps with the players, he would depart saying, 'Thank you. Now you can get on with your training.'

When he left, Struth would often climb into his chauffeur-driven car and make an exit from Ibrox, telling the players and training staff that he was off to make a business call. They noted that when he returned, generally before training was over, he would often be wearing a different suit. These trips became something of a joke among the players, who thought that he had more than likely driven around Govan a couple of times, then come back.

Struth enjoyed walking the track and would even go to the stadium on a Sunday morning to walk around with his captain – a routine that first started with Davie Meiklejohn. Each Sunday 'Meek' would report to Ibrox and he and the Boss would walk around and around the track, picking over the pieces and reviewing the previous day's game. This continued through to the days of George Young. It didn't assist Struth in his planning for the next game particularly, since the team essentially picked itself, but it did engender a close bond between the captain and his manager. It also helped to satiate the Boss's thirst for knowledge.

As he walked with the players, Struth would say, 'Breathe in deeply now, lads – it's good for you,' apparently oblivious to the stench from a nearby incinerator. On one occasion when the stench was truly obnoxious, Sandy Archibald turned to his teammates and said, 'Here we go again, breathing in all that shit.'

Rangers had closed off the twenties in some style, but the thirties would bring even greater success. The club was led from the front and centre by Struth, and the manager was not ready to ease up in the quest for silverware. His aim was to improve the side further and continue the success that Rangers fans now demanded. Certainly the new stand provided even greater substance to the claim that the club was the biggest in Scotland, but Struth was never a man to rest on his laurels or bask complacently in his own success. The construction of the stand was a bold statement from Rangers, but in the manager's eyes, there was much more work to be done.

If Rangers had made great strides off the park, they were also making some changes that would radically alter how the game was played on it. One player of the era, George Brown, recalled:

Until 1926, the rule was that you had to have three players between yourself and the goal or you were offside. This meant if you tried to burst through the middle, it only needed one full-back to step forward and you were offside. When the offside rule was changed, however, that trick was no use. In due course, we worked out our own way of coping with this. Then, about 1930, there was a charity match between a Hearts/Hibs select and a Rangers/Celtic select. Davie Meiklejohn was at right-half, I was at left-half and Celtic's Jimmy McStay was centre-half. Things didn't go well for us in the first half and by the interval we were a goal down.

So during half-time Meiklejohn said to McStay, 'All the trouble is coming through the middle because you're too far up the field. We play with Jimmy Simpson well back and this leaves the back free.' McStay agreed to try this and eventually we ran out comfortable winners. So from then on he played the same type of game whenever he played with Celtic and eventually everyone caught on to that style of defence. I feel I am on quite safe ground, however, when I say that it was Rangers and Jimmy Simpson who initiated the 'third back' formation, which was the accepted thing in football until recent years when teams started putting a sweeper behind the centre-half.

In the first season of the thirties, Rangers reached another milestone. When they clinched the Championship, that made it five successive titles. The win was not straightforward, however, and the team did not get off to the best of starts. To many, it seemed that the long summer tour of North America had taken its toll. They had played 14 games in just over six weeks and then had to endure the long trip across the Atlantic. After 25 league matches the team had lost five times, which was hardly title-winning form, but they rallied in a run of 11 victories and two draws in their final 13 games.

The Championship was secured on the last day of the season at Bayview against East Fife. Rangers went ahead through a Bob McPhail goal, and this was all the impetus that was required as the Light Blues proceeded to tear the home side apart with play that endorsed their claim to be the 'Untouch-ables' of Scottish football at that time. A second goal followed on 12 minutes, McPhail again the scorer. All that seemed to be required was for Rangers to play out the remaining 78 minutes. The team, backed by a vocal away support, had no intention of sitting back, though, and a third goal followed on the half hour when Marshall knocked home a rebound after the keeper failed to hold a fierce shot. Archibald completed the scoring in the second half. This turned out to be quite a momentous day for the club. When Struth, the first team and the directors returned to Ibrox, they found another celebration in full swing. The reserves had beaten Airdrie to clinch the Second XI Cup for the fourth consecutive year.

Chastened by the fatigue that had marked the season, the club decided that there would be no punishing close-season tour in 1931, in order to give the players a longer and well-earned rest. Struth was nothing if not a shrewd operator. He was well aware that he should not overwork the players, and that rest and recovery could be equally as important as the hard graft of training.

Olympians at Ibrox

The club may have had no tour to dwell on, but the Rangers Sports were once again held on the first Saturday in August. The event was a firm fixture in the athletics calendar and was by now attracting the very best of athletes, including Olympic champions and world-record holders. As a consequence of the esteem in which Ibrox was held as a top-notch athletics venue, famous Olympian Eric Liddell had no hesitation in accepting an invitation to train at the ground in 1931. Liddell is perhaps the best-known Scottish athlete of all time and his story was immortalised in the Oscar-winning film *Chariots of Fire*.

Liddell had left Scotland in 1925 to work as a missionary in China. Bill Struth was keen to ensure that Liddell was treated with the utmost respect and on the morning of his first visit, he sharply advised his players, 'Watch your language today. We're having a visit from Eric Liddell.' The visits became a regular occurrence and eventually a challenge was set up between the fastest player at Ibrox, Sandy Archibald, and Liddell. The race was held over 440 yards and, incredibly, Archibald triumphed! Struth was absolutely astonished, as were his players and probably Liddell himself. He took the defeat with good grace and congratulated Archibald on his victory. Archibald dined out on his win for weeks afterwards.

Bill Struth was now well settled into his accommodation in the new grandstand, and he would sit by the fireside for long hours, working through the administration of team affairs. To many, it seemed that he never went home. He was not alone. He had a companion that carved out its own little piece of history – a canary. The bird had flown in through his open window one day, presumably having escaped from a nearby house. Not too many canaries were to be found flying around Govan. The manager captured the lost bird and placed it in a cage that he hung by the window, suspended from a hook in the top frame. The hook remains to this day. Struth would occasionally give the bird a little tipple of whisky, which had it chirping merrily and appeared to have no adverse effect on its health, since it lived for a long number of years.

Football, of course, took up much of his time, but he had another labour of love – gardening. He grew tomatoes and flowers in a greenhouse that had been constructed at the west end of Ibrox, and the flowers would be displayed in the boardroom. Through all the years the greenhouse stood, never once was a pane of glass damaged, despite it being situated in an area of the ground that was traditionally used by Celtic supporters on Old Firm day. It is perhaps an indication of the levels of respect for property that football fans had in these days.

As the administrative duties mounted at Ibrox, Struth realised that he needed some assistance. Occasionally, he would take the short walk around to a little shop attached to Peacock's Bakery in Copland Road, and he got to know the office manager there. One day he asked the bakery office boss if he knew of anyone who could assist at Ibrox part-time, and he suggested Mrs Alice Dallas. Mrs Dallas agreed to take up the position and went on to become the heart of Rangers' administrative office for the remainder of Struth's management, and his companion in later years. While Mrs Dallas eased the burdens of the paperwork, Struth continued to nurture 'his boys', and to seek to push the club to new boundaries.

With the new stand in place, Struth was even more enthused to promote the ground for a wide range of activities. As well as the Rangers Sports, it was used by many other clubs keen to take advantage of its fine track and playing field. Struth was keen to increase the stadium's usage when any events came on the horizon, particularly if it could generate some decent income. During the summer close-season break of 1931, Struth engaged in talks with a Leicester boxing promoter with a view to arranging a heavyweight elimination bout between British Heavyweight Champion Reggie Meen and Robbie Scholey. A quick inspection showed that the ring could be placed in the area in front of the main stand, which, irrespective of the weather, could provide covered facilities for around 20,000 spectators. The parties could not reach an agreement, but it is significant that Struth was proactive in these discussions, which indicates that he had a growing influence in the wider administration of the club. It seems that the days when his responsibilities were limited to those of a trainer were long behind him.

The tragedy of Sam English and John Thomson

The close season did bring one significant arrival when, in July 1931, Struth signed a young fair-haired centre-forward from Yoker Athletic, Sam English. English hailed from Coleraine, but his family had moved to Dalmuir when he was just 14. The youngster worked in John Brown's shipyard, but had attracted attention while turning out on a Saturday for Yoker. In the three years before signing for Rangers, English scored an incredible 294 goals for the junior side. The signing was something of a coup since English was in much demand. Stoke City and Sunderland, in particular, were both keen to get the signature of the young Irish marksman. In fact, a Sunderland deputation arrived in Glasgow armed with plenty of cash and inducements, which far outweighed anything Rangers could offer, determined to get their man. Struth recalled, 'I sent a message to English asking him to meet me at Ibrox. When he arrived, I was clear about what we had to offer and the prestige involved in joining Rangers. He signed with little fuss. In fact, I am not even sure he was clear of the terms.'

Struth probably understated his role in the signing. He had clearly convinced English that there really there was no other team like the Rangers, and Ibrox was the only place to play. The opportunity to meet the formidable and impressive Struth at Ibrox, surrounded by all that grandeur, would have further convinced English that his career was best served at Rangers. The Ibrox boss had no hesitation about introducing the free-scoring Irishman into his attack. English rewarded Struth with a remarkable start to his Rangers career, scoring two goals on his debut, then grabbing five in a 7–3 win over Morton in only his fourth game. By the time Celtic came to Ibrox on 5 September 1931 for the first Old Firm game of the season, English had scored 12 goals in the opening eight league games.

The match was eagerly anticipated as always, but especially as it pitted the League Champions (Rangers) against the Scottish Cup winners (Celtic). After a largely uneventful first half the score stood level at 0–0. Sam English had never spoken to Thomson in the Celtic goal before, or even heard his voice, but shortly before the end of the first half he went close with a header. As the ball flashed past, Thomson was heard to remark to English, 'Hard lines, young fellow.' This was typical of John Thomson, who was renowned as a true sportsman.

Five minutes into the second half, English broke forward and rushed in on goal, following a Jimmy Fleming cross, preparing himself for a shot. Celtic's courageous young goal-keeper rushed out to block the shot. In a sickening collision, Thomson's head struck English's knee, leaving the Rangers player limping away in pain, while the goalkeeper lay motionless on the turf. Bob McPhail was close to the incident and later said, 'I was just two yards away. John's head struck Sam's knee and both players went down. Sam told me later that he hadn't felt any pain in his knee, but for several days after the incident you could clearly see tooth marks on the fleshy part close to the kneecap.'

Mrs Dallas recalled that when the players collided, there was a sickening scream from the stand. It came from Thomson's fiancée. Mrs Dallas took her away to the Rangers tearoom while events unfolded on the field.

As usual when any injury occurred in an Old Firm match, there was some unsavoury chanting – this time from the Rangers support. This was quickly silenced by the Light Blues' captain, Davie Meiklejohn, who ran behind the goal to suppress the crowd. After some treatment on the park, the goalkeeper was stretchered off and it was clear the situation was serious. The rest of the match did not seem to matter much to anyone and the players more or less went through the motions for the remainder of the game. The match ended, perhaps appropriately, in a 0–0 draw, because this was not a game for victors.

The 23-year-old Thomson was rushed to the Victoria Infirmary, but was pronounced dead later that evening, at 21.25, from a depressed fracture of the skull. English was devastated by the incident. After the match, Struth instructed English to get home to Dalmuir as quickly as possible, driven by Rangers goalkeeper Tom Hamilton, and told him that the club would take care of everything. Once it became clear how serious the situation was, Struth arranged for a car to be sent to collect Thomson's parents from Cardenden in Fife. Several weeks later Struth, Meiklejohn and English all visited Thomson's parents to pass on their condolences in person. How Sam English felt we can only speculate, but it must have been exceptionally difficult for him to face John Thomson's devastated parents.

In the aftermath, emotive words from Celtic manager Willie Maley at the fatal accident inquiry cast doubt on

English's intent, but newsreel footage later confirmed what just about everyone had accepted, that it was an accident. It had been the second serious injury suffered by the goalkeeper in similar circumstances. A year earlier he had sustained a fractured jaw in another courageous dive at the feet of an onrushing forward. On that occasion, Thomson survived. His luck ran out at Ibrox.

Interestingly, Jimmy Simpson – father of future Celtic keeper Ronnie – had shared a coffee with Thomson on Argyle Street prior to the match. Both were from Fife and were good friends. Indeed after the match, Simpson went to hospital with his family doctor to check on his friend. When he arrived, he was given the traumatic news that he should probably not go in, and Thomson was unlikely to see the morning.

The incident left a huge scar on the life of Sam English and although he continued his remarkable scoring rate – his record of 44 league goals in 1931–32 stands intact to this day – he never recovered from its effects. He was subjected to some cruel taunts from the terraces, and family members talked of the deep anguish he continued to endure until his death. His father even tried to encourage him to emigrate to Australia, but he wouldn't go, although the shadow of John Thomson was never far away. The Celtic players bore English no ill will and Parkhead full-back Chris Geatons was quoted as saying, 'The sympathy of every Celtic player is with Sam English. If there is one player who would have avoided that impact, if he could, it would have been English. He is not a rough player.'

The incident and its aftermath also affected Struth deeply. How could it not have? He refrained from any public antipathy towards Maley, who was a good friend, and provided comfort and support for English. He did not allow Sam to hide away, and encouraged him to play in a Glasgow Cup game against Third Lanark a few days after Thomson's funeral. Struth advised, 'Keep your eye on the ball and remember to play football.' They were the simple words, but much easier said than done.

Bill Struth did not forget Thomson. Some time after his own death, the club received a number of Struth's personal effects and included within a collection of old photographs was a sketch of John Thomson.

Rangers were heavily represented at Thomson's funeral in Cardenden and the memorial service in Glasgow, and then at the unveiling of the Thomson memorial in July 1932. English, of course, was in attendance, and was clearly distraught at what had happened. The burden was never to leave him. The torment of the Thomson tragedy forced him to leave Ibrox in an effort to make a fresh start. He had endured cruel terracing taunts and it seemed that the only way for him to gain some respite would be to move south. English sadly departed for Liverpool for a fee of £8,000 at the start of season 1933–34. One can only speculate on the scoring records English may have achieved had fate not intervened on that bright sunny day in September 1931 when his life changed forever. English never recaptured his form, his career sadly petered out and he retired at 27.

The honours flow for Struth

Struth put the trauma caused by the sad death of John Thomson behind him and continued to pursue the honours that the support so craved. The Old Firm, while huge rivals, also recognised that in many issues they were stronger together.

One issue that precipitated the two giants to join forces in the autumn of 1931 was the prospect of the SFA organising international matches in the close season. The ruling body claimed that under Article 29 of their regulations for members, they would have the right to call up players for these matches. This immediately created a conflict with the Old Firm, who felt that they were entitled to take their own players on tour. The matter had serious ramifications for Rangers in particular, who believed that any club tour would be diluted if they did not have the regular eleven available for selection.

At the SFA Council meeting, Struth was reported to have reacted pointedly, rising to his feet and voicing his opinion that it was a right of the clubs to have first call on players during the close season. He described continental visits for the SFA as 'holiday trips' for a select few, with no discernible benefit for the game as a whole. SFA chairman Robert Campbell stated that Scotland was regarded as at the top of the football world by continental nations, and in his opinion there was no use continuing these games unless they could field the best team. This was precisely the same argument put forward by Struth with regards to the club's tour. The SFA pointed out that the fact that a club had arranged to go on tour would not be considered a *bone fide* excuse for clubs asking to retain their players.

Struth would not be silenced and insisted that the SFA 'rights' be revoked. John Shaughnessy of Celtic backed up Struth by pointing out that in the forty-week playing season, eight dates were already set aside for internationals, and to increase this by the proposed three weeks in the close season was not acceptable. He also contested the meaning of Article 29, suggesting that it related solely to the playing season. In the voting, the Old Firm, despite being united, were defeated by a large majority. Perhaps in Struth's opinion, the holiday plans for some of the members of the SFA committee would now have been sorted out! An important consideration in the story is the strong role Struth took in representing the club. While Celtic had clearly put their trust in a director to represent their case, Rangers had turned to Bill Struth.

Despite Sam English's record haul of 44 goals, Rangers' quest for a sixth successive League Championship was thwarted in the 1931–32 season by a superb Motherwell side, who dropped just one point at home all season. As far as Bill Struth was concerned, the title was lost as early as October when the side slid to defeat by Queen's Park. Rangers had beaten the Spiders by three goals to nil at Hampden in the Glasgow Cup final a week earlier. Their dominance in that game was such that it seemed they could score at will. However, if the Queen's Park players felt any trepidation in the league game, it did not show as they took the lead and then held on despite incessant pressure and a barrage on their goal. Nothing went right for the Light Blues, who missed two penalties in the course of allowing the points to go to the south side of the city. While it was not the only game they lost that year, Struth was convinced that the Queen's Park upset was the turning point in the season. Even after losing to Third Lanark later that season, which effectively ended their title hopes, Struth trooped wearily into the dressing room and announced, 'Boys, do not let that trouble you. The Championship was not lost today; you lost it when Queen's Park beat you at Ibrox.'

Rangers found Motherwell to be their barrier again in the Scottish Cup. The Fir Park men had been one of Rangers' main rivals through the period, finishing in the top three in each of the five preceding seasons. When the sides were drawn together in the Scottish Cup quarter-final, the demand for tickets was incredible. The tie was to be played on 6 March, and when tickets were due to be released for sale at Lumley's on Sauchiehall Street, the queues started to form from 11 p.m. the night before. This was quite simply unheard of. By the time the shop opened the following morning, the crowd had grown to several hundred.

For the Rangers contingent, the wait was well worthwhile. The club triumphed 2–0, with goals from James Murray and McPhail, in front of 88,000 fans. Rangers marched on to the final and won the Cup by beating Kilmarnock 3–0 in the replay after a 1–1 draw. The combined attendance at the two fixtures was just short of 220,000. After the match, Celtic manager Willie Maley came into the Hampden dressing room and 'heartily congratulated the Ibrox players, with whom he shook hands all round, and told them they were the better team'. It was the way of things in these days, when rivalry was strong but there was always time for recognition of a worthy achievement. The gesture undoubtedly consolidated the relationship between the two Old Firm bosses.

Rangers added the Charity Cup that season, for the fifth year in a row, along with the Reserve (Alliance) League, which was also won for the fifth season in a row.

To prepare for the new season, Struth added Torry Gillick and Alex Venters to his squad while during the campaign, old war-horses Morton, Fleming, Buchanan and Archibald departed. Trainer Jimmy Kerr also left to take up the manager's post at Hearts. Jock Buchanan had been well respected at Rangers and Alan Morton paid this tribute:

He brought the punch to our side when we badly needed it. He seldom if ever failed to give his all. To have so resolute a fellow with you induced a feeling of wellbeing no matter how hard a task faced you.

The first foreign team at Ibrox

Rangers secured their sixth title in seven years when they wrestled the Championship back from Motherwell in the 1932–33 season. Despite suffering just two defeats in the campaign, several drawn matches maintained the pressure right up until the end of April with the 'Steelmen' close behind. A point against Third Lanark, at Cathkin Park, was enough to take Rangers over the line.

If there was celebration in the win, the club was sad to see Alan Morton hang up his boots in January 1933, in a match against his home-town team Airdrie. Fittingly, he scored the final goal in a 5–1 win. Morton was held in such regard by the club that he was immediately elevated to the position of club director. It is unclear what Struth's reaction was to one of his players being lifted to such status. However, it seems that he had as much control as he needed in the everyday affairs of the club. Besides, he did not seem to feel much antipathy towards the board.

Ibrox Park was renowned and some of the biggest clubs in the country had enjoyed the atmosphere at the ground. However, although Rangers had been touring overseas regularly, they had never faced foreign opposition on home territory. The opportunity to change that came on 21 January 1933 when Rapid Vienna arrived in Scotland. The clubs had been in communication, but the calendar date opened up by chance.

It was Scottish Cup third round day, but Rangers' scheduled match away at Arbroath had been postponed. Arrangements were hastily made to bring the Austrians over for a clash that was eagerly awaited. Two years earlier, Scotland (minus Rangers and Celtic players) had been routed 5–0 in Austria.

On the face of it, the match presented a serious challenge for the Light Blues on home soil against the continentals. The Rapid side contained several of the players who had taken part in the match against Scotland, including the Austrian captain Smistik. The Austrians, too, recognised it would be a tough game, but they highlighted that they wanted to see what they could learn from Rangers.

The visitors arrived against the backdrop of the Annual Students' Charity Day in Glasgow. The Rapid boss said that he expected 'flat football', which can be interpreted to suggest that he was of the opinion that Rangers would play the ball on the ground. Rapid started impressively and opened the scoring. Bob McPhail equalised before half-time. In the second half, Jimmy Smith scored twice and the match finally finished 3–3 in front of 56,000 spectators.

Quite what the Austrians made of the pre-match pitch invasion by students in fancy dress is not known but they added to what was something of a novelty for the fans. Moreover, the Austrians may have offered different opposition from the routine of Scottish football, but the roots of their game lay in Scotland and in Ibrox. *Evening Times* journalist 'Meander' reported that:

> The visitors are pleased to have displayed what they called Austrian football, which was more or less like old-fashioned Scottish stuff. Such pioneers as Jackie

Robinson of Rangers took it abroad and the visitors brought it back to the land of its origin.

Robinson was of the period before Struth arrived, representing Rangers from 1899 to 1905, when he left to join Chelsea as player-manager. He was once considered one of Scotland's best players and he took his skills and knowledge as a coach to Hungary and Austria. He is generally credited with playing a huge part in the footballing success of both those countries during the thirties and fifties.

A close-season tour of Germany and Austria was organised for the summer of 1933, following on from the success of the match against Vienna. In the three weeks of the tour, the club played five matches against a German select side, winning four and losing the final game 1–2. The last match of the tour was a return contest against Rapid in Vienna, which the Light Blues lost by the odd goal in seven. These defeats were significant because they were the first that the club had suffered abroad. In Germany, Adolf Hitler had been elected Chancellor and on the tour the Rangers party were actually present at one of his speeches.

Torry Gillick – a true character

At Rangers, as at every other club, when the door closes on the career of one player, it generally opens for another. As Sam English headed south in search of solace, 18-year-old Torrance 'Torry' Gillick walked into Ibrox. When Gillick signed, Struth announced that he had a high opinion of the youngster, and said big things were expected of him. He was not to be disappointed. Torry was one of the true characters of the time.

If he was perhaps a little rough and ready, and the antithesis of Struth, the manager had a real soft spot for him.

Gillick came from a humble background and found some aspects of the high standards demanded at Ibrox difficult to embrace. He would invariably turn up at Ibrox looking exactly what he was, a working-class lad from Lanarkshire, wearing a bunnet. The requirement to wear a 'bowler' gave Torry some anxiety and it soon became common practice for him to carry the hat in a paper bag. He would change hats once he got off the underground and before he came within sight of Mr Struth's flat on the corner of Copland Road. On the return journey back to Airdrie, the bowler would be returned to the bag and his bunnet would reappear once he was safely inside the underground station.

Gillick was a gifted inside-forward and a real fans' favourite, whose sense of fun came across to those on the terracing. He was the only player whom Struth signed twice. He was sold to Everton in the summer of 1935, and re-joined in 1945 before finally leaving to go to Partick Thistle in 1951. Many years after he left Rangers, Gillick remarked, 'Mr Struth gave me the impression that I wasn't signing for a football club, but that I had entered the most magnificent organisation in the world. I did not know or appreciate it then, but he was right.'

For all that Gillick thought Ibrox a magnificent organisation, he frequently fell foul of the voice of authority that was Struth. Perhaps that was what endeared him to the manager. He was forever being summoned 'up the stairs' and probably spent more time in the manager's office than everyone else combined. Often, he would make the trip of his own volition as a spokesman for the team. On one occasion, he took up the players' case after they received a bonus cheque from the Boss.

When the players received their reward, there was much talk in the dressing room that the amount was less than generous. Gillick was duly elected spokesperson and dispatched upstairs to raise the matter with the Boss. When he stated the reason for his visit, Struth was out his chair in a flash, telling him quite pointedly, 'You go down and tell the chaps that if they don't want the cheques, I will take them back, and yours, too.' Torry quickly left the room, crestfallen, realising that arguing was pointless. Struth later told that he had heard that Gillick had returned to the dressing room with his tail between his legs, bemoaning, 'I've never won an argument with the old man up there yet.' It seems, however, that Gillick was not afraid to confront the Boss, which is why he was probably selected as spokesperson by the others. These confrontations were few, though. In any case, Struth never harboured a grudge and Gillick remained one of his favourites.

Harmony in any football club is established within the dressing room and Struth always assembled players who could bring more than footballing skill to Ibrox. Jock Wallace used to highlight an indomitable ingredient, which he called 'character', and Bill Struth would have known exactly what he meant. In that regard, the two bosses were the same and when Struth signed Gillick, he added an enormous character to the club.

The sense of fun that the fans detected from the terraces was often at the forefront in training. It brought out the best in Struth, too, especially when the player strayed from the rules. Gillick was not the greatest timekeeper in the world to say the least, and was often caught out by the 10.00 a.m. training start. One particular morning, he was about fifteen minutes late, arriving into an empty dressing room. He knew that Struth was a stickler for timekeeping and his heart sank when he realised that the daily pre-training 'walk' was already under way. Fearing trouble if the Boss caught him, Gillick crept silently along the indoor track and through the tunnel. Struth was nowhere to be seen and with a palpable sigh of relief, he thought, 'I'll just wait for the boys here and join them, and no one will be any the wiser.'

When the players came round on their last lap, Torry prepared to join them, allowing himself a grin of self-satisfaction at his escape. Just as he was stepping out among his teammates, a quiet voice came from behind him, saying, 'Good morning, Gillick.' Struth had walked in quietly on rubber-soled shoes. Torry waited for the blast but it never came and instead of the chastisement, he was greeted with a knowing smile. Struth added, 'Well, you've watched what those fellows can do. Let's show them what we can do, Gillick.' The manager led him off at a cracking pace, which Gillick struggled to maintain. Poor Torry was never a particularly enthusiastic participant in the walking at the best of times. He was half a lap behind before they had completed one full circuit, to his great discomfort and howls of laughter from his teammates, gathered in the mouth of the tunnel.

Struth knew how to get the best out of all of his players and he was also aware of their limitations and idiosyncrasies. In Gillick's case, he knew when to apply a little psychology, particularly when he seemed debilitated by injury. Jimmy Smith, interviewed in the *Sunday Post* in 1954, recalled an occasion when Gillick reported injured, effectively ruling himself out of the match on the Saturday:

Torry Gillick came in and said, 'Ach, I'm no fit; jings, I'm crippled; I'll never be able to play the day.' I told him he better go upstairs to see Mr Struth. 'See Mr Struth? I couldn'ae crawl up the stairs.' I said, 'Oh, you couldn'ae? Well, you better try.' Off he went, and appeared back five minutes later. 'Listen, I'm playing. That auld bugger has ye fit unless the bones are sticking oot yer stockings.' Torry played and scored the winning goal.

Besides football, Gillick loved the dog track and walked his own animals. Towards the end of his career, rumours abounded that he was courting. Struth called him to the office and asked if the relationship was serious. Gillick acknowledged that he was quite taken with the young lady and that a proposal was on the cards. Fearing that he might never save enough money for a ring, Bill Struth said that he would dock Gillick's wages each week. When Torry decided to pop the question, he called on the Boss, who produced the money that he needed. That is another illustration of the caring attitude that Struth had towards his boys.

The good old Gunners

Struth's Rangers side swept all before them in season 1933–34 in the culmination of a remarkably successful three-year spell, in which the club won ten out of the twelve trophies it competed for. The season was also notable for the emergence of central defender Jimmy Simpson, and Willie Nicholson taking up the challenge of trying to replace the legendary 'Wee Blue Devil' on the left wing.

In the autumn of 1933 Rangers resurrected their jousts

with Arsenal. The clubs had last met in 1912. Both were League Champions of their respective nations and Struth instigated discussions with Gunners boss Herbert Chapman over a contest to be played home and away to decide which team was 'Best of British'. Obviously, there was a commercial aspect to the matches, but huge prestige was also at stake. The two men were great friends, but the prospect of being top dog was intoxicating. The clubs embraced the idea wholeheartedly and arranged to make their pre-match preparations together at the Turnberry Hotel.

Rangers were triumphant in the first game, played at Ibrox on 20 September, with goals from Jimmy Smith and Bob McPhail. The ease of Rangers' victory was a little surprising, given that the legendary Scottish international Alex James was in the Gunners ranks, but he was largely anonymous. In their match report, the *Glasgow Herald* recorded that the fans '. . . witnessed a keen and interesting game, brim-full of action and sprinkled liberally with passages of football of a standard higher than is generally seen nowadays'.

The Ayrshire coast was a favoured haunt for Rangers and it was not unusual for the team to go away for a change of scene before a big match. They had done so even before Struth arrived at Ibrox. Indeed, when Struth's Clyde defeated Rangers in the Scottish Cup in 1910, some were critical of the Light Blues for taking their players to the coast while the Shawfield side remained in Glasgow to work hard in preparation. Struth did not draw the same conclusion on the reasons for Clyde's success on that occasion and he remained a firm believer in the need to ensure the players were well rested physically and mentally before big matches. As such, Turnberry was to figure strongly in his time at Ibrox.

Struth loved the grandeur of Turnberry and its quietness was particularly attractive to him. By taking the team to a hotel of such quality, Struth was emphasising his philosophy that only the best would be good enough for his boys. The players would visit the resort three or four times every season to relax and play golf. Struth was a golf fanatic and one of the first things he did when he arrived was to go down to the Ailsa Course. His regular partner was Chairman Joseph Buchanan and the pair were noted 'sharks'. They would do everything possible to ensure that they defeated the players, although it was suggested that most knew this and grudgingly acquiesced to keep the Boss sweet. The players were all encouraged to play the game and fill their lungs with the good clean fresh seaside air. Long walks off the course before dinner were also the order of the day, but not universally popular. Struth's favourite route took him from the hotel towards Girvan, on to the road, through the fields and round behind the hotel.

These trips were vital to team bonding and while some aspects might not have appealed to everyone, overall the players loved getting away, too. Aside from serving to relax the squad, Struth acknowledged that Turnberry provided a subtle education for the players on how to behave in public. They were required to act as gentlemen in and around the hotel. He was teaching them the Rangers way, but importantly, it was the way in which he had always aspired to live his own life. The mallet and chisel had long been confined to the toolbox and the working-class Bill Struth was now firmly replaced by a gentleman of the middle class.

Rangers travelled to London to face Arsenal in the clubs' return fixture, with Struth's rallying cry ringing in the players'ears. Pre-match he was confident, saying, 'We have beaten the best teams in the world in the past away from home. There is no reason to suppose we should not overcome Arsenal.' The match was an enthralling encounter, played on 27 September in front of 46,000. According to press reports and the local police, two thirds of the crowd were Rangers supporters.

Arsenal went ahead through Lambert with Rangers equalising five minutes before the interval through Jimmy Marshall. Following the break and before an hour had passed, two Jimmy Fleming goals had put Rangers ahead 3–1 and in complete control. The remainder of the match was played out with an exhibition-type display from the Scottish champions, who could now add the crown of British champions to their remarkable success.

After the match, the Rangers party were entertained at the Café Royal, where all of the team members, manager and directors were presented with a pair of field glasses as a memento of the occasion. The match had a huge amount of prestige attached and two years later when the teams met once again, Struth promised his players that, if they won, they would not be forgotten. The players naturally assumed they would receive a bonus and when they prevailed against the Gunners, they waited excitedly to see how Struth would reward them. They were less than impressed when Struth presented each man with a canteen of cutlery. Once the manager had left the dressing room, there was some fevered discussion and no little unhappiness. Jerry Dawson recalled:

It was very clear that there was real disgruntlement around the bonus. I was a relative newcomer to the first team and was dismayed when the chief spokesman, Bob

McPhail, told me to come with him. McPhail had decided it was time to call a halt to this cutlery caper and I was going along for moral support. I went straight up the stairs thinking my career was going to come to a sudden halt. Imagine going up to tell Bill Struth what we wanted. As we went in the door I kept well behind Bob. McPhail went straight on the attack and declared the players were far from happy about the canteens of cutlery.

Mr Struth was genuinely surprised and began to explain that these were valuable prizes as the cutlery was the best on the market. Then McPhail could contain himself no longer and suddenly declared, 'There's not much use having a knife and fork, Boss, if ye cann'ae afford a steak.' Few of us can muster such perfect logic at the moment we need it most, but his masterly summing up of the players' attitude ended the discussion. As I fought hard against my instinct to applaud, Struth said he would look into the matter. In due course we learned we would be on a £20 bonus against Arsenal, and from then on the Boss made his offers in cash rather than gifts. In fact, he was a firm believer in incentives and would not hesitate to offer £20 or more for games he considered important.

What is enlightening about this anecdote is the fact that McPhail, like Gillick, was able to confront the Boss. McPhail had matured somewhat from the early days when he feared telling Struth he could not play on a Sunday. Struth generally kept detached from his players, but he had selected confidants. McPhail was one, and before him Meiklejohn, Cairns and latterly George Young. These were also his on-field generals.

He would quiz them about future opponents and how each game should be tackled.

The matches against Arsenal rekindled the long association that the clubs had with each other. Ironically, Bill Struth could have found himself at Arsenal on two occasions. The London club had considered taking him from Clyde when he was trainer, and when Herbert Chapman of Arsenal died on 6 January 1934, Struth was sounded out again by the Highbury board about taking up the post. Willie Maley, in a tribute in the 1954 *Supporters Association Annual* stated:

> When Woolwich Arsenal lost their never to be forgotten leader, Herbert Chapman, Bill Struth was sounded out on the matter of his successor, and the old tag of 'East, West, Hame's Best' worked on his feelings till he declined with thanks, and Willie [Bill] has never regretted it.

The news of Arsenal's interest caused considerable consternation in Govan and beyond, when a London newspaper carried a report on the front page on the morning of 3 May 1934 that stated: 'Mr Struth, Manager of Rangers Football Club, has been offered the Arsenal managership, and he is going to make his decision today. An emergency meeting of Rangers directors is being held and Mr Struth will be present'. The speculation led Struth to come out with a statement on his position to calm the fears of the Rangers supporters:

> I am not making any statement as to whether or not I have received an offer from Arsenal, but I will say that there are no conditions in which I would leave my present club. A number of people have been flying kites

about this particular job. I have been Rangers manager since 1920 and I will admit in the last few years I have received a number of offers. The Arsenal job is one of the plums of the football circle.

The job must have held a certain appeal as a fresh challenge, and naturally he would have been flattered by the Arsenal offer. However, in the cold light of day, and being pragmatic, he almost certainly posed the question of why would he want to leave a club like Rangers? He had all that he wanted at Ibrox. Moreover, there was still much work to be done and trophies to be won. His rejection of any move was the final word on the matter. However, he came into contact with the Gunners in subsequent years, facing them on eight occasions through his tenure. For two honourable clubs, the results could be described as 'honours even'. Rangers won three, lost three and drew on two occasions.

Rangers continued to be the dominant force in Scottish football, but if Struth ruled on the field, he did not always find that his ideas were in tandem with the SFA. Never afraid to speak out against the authorities in moments of perceived injustice, he crossed swords with the ruling body in April 1934. The source of his concern was distribution of gate receipts, particularly from the Scottish Cup semi-final and final. He raised some objections to the amount the SFA were taking as their share, insisting that, 'The money must come back into football.' Despite making his point forcibly, he did not succeed. However, again it is an indication that he was taking a lead in the strategic and financial affairs of the club.

Rangers clinched the title at Brockville in April 1934 with a 3–1 victory over Falkirk, and the Scottish Cup was secured with an emphatic 5–0 rout of St Mirren. Interestingly, the trophy presentation ceremony took place in the Hampden boardroom when the Cup was passed to the Rangers chairman, ex-bailie Duncan Graham. It was reported that:

> Just after the ceremony started, two prominent officials 'gatecrashed'. These gatecrashers were Tom Reid, chairman of the Scottish League, and Willie Struth of Rangers. Mr Reid penetrated the crowd and secured a place at the top of the table. Mr Struth stopped halfway to the dais. There he listened to the eulogies of the team. I'd like to have heard him speak about his eleven but the Ibrox manager seldom says much.

This says much about the times in that the manager of the winning team and none of the players were present at the ceremony. The comment also highlights that Struth was generally a quiet man, especially around the press or officialdom, except when riled.

Struth and Maley

Willie Maley was born in British army barracks in Newry, the son of a soldier. He played in Celtic's first-ever game, was capped for Scotland and became Celtic manager in 1897, a post he held until he was persuaded to stand down due to faltering health in February 1940. Maley was a staunch Royalist, whose business card included a picture of him shaking hands with the king. Maley and Struth were close friends and shared a mutual respect despite operating on opposite sides of the 'great divide'. They also shared a love of athletics, and Maley, like Struth, was no mean athlete, winning the Scottish Amateur Athletic 100-yards championship. In contrast to Struth, Maley appears to have favoured the amateur circuit.

The two are often compared, particularly by the fervent fans who sit on each side of the Old Firm. These comparisons are not wholly pertinent since they reflect different periods when the managers were in control. However, there was a reasonable period when their respective tenures overlapped. The statistics are interesting, particularly when examined before and after Struth's emergence as Rangers boss. Prior to Struth's appointment, Celtic had undoubtedly been the dominant force in the land, winning the League eleven times, to Rangers' nine. They were even more commanding in the Scottish Cup, lifting the trophy eight times to Rangers' two. To say the roles were reversed upon Struth's arrival would be an understatement of the highest order.

From Struth's first full season in 1920–21 to Maley's final season in 1939–40, Rangers won the League fourteen times, to Celtic's four. Their head-to-head statistics are even more impressive in favour of the Rangers boss.

Struth's Record in Head-to-head Matches with Maley						
	Pld	W	D	L	F	A
Scottish League	38	20	12	6	55	41
Regional League	1	0	1	0	1	1
Scottish Cup	2	1	0	1	4	5
Glasgow Cup	22	10	6	6	32	23
Glasgow Merchants Charity Cup	13	6	3	4	24	18
Rent Relief Cup	1	1	0	0	2	0
Benefit/Friendlies	5	3	0	2	11	8

The statistics are overwhelming, although circumstance should always be considered in such comparisons. A common argument put forward by fans of the greens is that during some of this period, Celtic decided not to continue with a reserve side for cost-cutting purposes. At the time, Maley commented in the *Weekly Record* of 4 November 1922, 'I would be quite happy if Celtic retained their First Division status so that the younger players would have a chance to mature and replace some of the ageing performers.' Rivalries were strong at this time, but it seems that the Celtic boss was prepared to sacrifice success for the breeding of new young players. Whether this was part of a long-term strategy or was a realistic view of their financial limitations is unclear. What is clear, however, is that Rangers were supreme through much of the period when the two bosses were in their respective offices.

Struth's reaction to Maley's ill-judged statement following the death of John Thomson would have undoubtedly caused some rancour with the Rangers boss. However, we have nothing to confirm his feelings and, if the two did have an exchange of views, their relationship appears to have been regularised. That apart, the only other time they were known to have come into conflict followed a late Bob McPhail winner in the 1933 New Year match at Celtic Park, overturning Celtic's early 3–1 lead. A disappointed Maley made his way down to the tunnel at the full-time whistle to watch his players come off the park, as he always did. He was agitated to see Adam McLean and Bob McPhail walking off the pitch with their arms around each other, engaged in cordial discussion. The pair were probably reflecting on the excitement of a game, which was later acknowledged to be a superb advert for the Scottish game. That was far from Maley's concerns and he sneeringly called out, 'Don't kiss him, Adam,' clearly frustrated at how events had unravelled. A short time later, Struth went into Maley's office, saying, 'I want a word with you.'

Struth was annoyed that McPhail had been dragged into a Celtic dispute in such circumstances. They talked and talked, becoming quite heated at times, as Maley pointed out that players should not be so 'pally wally' after a defeat. The Celtic boss considered that rivalry was healthy for the game and he would not stand for anyone who apparently accepted defeat so lightly. Struth agreed, but emphasised that players had to be able to accept failure in a sporting manner. Maley was not convinced. Struth may have argued that Maley had more opportunities to deal with the disappointment of defeat and should have learned how to manage it.

It was always something of a conundrum to Maley that Struth was so successful as a manager, but had never really played the game other than at local park level. When he raised the query with Bob McPhail, the player responded by highlighting that Struth put everything into being manager of Rangers and expected the same back from everyone else. There was no magic plan, or tactical nuance – it was simply a case of picking the best players, who would then work hard to deliver the required result. Of course, there was much more to it than simple hard work, important as that was – motivation, fitness, recruitment and delegation all played their part.

Whatever the depths of their relationship, Struth and Maley were sufficiently close that the Celtic boss felt inclined to give a Christmas present to Bill's granddaughter. This would appear to confirm that the two were good pals, despite the intense rivalry of the sides they managed. The gift that young Anne received was the children's novel *The Secret*

Garden by Frances Hodgson Burnett. The book is about a young girl who finds that the garden is a magical place. Anne may well have found that Ibrox had become a magical place, too, for the time that her grandfather spent there. Inside, Maley wrote, 'To a Young Ranger from an Old Celt'. The managers perhaps reflected a cordiality between the clubs over the period, which existed outside the intensity of their rivalry. Indeed, Rangers were invited to participate in a benefit match for legendary Celtic striker Jimmy McGrory and Struth was only too happy to agree.

The cascade of silverware continues

In season 1934–35, Rangers secured their twenty-second League Championship by a 3-point margin over Celtic, while previous rivals Motherwell slipped back and finished in seventh place. As the season moved towards its climax in April 1935, the populace read the newspapers warily. Amid news items of local interest, such as a report on Princess Elizabeth celebrating her ninth birthday at Buckingham Palace and the death of Glasgow comedian Tommy Lorne, were reports of ominous changes taking place in the heart of Europe. The League of Nations was protesting about Hitler's re-armament of Germany. For Rangers fans, however, distraction came in the shape of the forthcoming Scottish Cup Final against Hamilton.

Davie Meiklejohn had been ruled out through injury, but the final was to be another day of glory for the fans and for Bill Struth. Rangers won the match by two goals to one despite an early penalty miss by their captain for the day, Bob McPhail. After the match, it was confirmed that veteran Tully Craig would be released from his contract to allow him to take up the post of Falkirk manager, no doubt influenced considerably by what he had learned from the Rangers boss.

Bill Struth prepared for the new season by welcoming challenges to Rangers' dominance from Aberdeen and St Johnstone, both of whom had risen to contest honours among the bigger clubs on a regular basis. He said, 'We welcome the additional challengers and their time will come, but I am confident that the standard set by my players will be maintained in the coming season.' The challenge was perhaps more robust than he would have liked and Celtic took the title, but silverware continued to arrive in the shape of the Scottish and Glasgow Cups. Perhaps an early indication of Celtic's challenge for the title came in Rangers' defeat at the hands of their Old Firm rivals, who prevailed by 2–1 at Ibrox, in the same week as the Rangers Sports. It was Celtic's first win at the stadium in fourteen years. The annual Rangers Sports took place in front of around 40,000 spectators and they were treated to the traditional unfurling of the League flag.

Rangers lost the Championship that season but it was not through any lack of commitment from Struth or his players. Indeed, one of the players, right-half James Kennedy, showed the lengths to which some would go to play for Rangers. Kennedy was a replacement for the injured Davie Meiklejohn and he did not want to let down his teammates or, more importantly, his manager. Rangers were scheduled to play against Dundee at Dens Park and Kennedy, who lived in Greenock, missed the only train to Glasgow that would connect with the Larbert train. Kennedy's anxiety was compounded by his two-year-old son being taken ill and rushed to the doctor. The child was fine after some attention from the doctor, but Kennedy realised he could not get to Dundee on time through conventional public transport. Perhaps fearful of Struth's reaction, he chartered a plane and flew from Renfrew airport, landing in the public Riverside Park, Dundee, an hour before kick-off.

Struth was astonished and impressed in equal measure. He said:

> It was an innovation for my players to fly, and it was the first time Kennedy had been in an aeroplane but he enjoyed the experience, and it did not put him off his game. I did not know what had happened to Kennedy until I got to Dens. When he did not join us at Larbert, I thought he had travelled ahead on an earlier train and the majority of players were on the Special. He was not at Dundee station when we arrived, but we found him at Dens Park all right where we learned with pleasure how he had done things in style.

Kennedy's trip was not in vain – Rangers ran out winners on the day.

While the incident says much for Kennedy, the story also provides some insight into the players' commitment to the club, and to Struth. In the case of a lesser manager, or club, a player in Kennedy's position may have thought that he had enough justification for missing the connections. Struth was clearly appreciative and, by recording his thoughts, he showed the players that their efforts did not go unnoticed.

While the team battled to retain the Championship, Struth carried another fight to the SFA on behalf of the club in April 1936, again highlighting the fact that his interests extended far beyond the playing field. He was obviously assigned some degree of responsibility by the board to take up the official position. In this instance, Struth's contention was over the venue for international fixtures and Cup ties. In 1936, the City of Glasgow District Council had accepted that Hampden should stage big matches, based on a report they had received from Queen's Park on two schemes to extend the enclosure. Each option would cost in the region of £50,000 and Queen's members would make the decision on which scheme to choose.

Serious concerns had been raised about whether, under either of the proposed new plans, lock-outs could be avoided, which Hampden had experienced in the recent past, and several Council members objected to inconsistencies within the report. Struth added his own contribution with a few pointed questions, although acknowledging that he had a vested interest through the availability of Ibrox as an alternative. He also responded to objections from both the police and the railway companies, who favoured Hampden over Ibrox. When the Council realised that Queen's Park would fund any ground improvements themselves to secure the big fixtures, they endorsed the selection of Hampden. Again, however, Struth was representing the club in a role that seemed to be assigned to him by his directors. He clearly had their support and trust.

As Struth conceded the Championship to Celtic, he showed the kind of sportsmanship that had been the substance of his argument with Maley two years earlier after the sides' New Year encounter. He was truly magnanimous in defeat, which was particularly gracious since he was not accustomed to being in this position in his encounters with Celtic:

We heartily join in the congratulations which have been extended to the Celtic club in again becoming League

Champions after a lapse of ten years. Their record during the season proved their right to that title. During the past few years honours have not been as plentiful at Parkhead as in former years and no club welcomes the reincarnation of Celtic more than we do.

The League may have been lost, but Rangers took great satisfaction in winning the Scottish Cup at Hampden against Third Lanark. It was, after all, the premier trophy in the country. Bob McPhail, who grabbed the goal that clinched victory, was especially entitled to feel a degree of personal satisfaction since there had been a strong chance that he wouldn't play in the game. A groin injury nearly forced him out of the contest. Struth supervised the strapping up of his leg, which, although it helped, certainly didn't clear the injury. McPhail told Struth, 'I can only lift my leg a small distance off the ground.' Struth replied that he knew that, '. . . but the opposition didn't!'

It was by no means a one-sided final. Jerry Dawson in goal put in one of his best-ever performances to keep Thirds at bay. What was of particular significance was that this was Rangers' third Cup triumph in a row, the first time the club had ever accomplished such a feat. Struth could not hide his delight at the achievement:

Overall we consider to have had an outstanding season because of our winning of the Scottish Cup for the tenth time. In the winning of this trophy this year we set a new record for the club by making it three wins in succession. While Queen's Park won in 1874–1876 and 1880–1882 and Vale of Leven 1877–1879, there can be no comparison whatsoever regarding the merit of our performance in the season just past and those. Under modern conditions it is a noteworthy fact and one which may not be equalled in our time. Our success this year was our sixth during the past nine seasons, which also represents a performance never before accomplished within the ken of the present generation, which may well stand unsurpassed for many generations to come.

McPhail had struggled with several injuries that season and, always keen to embrace pioneering techniques, Struth referred him to a medical contact to try to get to the bottom of the problem. McPhail took up the story in his autobiography:

Having got myself stripped and laid out on the treatment table, I was horrified to see the beaming talkative practitioner begin to heat a large needle over what looked like a Bunsen burner. Mr Struth smiled encouragingly as the confident consultant described what he was going to do. He was going to heat the tip of the needle until it was red hot, then jab it into my groin. Apparently this, what seemed to me, barbaric treatment would eliminate the dead tissue in my groin area and I would soon be as fit as a fiddle. I could feel the perspiration on my forehead and the old knees began to tremble a bit. Sure enough, in went the red hot needle into my groin area. Was it twice or three times he struck it into my body? I am not sure because I didn't feel a thing.

Having received a cheerful farewell from this medical man of mystery, the Rangers manager and I set off back to Ibrox, but *en route* Mr Struth fancied an apple so he stopped at a fruit shop and left me sitting in the car, and then the reaction set in. When he returned he must have thought he was looking at a ghost. I had gone chalk white and I just couldn't stop my hands from shaking. He was concerned, very concerned. He apologised for leaving me alone in the car and that it was thoughtless of him, and quickly took me back to Ibrox. Though I thought the treatment had been a bit primitive and a bit unnerving it worked. My fitness improved considerably and, of course, Bill Struth had come up trumps once more.

We believe the man of medicine to have been Thomas McLurg Anderson, as we know Rangers utilised his services. Anderson had a physiotherapy practice in Glasgow City Centre and pioneered the development of ergonomics or human kinetics. He had been a professional boxer and athletics and sports coach in the 1920's before setting up in private practice from 1928 to 1964. He was responsible for training Tommy Craig, who went on to become the Rangers physio from 1970's until the early eighties. In using Anderson, Struth had identified a kindred spirit, enthused by the attempt to try new ideas and treatments.

The club may have finished the season on a high, but it also marked the end for Struth's perhaps most trusted confidant on the pitch – Davie Meiklejohn, who played his last game for the club on 22 April 1936. The great general was Govan born and his career had been virtually in step with Struth's managerial period. He joined the club in 1919, just a year before Struth took the reins, and he had shared in 18 years of glory at Ibrox, winning 13 league and 5 Scottish Cup winner's medals in 686 appearances for Rangers. A measure of the man was that, despite being in the twilight years of his career, he gave a remarkable performance in his final New Year derby on 1 January 1936 at Celtic Park. Rangers had found themselves 3–1 down and in big trouble, but this only seemed to inspire Meiklejohn, who almost single-handedly dragged Rangers back into the game. The team eventually secured a 4–3 victory.

Such was Meiklejohn's impact in the match that the 'Man in the Know', who was a correspondent of the *Observer* – the Catholic newspaper of the time, which was considered to have a strong Celtic bias – conceded that 'Meiklejohn was great enough to be a Celt.' That was quite an accolade for the *Observer*, but perhaps not one that would sit well with Struth, or the Rangers contingent.

Former teammate Andy Cunningham also paid tribute to him, saying:

Meek has earned an immortal place among the all-time greats of Scottish football. He was a member of that wonderful half-back line of Meiklejohn, Dixon and Muirhead, and only someone who played directly in front of him, as I did, can appreciate what a magnificent player he was. He was, in my opinion, unsurpassed at wing-half and later at centre-half.

George Brown had this to say:

He was always in control of himself. You never saw him rattled. He took command of a game and in later years the only player of Meek's calibre I can think of was the brilliant young Manchester United wing-half Duncan Edwards, who was killed in the Munich air crash.

These were wonderful testaments to a player who embraced the qualities that Struth sought to instil in his boys. In Meiklejohn, he had a player on whom he could rely.

As club legends departed, aspiring stars arrived as replacements and, in time, would tread the same path into Ibrox folklore. Struth was again proving adept at uncovering the right players at the right time. In 1936, he signed a 16 year old from Winchburgh, Willie Thornton. Rangers were alerted to the young striker after sending a scout to watch Winchburgh Albion. Their interest was in another player, but the scout was sufficiently impressed to offer a trial to Thornton. The youngster played against Kilmarnock and scored two goals that afternoon, before heading home where he was to find a Hearts scout waiting to entice him to Tynecastle to meet the manager. However, Thornton's brother Jim was a Rangers fan and he promptly got the local club secretary to phone Bill Struth that very Saturday night. The result was that the next day – Sunday, 7 March 1936, just four days after his 16th birthday – Willie Thornton signed for Rangers.

Thornton was still at school, so the form was put away in a drawer until he could officially join Rangers, and then he was taken on at £1 a week. Not for the first time, Struth was to show his amazing capacity for winning the hearts and minds of his players. As Thornton prepared for his big day, Struth walked round the dressing room from player to player, stopped in front of the youngster and asked him, 'How much am I paying you, boy?' When he was told £1, the Rangers boss replied, 'Anyone who keeps his boots as clean as you do deserves double that.' This sent the teenaged Thornton out in a jubilant mood and, sure enough, his pay packet contained £2 the following week. Willie Thornton never did have the heart to tell Struth that it was his mother who kept his boots in such pristine condition, although he did make sure that the extra cash was passed straight on to the rightful recipient – his mother!

Thornton, in later years, paid his own tribute to Bill Struth:

He was a remarkable man. He instinctively knew how to get the best out of people. He was like a second father to young players and influenced and helped shape the lives of so many of us. You never wanted to let him down. He convinced us for years that we were better than any other side, and we believed him. We stepped out on the pitch week after week absolutely sure of our own superiority. There were so many good players at other clubs you couldn't be complacent, but we were confident. Struth had instilled that in us. We felt fitter, stronger than the rest.

Thornton also highlighted one of the idiosyncrasies Struth had about travel:

He hated cars. He wouldn't let the players travel to training in them. He had a flat right at the corner of Copland Road and used to watch for the players arriving by underground or bus. If he was suspicious, he would send the doorman round the streets in the district to check to see if there were any players' cars parked nearby.

It is a curious story and Struth obviously changed his views, because he eventually had a car and even ordered some for senior players towards the end of his tenure.

Thornton also highlighted that, by the time he arrived, little had changed in Struth's regime at training:

> When you got in the ground, you went straight out on the track in the clothes you arrived in and did a few brisk walking laps of the stadium. Then it was in to change and start the real training. Every week there was a routine known as getting your medicine. I think the Boss believed the players would go out every weekend and have a right good time to themselves. So he believed in clearing you out. That involved a dose of laxative, either castor oil, liquid paraffin or black draught (which was liquorice based). I'll tell you there was many a hasty exit from the subway on the way back from training.

Champions again

In season 1936–37 normal service was resumed and Rangers returned to their rightful spot as champions, comfortably winning the title by 7 points from Celtic. This season also highlighted another vagary that managers all those years ago had to contend with. Not only could injury affect your team selection, but the 'Cooncil' could, too. Rangers found themselves in dispute with Glasgow Corporation in November 1936 due to issues relating to the release of George Brown from his job as a schoolmaster for a midweek match. Again, Struth took it on board to deal with the matter, which ended up in the public domain.

The Corporation released a statement through the Treasurer of the Education Committee stating that no official request had been received for Brown's release. Struth countered by advising that a request *had* been made to the Director of Education and that it had been turned down. The Rangers manager stated that, having been refused by the proper authority, the club was astonished that any suggestion should be made that they should have gone beyond the Director of Education and applied to the Education Committee. Struth also pointed out that when Brown was released to play for the Scottish League at Liverpool, it was the League Management Committee who appealed to the Education Committee after a refusal had been made by the Director of Education, and not Rangers.

> We feel we took the proper course of action in making our request to the Director of Education and accepted his decision without further comment. I do think, however, that where Corporation employees who play football are concerned there should be equality of treatment. That is all we ask for.

During the summer of 1937 Rangers made improvements to the ground with a view to making Ibrox the most up-to-date football arena in Britain. They introduced an elaborate broadcasting station with state-of-the-art equipment and a broadcasting hut overlooking the pitch. All around the ground, plugs were fitted so that portable microphones could be used from any part of the stadium. A mike was even set up in the manager's office, apparently to allow Struth to make announcements to the crowd, or was it to keep the players on their toes during training? The Rangers Sports in August would present an ideal opportunity for the system to be tested and used for the first time.

As Rangers, led by Struth's initiative, continued to modernise, they mooted the idea of floodlights. The Ibrox boss was keen to stage minor events, such as Alliance matches, in the evenings during winter, under artificial lighting. The initiative would require SFA approval, but the considered opinion was that such a move would be very popular. It was not until the 1950s that floodlights were first used at Ibrox but Struth had instigated the planning, and he continued to explore ways of improving the club on all fronts.

Through season 1937–38, the club was in something of a transitional period, and Struth admitted as much. With the exception of the Glasgow Cup, the cupboard was bare. For only the third time since the Great War, Rangers failed to win either the League or Scottish Cup. The side was heavily dependent on the talents of Dawson, Gray, Simpson, Brown and McPhail, but the years were catching up on these players.

The season was not entirely uneventful, however, as the club were invited to play Stoke City in a benefit match in respect of the Holditch Colliery Disaster, on 19 October 1937. Rangers had previously turned down a request from Arsenal for a challenge match due to the congested fixture list, but Stoke manager Bob McGrory made a personal plea and, of course, Struth had no hesitation in accepting the request in the circumstances. The match finished 0–0 in front of 30,000 spectators and £1,500 was raised towards the relief fund. After the match, players and officials were guests at a function in Stoke City Hall where the Stoke president, Sir Francis Joseph, presented Rangers with his own Loving Cup – one of thirty that had been specially commissioned by him to commemorate the coronation of George VI. He requested that the cup be used to toast the monarch at the first home match of every New Year, a tradition that continues to this day.

Rangers were integral to another piece of history-making during this season when on 19 March 1938 they took part in a Scottish Cup quarter-final against Falkirk at Brockville. This was the first all-ticket fixture for a club tie, outwith of Glasgow based matches. Falkirk's greed got the better of them, however, and they doubled admission prices for the tie. The crowd numbered around 4,000 fewer than had attended the league clash earlier in the season. Prior to the kick-off Struth wrestled with a dilemma – should he start with the youngster Willie Thornton or the veteran Jimmy Smith? He marched around the rain-sodden pitch, testing it with his foot for several minutes, before deciding to plump for youth. The decision paid dividends. The match ended 2–1 and Thornton scored the winning goal.

If the side was in transition, one possible signing captured the imagination of the fans and press alike. The speculation was that Stanley Matthews was to sign, a bold move that would surely have appealed to Struth. However, the asking price of £13,000 was just a little too rich, even for Rangers. Matthews did eventually turn out for Rangers during the war, but as a guest.

While Rangers struggled, one of Struth's boys had a better time of it. Sandy Archibald, by now boss of Raith Rovers, helped the Kirkcaldy side to the Second Division title. Struth, showing great pride in the achievement of one of the players who had been vital to his own success, sent the following telegram to congratulate his 'boy': 'Please convey to all the heartiest congratulations on your splendid performance, and sincerely wish you continued success in your new sphere. From officials and players of Rangers Football Club – Struth'.

Another arrival that season was teenager Willie Woodburn in October 1937. He lived in Gorgie Road, right next to Tynecastle and close to where Struth once resided, but he got fed up waiting for the call from Hearts. His Ibrox adventure did not get off to the best of starts, though, in a trial match against Third Lanark. Such was his excitement that he forgot his boots, realising it while sat on the Edinburgh to Glasgow train. He had to borrow a pair of Jimmy Simpson's, which were a size too big. Then, in the match, he conceded a penalty.

After the game he was very downcast, and climbed the stairs to the manager's office when he was summoned, fearing the worst. He recalled:

> The trainer Arthur Dixon came up to me and said the Boss wanted to see me upstairs. I had just given away a penalty in the game and, quite honestly, thought that was me out of the window. The first words Bill Struth spoke to me were, 'How would you like to be a Rangers player?' I blurted out an apology for the penalty, and all he said was, 'The man who never made a mistake, never made anything!'

Struth then went on to detail the terms of £4 a week in the reserves and £6 in the first team. Woodburn was also given a signing-on fee of £20. He was working as an apprentice plasterer at the time and Struth, with pragmatic sense, ensured that Woodburn served his time, although his meagre earnings of just 18 shillings (90p) per week made a career in football much more attractive. Woodburn's father, a staunch Hearts supporter, was less than pleased with the news. He knew nothing about this major development in his son's life until he read it in the paper the following day. Father and son did not speak for two days such was his rage. He came round, though, no doubt helped by the fact that he knew Struth through the building trade. They had worked together in Edinburgh many years earlier.

When Woodburn first moved to Glasgow, he stayed in digs, and if he wasn't in bed by ten o'clock the landlady would be on the phone to Bill Struth the following morning. He recalled, 'It was a bit like the army under old Bill, all that hard work and discipline, for £4 a week, too.' Struth, although not a great football man, did pass on words of wisdom to Woodburn, who, himself, admitted he had a tendency to hold on to the ball and play too much football in and around the penalty area. The advice was brief and concise: 'A centre-half cannot afford to take chances in the penalty area. Your job is to clear your lines. Let the other fellows play the football.' Simple advice, yet it made Woodburn a better player.

Rangers' assertion that they had a stadium fit for royalty was confirmed when George VI and Queen Elizabeth were welcomed officially to open the 1938 Empire Exhibition at Ibrox on 3 May 1939, in front of a crowd reported to be in excess of 100,000. The king's opening address, edited sympathetically by *Pathe News*, is available from their archives. George VI's difficulties with a stammer were covered in the Academy Award-winning film *The King's Speech*. The visit from the royal party was a source of immense pride for Rangers but no photographic records survive showing Struth's part-icipation, although he would undoubtedly have figured in the arrangements. The main exhibition was sited at Bellahouston Park and a football tournament was scheduled to be played at Ibrox. During the course of the exhibition, which ran for six months and was intended to help boost the economy after the austerity of the 1930s, a total of 12,593,232 visitors attended the many events, despite the summer being one of the wettest on record.

The cream of British football came to Ibrox for the tournament, giving spectators a feast from May to June. Among the sides who took part alongside the hosts were Celtic, Sunderland, Aberdeen, Chelsea, Everton, Hearts and Brentford. Brentford's involvement, while puzzling, came about because Arsenal, Aston Villa and Manchester City all declined invitations to be involved, and Brentford filled the void at short notice. Rangers opened the tournament against Everton but there was to be no glory as the Toffeemen ran out deserved winners 2–0, ironically, with one of Struth's favourite sons, Torry Gillick, in the ranks. Celtic went on to win the tournament, beating Everton in the final.

Failure to win the tournament must have been a source of some frustration and disappointment for Struth, especially with the prestigious trophy ending up at the home of the club's greatest rivals. It was one of the quirks of the Old Firm rivalry of that time that, despite Rangers being the dominant force, Celtic always seemed to be able to raise themselves for these one-off competitions. The Coronation Cup many years later is another example of this.

After a season of general disappointment, Bill and Kate headed off to Kinghorn in Fife where they had had a holiday home for a number of years. There, Bill had the opportunity to recharge his batteries and to indulge in some golf, which he greatly enjoyed. By all accounts, however, Struth was always immersed in all things Rangers and he was never able truly to relax on holiday. Indeed, it was suggested that he only appeared to enjoy himself towards the end, when he knew a return to Ibrox was imminent. There is no great surprise in this, since his life was almost wholly devoted to the club. By then, Kate had probably come to terms with the fact that his devotion to Rangers was all-encompassing.

When Struth returned from the Fife coast, he quickly got back into football business, acquiring some new players for the 1938–39 campaign. The club was still in transition. Club legends, such as Dougie Gray, Bob McPhail, Jimmy Simpson, Jimmy Smith, George Brown and Bob McDonald, were all in the twilight of their careers, and few faces continued to arrive. As well as Woodburn, Willie Waddell, Scot Symon and Jimmy Duncanson came to Ibrox. Struth recognised the need to freshen up the team and he had an uncanny knack of replacing one group of legends with another set of potential stars.

One area that had been a problem to him ever since Bob McAuley left for Chelsea was the left-back position. Several different players, including Russell, McDonald and Cheyne, had been tried with no really consistent success, and in the light of this, Struth moved for a player who was to become one of his best-ever signings – Jock 'Tiger' Shaw. Shaw was acquired from Airdrie in July 1938 for a fee of £1,500. He was great value, ultimately serving the club on the field until he was 42 and becoming club captain. Struth later spoke of how he remembered Shaw hardly ever being injured, which he accounted for by his fierce tackling. He said, 'Shaw went into every tackle with perfect timing, braced and ready for it. The chaps who get hurt are those who go in half-heartedly with the leg loose and flabby.'

He may have had a new talisman in the side, but the start of season 1938–39 scarcely gave Struth or the Rangers supporters a hint of better things to come. They were soundly thrashed 6–2 by Celtic in the League. However, the team got back on track and reversed the defeat in the Old Firm fixture at Ibrox. By then, a new young star had emerged to wide acclaim – Willie Waddell. Waddell made his debut against Arsenal in August 1938 aged just 17 and it was, indeed, the stuff of dreams as he scored the game's only goal. Not unnaturally, he made all the headlines, and the news hack Waverley, writing in the *Daily Record* noted, 'One can readily understand manager Struth not wasting any time in making this youngster an Ibrox fixture. He is too good a proposition not to take risks with.' Struth was of the mind that if you are good enough, you are old enough, and he never had any hesitation about giving youth a chance. These same youngsters would play a key role in the rebuilding of the Rangers.

The team, though, rallied for one last hurrah and the League was won in emphatic fashion. Rangers finished 11 points clear of Celtic, scoring 112 goals in the 38 games.

Attendances continued to rise and in 1939, a record 118,730 were attracted to the Ne'erday Old Firm fixture at Ibrox. We can speculate that numbers may well have been considerably higher, since it was quite common for fans to skip the turnstiles, go through in pairs, or lift children over. Incredibly, the match was not all-ticket, and the newspapers were full of complaints, including one from a member of the public who said he was going to write to Bill Struth to point out that he could not actually see the game other than when the ball was in the air. Interestingly, he said that he would write to the manager, not the board.

Many fans said the gates should have been closed, but

secretary J. Rogers Simpson stated that there was still room for another 15,000. People were commenting on how they had to scrape, scramble and scuffle, just to see the ball in the air, and how they gave up to wander about hopelessly at the bottom of the terracing rim. Some suggested that it was not right to boast of such a high crowd when many could not see. While there was a measure of pride in having such a great crowd inside the ground, the consensus was that it shouldn't happen again. It is worth noting that, despite all the adverse comment and publicity, the architect's measurements showed the ground could hold 136,940.

Some may have considered limiting the attendance through ticketing. Struth went completely in the opposite direction. When questioned about the events, Struth responded that 'There will be no trouble next time. We have alterations going on which will give accommodation for 20,000 more.' George Graham, secretary of the Scottish Football Association, also suggested there would be great difficulty with the all-ticket proposal because administration and management at the present grounds could be undertaken only at great cost to the clubs. On the same day, Prime Minister Neville Chamberlain was reported as saying, 'I think 1939 will be a more tranquil year than 1938.' As we entered the second half of 1939, events elsewhere were about to change the world forever.

THE FORTIES – NEW CHALLENGES

A world in strife

On 3 September 1939, the uncertainty over Germany's territorial ambitions was ended when Prime Minister Neville Chamberlain announced, 'This country is at war.' Britain had issued an ultimatum to Germany, insisting that unless their troops were withdrawn from Poland by 11.00 a.m. a state of war would exist between the two countries, but Adolf Hitler had dismissed it. For the older citizens, including Bill Struth, who was just three weeks short of his 64th birthday, the memories of the wasteful carnage of the First World War were all too vivid. George VI, broadcasting from Buckingham Palace, called for his people to ' . . . stand calm and firm and united'. In football, the mood was anything but united.

The day before the momentous declaration of war, over 30,000 fans watched at Cathkin Park as Rangers waved goodbye to the normality of peacetime with a win over Third Lanark. Goals by Thornton and Gilmour were enough to counter Jimmy Mason's goal for the 'Hi-Hi'. Now the football authorities in Scotland were about to be plunged into disarray. The Scottish League was immediately suspended with just five games played. Confusion reigned as the League announced that all players' contracts would be suspended, while the

Scottish Football Association issued an edict that all players' contracts would be cancelled, not banned, but players would remain registered to their clubs. The incongruous positions taken by the two football authorities were all the more surprising since the posts of vice president of the SFA and president of the Scottish League were held by the same man, the Rangers chairman James Bowie. He was at the league meeting when they reached their decision, but not at the table when the SFA reached their position.

The SFA's decision would have a huge impact on professional players, who would have to revert to amateur status *and* be tied to their clubs except when selected for sides operating under the armed forces' jurisdiction. For those players who enlisted for the services, the opportunity to play at weekends with their clubs remained, but only under the authority of their commanding officer.

The concern of professional players was natural because the cessation of contracts would block any income. Some degree of sanity was reached when the authorities agreed that the players could be paid, but their wages would be capped at £2 per week. The remuneration of football players was not a concern for Glasgow's citizens, who were more worried about the plunge of the country into the abyss of war. However, sections of the media were preoccupied with speculation over the impact that the war would have on sport and, particularly, football.

One consideration in the reorganisation of football was the susceptibility of grounds to aerial attack – a danger that did not arise in the First World War. In the early days of the war, the home secretary banned football from Glasgow, Edinburgh, Dundee, Dunfermline and Clydebank because of concerns that large crowds would make the grounds easy targets for German bombers. When the restrictions were lifted, the government placed a limit of 5,000 on the capacity of grounds, which the football authorities declared to be 'inoperable'. Eventually, the restrictions were lifted and football could continue, but Ibrox remained identified as the most critical of all the grounds in Glasgow. The stadium was designated a 'dangerous zone' since it had been handed over to the Air Raid Precautions (ARP) authorities, quite apart from its proximity to the shipyards.

Under the guidance of the Home Office, football resumed three weeks after the declaration of war. At the beginning, there were friendly matches before a league competition was initiated on a regionalised basis. Regionalisation had worked effectively through the First World War and the same model was employed again. Two leagues were established, with the clubs in the west and south of Scotland forming the Southern League and those in the north and east comprising the Northern League. It was not a popular arrangement with the Edinburgh sides, who would be hit financially through the loss of matches against the Old Firm, and they lobbied for a rethink. Eventually, they were incorporated into the more formidable Southern League.

As football specials were cancelled and children were evacuated by train and by boat from the cities, Britain readied itself for a long and arduous war. Unlike the early years of the First World War, when the army was mobilised with volunteers, enthused by Kitchener to take the king's shilling, conscription for men between the ages of 18 and 41 was established quickly by the government and enshrined in the National Service (Armed Forces) Act. Cognisant of the need to maintain momentum in its industries and wider economics, the government had, a year earlier, enacted another piece of related legislation – the Schedule of Reserved Occupations. This sought to address a problem experienced in the First World War when indiscriminate recruitment removed key employees, destabilising the industrial machine. The reserved occupations included farmers, miners, shipbuilders, train drivers and many jobs in heavy industries. Although sport had its role to play in maintaining public spirit and a sense of normality, sportsmen were not included on the schedule.

Professional players were placed in an invidious position. Their income had been slashed through wage restrictions, forcing them into secondary employment, although a large number entered the services. For several of the Rangers players, work was available on the Clyde or in the heavy engineering factories around Govan. This placed them in reserved occupations, but many of the players also went to war. Bill Struth was clearly well beyond the age of conscription, but his charges were fit young men who were conscripted or joined voluntary reserve units at various stages through the conflict.

The list of those Rangers players who served in the war is lengthy and includes a number of notable conscripts who were decorated for their gallantry. Among them, and probably most celebrated, is Willie Thornton, who was a gunner in the 80th (The Scottish Horse) Medium Regiment of the Royal Artillery. He was awarded the Military Medal for gallantry during the Battle of Sferro Hills in Sicily. On the evening of 31 July 1943, he was engaged as a signaller and, despite being under heavy shelling and mortar fire, maintained communication for eighteen intense hours, directing the Allies' response. His award was given for 'coolness and devotion to duty'. On his return to Ibrox at the end of the war, he was given a hero's welcome by his teammates and Bill Struth – a moment captured on camera when he was received in the Rangers dressing room.

Of the eleven players who played in Rangers' last match before Britain entered the war, at least three went into the armed services. Willie Thornton was one, and Jimmy Simpson and Chris McNee joined the RAF.

The New Year Old Firm match of 1940 attracted 40,000 fans to Ibrox, in contrast to the previous year's record attendance of 118,730. At the end of the match, Celtic announced that Willie Maley would relinquish his post from the beginning of February. His health was failing and the Parkhead club felt they needed a change to allow them seriously to challenge Rangers.

The previous year's Old Firm fixture, with its huge attendance, precipitated a claim from one fan who had sustained an injury that he attributed to poor crowd control. The war had delayed the action reaching court, but when it was heard by the Sheriff in March 1940, the claimant told of the crushing in which he sustained a broken rib. He claimed £300 in compensation for the injury.

The case was interesting in that it relied in part on the evidence of the secretary of the SFA, George Graham, and, more particularly, Willie Maley, who had been forced to retire from his Celtic role two months earlier. In his evidence, Graham spoke in support of the Ibrox club, mentioning his experience and observations of safety for crowds at Ibrox. Maley, who was a star witness for the defendants, advised that 'the safety arrangements at Ibrox were first class'.

Struth was also called to give evidence and he took the opportunity to offer his own support for the police, noting that their handling of football grounds was 'second to none'. Maley was under oath and his evidence can be considered to give no less than a truthful account of his views on the ground, but the enthusiasm of his support for Rangers' position highlighted the affinity he had with his Old Firm foes, despite the long years of rivalry. Indeed, his words consolidated the close personal relationship he had with Bill Struth.

If anyone disputed that Maley was popular with the Rangers hierarchy, any doubts were dispelled when the Ibrox club organised a dinner for him on 17 January 1940 and presented him with a silver salver, following his retirement from Celtic. He was also invited to Ibrox to take in a match against Airdrie a month later, seated alongside Struth in the directors' box. He observed, 'The marked antipathy, which used to greet me, was noticeably absent.' The Celtic boss had ended his fifty-year association with his club, but Struth continued. He had many more honours to win, despite the war.

When the season ended in 1940, Struth set about gathering a solid field for the Rangers Sports meeting, scheduled for August. While he could not assemble the all-star field that had characterised the meeting in peacetime, the event remained a big attraction, headlined by world mile record holder, Sydney Wooderson. There were 40,000 inside Ibrox to watch the great English middle-distance runner set a Scottish all-comers record. For a time, they could set aside the anxieties of war.

A few weeks later, the war in the skies over the south-east of England intensified as the country fought to avert a threatened German invasion. Amid daily reports of the RAF taking on the Luftwaffe in the Battle of Britain, football was very much incidental. Attendances that had averaged over 27,000 in the season before the outbreak of war fell to around half of that number in 1940–41. Still, Rangers continued to dominate, winning the Southern League Championship and the Southern League Cup, despite an increasing number of players heading off to war. The war had reached the Clyde with the aerial blitz of the Clydebank in March 1941. Bombs also fell on the Gorbals, Tradeston and Bridgeton, but Ibrox remained intact, as did the Govan shipyards. In fact, bombs did fall near the stadium during the earliest stages of the war, the first cluster landing around Benburb FC's Tinto Park.

One of the highlights of the season was the appearance of Stanley Matthews when he finally played in a Rangers jersey. He represented the club in the Charity Cup Final of 31 May 1941 against Partick Thistle at Hampden. It was a pleasant distraction for the fans of the Light Blues, away from the battle at sea. Britain's flagship HMS *Hood* had just been sunk by the German destroyer *Bismarck*, which was in turn sunk by British forces.

The death of Kate Struth

As 1941 drew to a close, the flames of war enveloped more and more countries. Finally, on 7 December, they reached the United States. Japan's devastating attack on Pearl Harbor incurred the wrath of a nation that, until then, had maintained some neutrality. In Russia, the Germans were on the retreat and the British army was reporting considerable success against Rommel in the North African desert. Three weeks later, Bill Struth readied himself for a busy spell over the festive period. Rangers would play Hibernian, Celtic in the Ne'erday fixture, then Third Lanark, all within a week. However, football was furthest from his mind on Monday, 22

December 1941. His wife Kate was found dead at 12.15 p.m. at their home at 193 Copland Road. It is not clear if it was Bill Struth who found her, but the timing suggests that he probably did. Certainly, the time of her discovery would coincide with the end of training, when he would normally walk to his home across from Ibrox, for lunch.

Kate's death certificate stated that she died from 'irritant poisoning'. The symptoms are generally vomiting and severe abdominal pain. The records provide no indication of what poison caused her death, but the mere fact that the doctor who attended her after death noted this on the certificate suggests that she was known to have taken some substance that would harm her. The Struths had a telephone at their home in Copland Road and if she called to summons help, assistance obviously arrived too late. More than likely, she was so severely debilitated and so much into the last throes of life that she could not summon the energy to make a rescue call. Whatever the circumstances, she died alone at home while Bill was a short distance away inside Ibrox.

The death notice in the *Glasgow Herald* next day reported simply that she died suddenly and that the funeral would be private. Indeed, the newspapers carried no further comment in the following days as Struth maintained the veil of privacy around Kate's death.

While Bill and Kate appeared to share many happy times, especially on holiday at their favourite retreat in Kinghorn, she also had some sadness and torment in her life. Her marriage had not been blissful from the earliest years. She had to come to terms with Bill's betrayal and the birth of young William. We can only imagine how deeply this cut into her heart and how lasting the scars were. However, she seemed to put this aside, and when they could care for the youngster, she took him under their roof and treated him as her own son. Destined never to bear a child, she had also cared for her deceased sister's son, Alex, as if he were her own, only to see him torn from her in the Great War. Steadfastly, she stood by Bill through these troubles as he chased fame and fortune in sport – perhaps his true love. Kate was laid to rest in Craigton Cemetery, aged 65. After the funeral, Bill Struth returned to Ibrox. His life would now be in Rangers – arguably, nothing had changed in that respect.

After Kate died, Struth found increasing companionship with the Dallas family. Among those who worked inside Ibrox, including the players, the speculation was that his relationship with his secretary, Alice Dallas, was more than professional, despite her husband Charlie also working at the stadium. They were certainly close and their relationship strengthened in his later years, but it would be unfair to suggest that they were in the depths of romance. In court parlance, the evidence of an affair between Bill Struth and Alice Dallas could best be described as no more than circumstantial. Struth himself did nothing to dispel the rumours and, in later years, he consolidated the view of many that he was in a relationship with Alice Dallas, often being seen in her company.

Rangers 8 – Celtic 1

Rangers continued their march through the Scottish game and achieved perhaps the most remarkable result of the war years in the New Year fixture of 1943. The match is rarely recalled by those with green tendencies, but is certainly held in great reverence by the Light Blue legions. It was in this match that Rangers achieved the biggest win in an Old Firm derby, defeating Celtic by eight goals to one at Ibrox in front of a crowd of 30,000. Prior to the match, Celtic were not favoured but were considered to have a 'strengthened side at their disposal'. However, two of their players were dismissed shortly after the interval – one for contesting a 50-yard goal by Young. When they were down to nine men, the score was 4–1 and Rangers easily added another four to their total.

Rangers continued to dominate football in the war period and secured every form of league title on offer. They won the Southern League Cup on four occasions, the War Emergency Cup and, at the end of the war, the coveted Victory Cup. They even won a competition held in a PoW camp in Germany on 1 November 1942! The prisoners assembled fourteen teams, all named after Scottish and English sides. Rangers came out on top, closely followed by Preston North End. It was really no big surprise that Rangers should win a competition played behind 'closed doors'. They had won just about every other tournament they played in. They had exhibited complete dominance of the game in Scotland. Who else would there be to play? Who could offer decent competition?

The post-war era and Moscow Dynamo

When the war ended, Rangers and, in particular, Bill Struth had plenty of reasons to celebrate. As well as revelling in the joy of the cessation of hostilities, along with the rest of the country, the club could reflect on the fact that not only had the team performed well on the field, but had also made a great contribution to the war effort, as had many other clubs. This was highlighted by Struth in Britain's celebrations of VE Day. He commented:

> We on the home front, charged with a duty to maintain the morale of the workers in the factories, shipyards and other branches of industry, can claim to have played our part in the victorious end of the German war and, as far as football is concerned, it may be truly said that no request made to the clubs for any war object was left unanswered.

Within a few weeks of the war ending, a special joint committee, including representatives of the Scottish Southern League, the North-eastern Football League and clubs that had ceased playing through the war, convened in Glasgow to agree a league structure for season 1945–46. They resolved to form two 'Southern League' tables, with an upper 'A' Division of sixteen clubs including the Glasgow and Edinburgh sides, and a lower 'B' Division of fourteen. It was agreed that the normal league structure that had been in operation before the war could not commence before 1946–47.

Before the year was out, Rangers would be drawn into a match that carried a greater significance than the clash of two great football teams. The Football Association in England invited Russian champions Moscow Dynamo to play some challenge matches over a month-long tour. It would be a rare opportunity for the British public to see a European side in action, long before UEFA had been established. After due deliberation, the Russians accepted amid some speculation that the tour had taken on a political dimension. In front of huge crowds, Dynamo drew 3–3 with Chelsea, slammed a weak

Cardiff City side 10–1, and then defeated Arsenal 4–3. In the game against the Gunners, they faced a side strengthened by the addition of guest players Stanley Matthews, Stan Mortensen and Joe Bacuzzi.

By the time the Russians reached Glasgow, interest was at fever-pitch, unprecedented for a game that would be played on a Wednesday afternoon. Some early Rusian arrivals took in a Rangers match against Motherwell. Next day they attended a dinner and the theatre, while some went on a tour through the Trossachs.

Rangers had decided to make the match all-ticket and set about preparations with a will. Struth coordinated players, trainers and the Dallas family to check every ticket as it arrived from the printers. On the Saturday before the game, thousands of fans endured an all-night vigil at Ibrox to secure a ticket. By 3.30 p.m. on the Sunday, all of the tickets had gone.

Struth's difficulties with the game were not limited to tickets. The Russians were agitated by Arsenal's inclusion of guest players and denied Rangers the opportunity to field their new signing, Jimmy Caskie, recently acquired from Everton. Such was the strength of their feelings that the Russians warned, 'If Caskie plays, we go home.'

In front of 92,000, the teams played out a 2–2 draw, with Rangers coming back from a 2–0 deficit, despite Willie Waddell uncharacteristically missing a penalty. Dynamo had insisted that substitutes could be deployed in games through the tour. Curiously, they used this to their advantage against Chelsea and against Rangers when, for a brief spell, they had twelve men on the field of play. Were it not for the attention of Torry Gillick, they may well have finished the match with the extra man.

At the end of the match, chairman James Bowie presented a silver bowl to the Russian Commissar for People's Sport and a pipe to each of the players. One of the Dynamo players commented on the friendship they had received from Rangers and the city. He said, 'We thought Glasgow was a drab and dirty industrial place. You have a fine city and you have warm-hearted people. We go back to Russia with a very different idea of Glasgow from what we previously had.'

The tour had been a huge success for Dynamo, who returned home undefeated. Many of the players received the honour 'Master of Sport'. The encounter with Rangers was a physical affair, but the Russians left with enormous respect for a team they believed to be the fittest they had faced. Once the tourists were back home in Moscow, celebrated author George Orwell entered the political arena, writing to the *Tribune* newspaper:

> Now that the brief visit of the Dynamo team has come to an end it is possible to say publicly what many thinking people were saying privately before the Dynamos ever arrived. That is that sport is an unfailing cause of good will, and that if such a visit as this had any effect at all on Anglo-Soviet relations, it could only be to make them worse.

It may have been a popular opinion, but Rangers had much to celebrate. The game was a glimpse of a different style of football, but an encounter from which they had emerged with huge credit. For Struth, the game was of enormous significance. His club had more than matched opponents who had gained the plaudits of correspondents in England, in front of the biggest crowd of the tour. Rangers were the pre-eminent football side in the country and the contest with Moscow Dynamo maintained the club's profile at the highest level. It was not the first time by any means that Rangers had faced foreign opposition at Ibrox. They had played Rapid Vienna in January 1933, but the match with the Russians was somewhat different. It was an introduction to competitive European football, and a new challenge would soon emerge upon the horizon.

As the country strove to return to normality, economic challenges and unrest faced Prime Minister Winston Churchill. Many workers sought higher wages and football players were no different. A professional players committee was formed to pursue improved pay. Assembled with representatives from many of the top clubs, including Jimmy Caskie of Rangers, the committee showed some militancy and threatened strike action on 1 January 1946, targeting the New Year derby matches, if their demand for a £6 per match fee was not accepted by the Southern League. When Caskie returned to Ibrox, the mood was quite different from the belligerency that had brought the players into conflict with the league administrators. Undoubtedly with some persuasion from Struth, the Rangers players declined to become involved with the strike and Caskie withdrew from the professional players committee. The strike collapsed and the players accepted the original offer to them of £4 per match plus a bonus of £2 for a win, £1 for a draw.

Ironically, Rangers had posted very healthy profits a week earlier; £1,000 had been transferred to reserves, £1,000 to the transfer kitty and a 10 per cent dividend applied to shareholders. Rangers had no control over the wage levels determined by The League, but they would have been happy with the levels finally agreed. The increase of £2 per match proposed by the players could have had a marked effect on the club's profitability as it tried to repair its balance sheet after the losses caused by the war. The top fifteen clubs considered that they had lost, on average, around £22,000 through the conflict.

As Rangers signed off in season 1945–46, Struth prepared for the Ibrox Sports. Once again, the Boss pulled out all the stops to ensure that he had the best of fields. His prize catches were E. McDonald Bailey and Arthur Wint. Bailey was a top-notch sprinter, who held the 100 m world record from 1951 to 1956 and won Olympic bronze in Helsinki in 1952. Wint won Olympic gold at both the 1948 and 1952 Olympics.

Struth convinced them to come to Ibrox and, despite it being a bank holiday, it was reported in the *Scottish Athlete* that Rangers arranged to fly Bailey and Wint from London and back in time for an international meet. Bailey would return to Ibrox again to compete and he built up a great friendship with Bill Struth. On one of his visits, he presented a picture to Struth in which he was dressed in kilt and Glengarry. He endorsed it, 'To A Grand Sportsman, From: McDonald Bailey'.

Big names and nicknames

By the end of the war, Bill Struth was the elder statesman of the game in Scotland and revered both inside and outside Ibrox. His control and influence were without question and he had every right to the title of 'The Boss'. Strangely, however, it was not a name that sat well with him. One of Rangers' most celebrated players, Andy Cunningham, reported that Struth hated the term:

He was far from the tyrant or dictator the outside world perceived him to be, but perhaps more surprisingly, a sentimentalist. He was never much of a talker but was incredibly proud of his record and jealously guarded the Ibrox traditions.

Struth may not have liked the name, but at least it was less colourful than some of the nicknames that were applied to his charges. Alan Morton had been known as 'The Wee Blue Devil' in his playing career, although to some he was known as 'The Wee Society Man' due to his impeccable dress sense. Nicknames such as these were actively encouraged by Struth and he entered into the spirit from the earliest days of his time at Ibrox by first christening Sandy Archibald 'Handsome Henry'. He considered that 'Nicknames are a sign of good fellowship among the players, and I always encouraged it. These things are part of the background. Until a player has been absorbed into it, he isn't a true Ranger.'

If Struth didn't like 'The Boss', he probably enjoyed being known as the 'Beau Brummel of Football', attributed through his apparent infatuation with fine clothes. Adam Little is the only player we have known to offer any kind of disparaging remarks about the manager and he called him 'Struthie'. Most others referred to him simply as 'Mr Struth' – unexciting perhaps, but certainly respectful. The names attributed to some the players of the Struth era are more intriguing. The sobriquets of some of the players included:

Andy Cunningham, 'Big Sone'. Struth reportedly never called him 'Andrew' or 'Andy'.

Bert Manderson, 'Burlington Bertie', because he was always immaculately dressed.

Billy McCandless, 'Bucky', through his weakness for buckskin shoes.

George Henderson, 'Webb'. He made a huge splash when the team went swimming at Turnberry, and so was named after a famous cross-channel swimmer of the time.

Tom Hamilton, 'The Drummer', because he lifted his arms as if he was playing the drum.

Tommy Muirhead, 'Horace', because he was the only player whom the bowler hat suited. He also wore spats and, in general, looked a bit of a toff.

Jock Shaw, 'Baas', after the South African term for Boss, or, more commonly, 'Tiger', because of the ferocity of his tackling.

Willie Waddell, 'Deedle Dawdle'.

Billy Williamson, 'Sailor', because he served in the Royal Navy during the war.

Willie Thornton, 'Scoop', because he was a newspaperman.

Jimmy Duncanson, 'Sammy', after golfer Sam Snead, due to his outlandish golfing outfits.

Eddie Rutherford, 'The Thin Man', for obvious reasons at the time.

Sammy Cox, 'Plum', due to his fondness for the fruit.

INTERNAL BLOOD-LETTING – THE BOARDROOM COUP

The Struth revolution

If the club displayed some caution over their finances in 1946, the following year brought healthy profits as crowds rose markedly in a real boom time for football in Scotland. Attendance figures averaged over 30,000 and the club declared a profit of £12,000. Outwardly, it seemed that everything was in fine fettle at Ibrox, but behind the great oak doors there was some unrest. This was manifested in one of the most important events in the club's history.

It is clear from press reports of the period that Struth was the authoritative voice from Ibrox, and he was even consulted by one newspaper about his views on the chancellor's budget and its impact on football. He said that financial pressures on clubs were increasing and the chancellor's fanciful idea that a reduction in entertainments tax would result in a reduction in admission prices was far off the mark. By becoming involved in this debate in the press, it is clear that Struth was not only acutely aware of the economics of the club and its budgeting, but that he was acting as its spokesman on these financial matters. Whether this was irksome to Rangers' three-man board of directors, James Bowie, Alan Morton and George Brown, is a matter of some conjecture, but Struth was clearly seen by the press as their main point of contact on strategic as well as team matters.

The dynamics of the Rangers board at that time was curious. Jimmy Bowie had joined Rangers as a player in 1910, long before Struth came to Ibrox. In contrast, both Brown and Morton were signed by Rangers in the Struth era. Morton, who had suffered some heart problems in the early part of 1947, was a quiet man, although undoubtedly one of the best players to represent the club. The 'Wee Blue Devil' had been one of the most influential in the side in the early years of Struth's management and carried a healthy respect for the man who introduced him to Ibrox. Brown, who had joined the board just four years earlier, was considerably younger than both Bowie and Morton and was a schoolteacher by profession. Although a confident and occasionally opinionated man, Brown was very much subordinate to Bowie, who was the chairman and leader of the triumvirate.

Jimmy Bowie had shown an inclination towards administration ever since his appointment to the Rangers board in 1925. He had been president of both the SFA and the Scottish Football League and had served in various positions with both for several years. There is nothing in the Ibrox archives to suggest that the relationship between Bill Struth and his board was anything other than sound. However, Struth's life revolved around Rangers and he spent every minute of the day, and often late into the evening, working at Ibrox or on club business elsewhere. It would be natural for him to feel that the directors, whose visits were more occasional, were detached from the day-to-day business of the club.

Struth was completely enveloped by his role as manager of the club. He had already given thirty-three years of his career to Rangers when he was approached by Bowie at the end of the 1946–47 season. Rangers had won the Championship, but had exited the Scottish Cup in the second round at the hands of Hibernian. Stalwarts Dougie Gray and Jimmy Smith were given free transfers and Scot Symon retired to take up the role of manager of East Fife. However, the team remained in good shape and had some fine players in the ranks. Indeed, Rangers would regularly field an eleven who would be revered for many years: Brown, Young, Shaw; McColl, Woodburn and Cox; Waddell, Gillick, Thornton, Duncanson and Rutherford.

Symon's departure was pivotal to the subsequent events that were to create turmoil at the very heart of Rangers. He was young, intelligent, and showed both an aptitude and interest in football management. At 71 years of age, Struth was seen by the board as a man whose best days were behind him. The message from Bowie, representing the three-man board, was that they believed it was time for Struth to retire. The Chairman also suggested that there might be a position on the board for the manager if he relinquished his position.

Bowie's reasoning was sound and entirely constitutional. Article 74 of the Memorandum and Articles of Association for The Rangers Football Club Limited stated quite unequivocally: 'No paid official or servant is eligible to hold the office of Director.'

The directors countenanced a position for Struth on the board, but not while he remained manager. Bowie went further in attempting to sweeten the proposal. He suggested that Struth could procure an assistant, who would be groomed to take over the manager's position when he moved along the corridor into the boardroom. In fact, he asked Struth if he knew who would best be suited to taking over. The Boss replied that there was one man capable of assuming the responsibility of running the club, but that he had taken up an 'important job in football'. That man was almost certainly Scot Symon.

Struth knew the standards that had to be maintained by Rangers and he himself had been schooled by Willie Wilton in the great traditions of the Ibrox club. The fact that he had highlighted that there was 'one man capable' of taking over, implies that he considered most other possible candidates incapable. However, Struth had no intention of stepping down from a role he felt still remained well within his capabilities. Moreover, the mere suggestion that he should step down was not only a challenge to his long-standing control of the club but, in his mind, an affront. He told Bowie that not only would he not consider resigning, but that he would relinquish office when he himself chose to do so!

Although the offer of a possible position on the board was floated with the intent to woo Struth, the move had a quite different purpose. It was designed to split the bond that Struth shared with the club secretary, W. Rogers Simpson, who was himself pressing for a position on the board. Struth more than rebuffed the offer from Bowie. He unleashed a chain of events that would precipitate a challenge to the directors and, more particularly, James Bowie.

Simpson and Struth both wanted positions on the board, but they also wanted to maintain their offices as secretary and manager, respectively. Simpson raised the suggestion that Article 74 be changed, but this suggestion was not well received by Bowie, Morton and Brown. Concerned at the split,

John F. Wilson, a friend of both Struth's and Simpson's arranged a meeting with the Rangers chairman, Bowie, in the interests of mediation. Wilson later said that he had been mobilised by concern at rumours that Struth had been asked to stand down. The fact that he took up the baton himself to approach Bowie, suggests that the two factions had descended into their trenches and relationships were strained. The meeting proved to be fruitless. Bowie repeated that Bill Struth would have to resign if he was to be considered for the board, but Simpson would not be accepted 'at any cost'.

Bowie's suggestion that a board position would be made available for Struth was based on an assumption that one of the incumbents would surrender his chair or that the board would be increased. It was clear, however, that the board were intent on retaining Article 74 and that the only way that Struth would be elected to the board would be through his resignation as manager.

The rebels realised that they could only effect change on the board if they succeeded in changing Article 74. They would also need an amendment to the Articles in respect of the number of directors accepted to constitute the board. When the club was incorporated in 1899, there had been nine board members but this had been reduced to three in 1935. The only way that Struth and Simpson could take a seat at the table was if the number of directors increased, or two resigned. There was no suggestion that any would resign, although Bowie was up for re-election at the Annual General Meeting.

With the board reluctant to relent on the desires of the rebels, Struth and Simpson realised that change could only be effected through the shareholders at an Extraordinary General Meeting. Quietly they worked in the background, gathering support for an EGM at which the motion would be to effect constitutional change. When Struth and Simpson believed they had harnessed the backing they needed among shareholders, they called for the EGM to be held a few days before the club's planned AGM. In fact, the meeting was eventually arranged for 12 June 1947, immediately prior to the scheduled date of the AGM.

The EGM would seek a change to Article 74 and would also challenge the restriction on the size of the board, seeking to increase it to five from three. The challengers were Struth and Simpson, but another candidate emerged seeking a place on the board – Mr John Fraser Wilson! If the constitutional change was to succeed, three people would be available for election to the board, with only two vacancies. If all the new candidates were to be elected, one of the existing board members would have to drop out as a consequence. Bowie was clearly the target and he knew it. He was the only one of the three due to retire, and he intended seeking re-election.

The planning in what was to become known as the 'Boardroom Coup' was meticulous and, crucially, entirely constitutional. The dissenters had done their homework quietly and Bowie feared the worst. Following a hastily convened meeting with Brown and Morton, the board released a statement to the press. They said that they had learned that proxy cards had been issued to shareholders along with a letter signed by both Bill Struth and W. Rogers Simpson. The letter called on the shareholders who were unable to attend the meeting to align their proxy votes behind Struth, Simpson and Wilson. The letter to the shareholders also highlighted that there were to be changes in the directorate and added ominously that 'they were needed'. Struth added to the condemnation with further sharp criticism, '. . . the efficiency of Rangers has not been achieved because of the directors of Rangers, but in spite of them.'

The contention from the board was that the move was 'threatening the future prosperity of the club' and they called members to a meeting on 11 June 1947, the night before the EGM and AGM, when they could explain the 'facts of this unexpected situation'. They also intimated that new proxy cards would be made available. Bowie said this meeting was 'one of the most important in the history of the Club'. It was a desperate move from a man who had been, quite clearly, outmanoeuvred. His hope was that those who had already signed proxies in support of the rebels would change their voting preference and align behind the board.

The rebels reacted by condemning the move and highlighting that the business was a matter solely for the shareholders, who would have the opportunity to consider the proposed constitution changes at the scheduled EGM next day. Struth entered the fray with an endorsement of his own position as well as that of W. Rogers Simpson, stating that neither had 'ever let the club down' and that regardless of the outcome, they would continue to be 'good and faithful servants'. It was a personal plea based on his popularity and, in this, Struth knew that he was on firm ground.

The rebels were correct in condemning the board's release of information to the wider media and their call for the meeting, but Bowie and his fellow directors took the only course open to them if they were to avert the result they feared.

The newspapers reported that the new candidate, John F. Wilson, was a well-known member of Glasgow Corporation and held 1,043 shares. Simpson held 744 shares, while Bowie and Morton could muster just 345 and 400 respectively. The most surprising revelation was that Bill Struth held the greatest shareholding of all of the competing parties, with 1,097 shares. Records show that Struth had begun accumulating shares as far back as 1923 and possibly earlier. Working in tandem with the secretary, Struth had acquired shares as they were offered by executors for sale back to the club.

In keeping with the duties of a company secretary of the period, Simpson valued shares when consulted by executors. Club correspondence from the time shows that in one transaction, thirty £1 shares were offered to Simpson for valuation. He considered that these should be valued at one shilling (5p) each, or 5 per cent of their original 1899 value. The thirty shares were duly transferred to Struth at a cost of thirty shillings (£1.50)! Interestingly, these shares were valued at 65 shillings (£3.25) two years earlier and, by the fifties, were valued at over £6.

On the face of it, the transaction seems to have been to the great detriment of the executors and to the enormous benefit of Bill Struth. However, researches have shown that Simpson's valuation was competent. The Articles provide no mechanism for valuation of shares, which was quite normal for the time. Indeed, even executors had no great interest in the valuation, when they were tying up the estate of the deceased. The decision on valuation would have been made by the secretary, based on his own personal assessment, relative to their previous value and the financial state of the club. It appears that Simpson's valuation was generally reasonable.

In showing interest in acquisition of available shares, often in lieu of other salary entitlements, Struth displayed great vision. He knew the club would increase in value and he was mindful of his pensionable wealth. He continued the practice of acquiring shares in lieu of wages throughout his management and this acute business sense was to prove an invaluable asset in the ultimate showdown of 1947.

Around 150 shareholders assembled at Ibrox for what the newspapers and Bowie called a 'crisis' meeting. Alan Morton could not attend, but he signed over his shares in proxy to his chairman – interestingly, showing support for Bowie rather than the man who had brought him to Rangers in the first place. Bowie spoke from the chair with great passion, stating that the very future of the club was at stake, reflecting that the changes could put control of the club in the hands of those with 'block financial interests as against an admini-stration solely concerned with maintaining the high sporting traditions [of the club]'. In many ways, his fears were pro-phetic of the dangers that would ultimately cause the club such grief in more recent times. Bowie had reasoned that, through the management of proxies, the ordinary shareholder would lose control to the large consortium assembled by Struth and Simpson.

He then handed the chair to George Brown to 'secure impartiality'. In essence, he realised that the meeting was not a battle between the rebels and the board, but that the target was himself. Brown provided his wholehearted support to Bowie, highlighting that the rebels had surreptitiously gained the support of the members without giving the chairman a chance to mobilise his own support. In effect, Brown acknowledged that they had been outmanoeuvred. Simpson responded, condemning the board for making public the affairs of the club.

Bowie was well aware of the implications of losing the battle over Article 74. It would open up the way to Struth, Simpson and Wilson being introduced to the board, especially with the proposal to increase the directorship to five positions. Based on his intelligence, Bowie knew that even if he won the vote on a show of hands, the mobilisation of proxy votes by the rebels could be used to usurp ordinary decisions. This battle was not just about the future administration of Rangers. It was a battle for survival that Bowie seemed destined to lose. He introduced an amendment to the proposal for constitutional change that would potentially block Struth's and Simpson's elevation to the board. The amendment gained significant support within the hall and it was carried in a show of hands by 84 votes to 31. However, when Simpson called for a poll vote, the huge weight of the proxies defeated the amendment by 13,286 votes to 3,787.

With the failure of the amendment, the motion was carried unanimously and the news was relayed to the press hacks assembled outside the ground. While the press men rushed away to file their reports, Struth and Simpson were elected to the board at the Annual General Meeting that immediately followed the EGM, deep into the evening. The change also allowed Struth to remain as manager and Simpson as secretary.

It seemed that the battle had been lost by the beleaguered board and, if the motion was indeed unanimous, by voting in its favour, they had effectively conceded defeat. The one issue that remained was that of the chairmanship. James Bowie was proposed for re-election and this was immediately challenged by John F. Wilson, who was counter-proposed by Simpson. On the call for a show of hands, Bowie's election was favoured by a majority of 45 to 27. Four and a half hours into the meeting and with midnight approaching, there was a demand on behalf of the proxy holders for a poll. By the time the meeting ended at 12.30, Bowie had been ousted. The final count did not emerge until later that day, but it was a foregone conclusion and Bowie had already conceded defeat as he departed the stadium, never to return. When the final tally of votes was assembled, it showed that Bowie's camp could muster only 2,852 votes against 13,486 for Wilson. The motion needed at least 75 per cent of the vote and it achieved this, providing the mandate for the change.

The outcome of the meeting that Bowie had construed as being the most important in the history of Rangers Football Club was reported in half a column in the *Glasgow Herald* and just twenty-one lines in the *Scotsman*. The Bowie camp lamented that the issue was of passive interest to the fans and not one supporter awaited the outcome at the doors to Ibrox. In contrast, as one reporter pointed out, if the team played a practice session, 30,000 would gather at the stadium.

The affair showed that what mattered to Rangers fans was the performance of the team. In that, they had every reason to be well pleased with the club at the end of the 1946–47 season. The Championship had been secured along with the newly created League Cup and the Glasgow Merchants Charity Cup. Bill Struth was a legendary figure and now he was a board member. Few would dispute that he had earned the accolade and to the vast number of supporters in the Light Blue legions, the Boardroom Coup was a non-issue.

The whole episode surrounding Struth's elevation to the board provides some insight to his character at the time. He had dedicated his life to Rangers and the suggestion that he might relinquish his position as manager threatened to remove more than stewardship of the day-to-day affairs of the club. Rangers had become his life and he was not the kind of man who could mull away the rest of his days in retirement. He was not ready to exit the office, which had become almost his living quarters at times, at the top of the marble staircase. The suggestion from Bowie that he should contemplate resignation was an affront to a man who had never countenanced any question of his authority and capabilities. To Struth, it was a personal attack and a challenge to his position that he repelled through both intense hurt and anger. His response in supporting the challenge to the board by the disaffected W. Rogers Simpson was retaliatory. It unleashed a sequence of events that not only removed any suggestion of his departure from the agenda, but led to the systematic dismantling of the board and Bowie.

Struth had long advocated that 'the club is greater than the man', but this maxim would have sounded hollow to Bowie. By seizing control of the club through the mobilised proxy votes, Struth had not only consolidated his own position, but formalised what many fans already believed – *he* was Rangers. However, Struth would vehemently disagree that he had seized control with his little consortium for his and their benefit alone. His argument, as publicly recorded, was that the board under Bowie needed to change for the benefit of the club. That the challenge was precipitated by a threat to his own position displayed an acute sense of self-preservation. His conduct through the crisis was uncompromising and both he and Simpson showed no mercy as Bowie succumbed. Having achieved their initial objective of a place on the board, both men could have reached compromise. However, this was never an option. They considered that Bowie had to go, although the club was financially sound and the team successful.

It was a harsh end to the career of a man who had served the club well as a player, director and ultimately chairman. The club may well have proven to be greater than the man, but Struth had won the battle of the mortals. His position would never be challenged again.

THE TWILIGHT YEARS

Massive crowds, a new challenge – and a treble

Bill Struth did not celebrate a Championship win in his first season as both manager and director, but the Scottish Cup was captured for the eleventh time after a thrilling replayed final against Morton. Hibernian took the title by 2 points as the Light Blues succumbed at the last hurdle, defeated by Hearts at Ibrox. Despite his disappointment, Struth could not have been more magnanimous in his praise of the new champions when he addressed the shareholders at his first AGM six weeks later. He lavished praise on Hibs, who had become the new challengers to the Ibrox side in the post-war era, adding that the title could not have gone to a worthier club. For Struth, injuries had affected Rangers' challenge and he highlighted to the meeting that 63 per cent of the players were working, which inhibited their recovery from injuries sustained on the field.

Aside from the mixed success they achieved on the field, the club was enjoying a massive resurgence in attendances. In the Cup Final, the crowd over the two games it took to separate the sides amounted to a stunning 265,725, and a midweek-record was established by the 129,176 who attended the replay. The Rangers shareholders had no reason to be anything but satisfied with the first year of the new board. Each of the directors was voted an honorarium of £200 and both Alan Morton and George Brown were successfully re-elected. The Boardroom Coup of 1947 was well behind them and the club looked forward to the post-war era with quiet confidence.

Ironically, William Rogers Simpson, Struth's faithful ally in the coup, did not have much time to revel in his newly elected role of director, then chairman. He died on 29 April 1949 while in London for the England v. Scotland Home International.

The treble success of 1949 consolidated Rangers' position as the biggest and best club in Scotland, and the fans had every reason to be proud of the team that Struth had assembled. The new decade was one of change, however, and no one was more aware than Bill Struth that his tenure would not be everlasting. The organisation within the club had gradually changed to accommodate Struth's advancing years as he found himself more and more restricted. John Wilson increasingly handled press enquiries while Jimmy Smith and Joe Craven handled matters at training. No matter the increased assistance from those around him, Struth was still the manager and in this regard, at least, was considerably more than a figurehead. His role and the manner in which he discharged his duties are clear from the circumstances surrounding the arrival of the little South African winger Johnny Hubbard. Hubbard recalled:

Rangers' interest in me came through Willie Allison, who was Sports Editor of the *Sunday Mail.* I gathered that he was a good friend of Mr Struth and it was the Rangers boss who arranged my passage from Pretoria. Mr Struth told Allison, 'The boy will be well looked after while he is with us. If he makes the grade, he will, of course, be well paid by the Rangers, but if he fails to come up to their standard, they will see to it that he has his passage paid back to South Africa.'

I was offered £100 signing-on fee and a wage of £12 per week, return flights, and a 3-months trial with my digs paid. I travelled to Scotland in July 1949 and was met at the Airport by Mr Struth. Tom Petrie, the chauffeur, then drove Mr Struth and myself to the St Enoch Hotel in Glasgow. Mr Struth told me that we would have dinner there and then I would spend the evening at the hotel, before being picked up by Mr Petrie in the morning. The next morning I went in to Ibrox for training, where I met the trainer, Jimmy Smith. Mr Struth watched me on the pitch, then training by myself and playing keepie-uppie.

After an hour, I went for a bath and then Jimmy Smith came in to tell me the Boss wanted to see me in his office upstairs. I went up the marble staircase, knocked on the manager's door and heard him call me to come in. He said, 'I was in the directors' box watching you and you will do me just fine. I'm signing you on for the rest of the season.' He gave me a £300 signing-on fee, which was three times the amount initially promised and my 'trial period' was obviously now longer than three months.

Hubbard's account on his arrival in Scotland for the first time provides an important insight into Struth's means of operating at that time. Firstly, the correspondence with Willie Allison highlights that Rangers had 'agents' far and wide looking for players. In fact, Allison's initial identification of Hubbard came from another Scot in South Africa, Alex Prior. Importantly, despite his growing years, Struth was still seen as the main point of contact for the acquisition of new players and by simply being at the airport when Hubbard arrived, he showed a personal interest that impressed the young South African. Struth's control of the club is further highlighted by his decision to offer Hubbard a contract immediately following training. The Rangers boss had the mandate to identify and sign players, with the costs apparently entirely at his discretion.

Hubbard was just 18 when he arrived in Scotland and it took four seasons for him to make a real impact on the side. However, although their meetings would be fleeting, he had enormous respect for a man he called simply, 'Mr Struth'. To him, Bill Struth was more than a manager – he was a father-figure.

The recollections of another Rangers star of the period, Billy Simpson, are similar, although the Ulsterman arrived on the back of a record transfer fee of £11,500. He recalled the thrill at meeting Struth when he was first driven to the stadium, even though the Rangers boss then 'laid down the law', telling Simpson that he had to '. . . conduct himself properly on and off the park as a Rangers player'.

These recollections of players acquired at the end of the forties and beginning of the new decade highlight the control that Struth exercised over the players. They were in no doubt who was the Boss, but they were also taken by the aura surrounding the Rangers manager.

Examinations of the club records for the fifties show that Struth maintained tight control in the decision-making process, while relying heavily on James Rogers Simpson, the newly-appointed Director/Secretary and son of William

Rogers Simpson, to deal with the day-to-day business of the club. There was regular correspondence from charitable institutions seeking donations or benefit matches and letters from other clubs asking Rangers' assistance in one way or another. The responses to these requests invariably came directly from Struth in the form of a brusque handwritten instruction at the bottom of each letter received. These would be signed off 'no' or 'yes' and in the case of donations, values ranging from £10 to £100 were offered. Despite the often curt responses suggested, Rangers were anything but abrupt in dealing with these regular requests. Indeed the club, through Bill Struth, was extremely charitable and there was no suggestion of anything other than even-handedness across the community – regardless of creed.

What the correspondence also revealed was the great respect in which he was held by all who dealt with him. However, through the fifties his role in the administration of the club had diminished markedly with J. Rogers Simpson assuming increasing responsibility. Struth also found the other directors taking a more proactive role in dealing with matters of political importance with the football authorities. This was never more evident than in February 1950, when the club received notification from the SFA that some of the Rangers players would be required for the Scotland side in May.

FIFA had created the opportunity for the winners and runners-up in the Home International series to qualify automatically for the World Cup in Brazil in May 1950. The SFA made the bizarre decision to accept the qualification only if Scotland were crowned champions. However, Rangers had other ideas for their players with an end-of-season tour to Denmark and Sweden planned. Although the date of the

Rangers tour did not clash with the World Cup, the SFA was determined to invoke a requirement for clubs to release players for international matches.

The club's refusal to accede to the demands of the SFA would normally have been carried to the governing body's Carlton Place headquarters by Struth. However, it was the Rangers chairman, Bailie John Wilson who led the club's opposition, insisting that if the SFA enforced their restrictive conditions, Rangers would be unable to tour Denmark and Sweden. With the Ibrox side requested to release seven players to Scotland – Young, Cox, Woodburn, Waddell, McColl, Shaw and Brown – it was unsurprising that they felt unable to tour with a weakened side.

The club records show that Rangers prepared for their challenge with an initial legal review of the SFA's conditions of membership. The advice from the club's solicitors was that there was some ambiguity in the clause that the SFA were invoking. Regardless, the SFA's ambitions were dependent on them winning the Home International Championship in April. Come the Championship, victories over Northern Ireland and Wales inspired some confidence that they would succeed against the Auld Enemy at Hampden Park, but a second-half goal put paid to any dreams of Rio.

Ultimately, there was no clash of the calendars, and Rangers proceeded with the tour before releasing their players for friendly internationals over the summer. The battle over the release of the players barely materialised, but it was one that a younger Struth would have relished. By 1950, the manager's ability to deal with such conflicts had waned and he became increasingly reliant on those around him.

If he had passed some responsibilities on to others, he was

very much regarded as the man in control by the players, and he continued to exercise his influence over them. George Young was a Rangers captain and played for sixteen years. During that time, he ran up a total of 97 appearances for Scotland and Scottish League sides. He talked about Struth's influence on the side during his era:

> He was a master of psychology. He could read and understand people like no one else. So when he came into the dressing room, he knew exactly what to say to make you feel better. If we had struggled in the first half because of the wind against us, he would say, 'You'll be all right now because the ball will run with you this half.' A fortnight later, if we had been troubled by a strong wind at our back, he would say at half-time, 'Well, lads, you should find it a lot easier this half with the wind holding the ball up for you.'
>
> He said these things with such confidence, so you believed him. He never tried to tell you how to play the game. The nearest he would come to talking tactics would be to point out when we were playing on a narrow pitch. Then he would suggest that since there was hardly room for five forwards to be spread across the field, it would be better to have one drop back to give the other four more space. Then we took it from there.

On the field, Rangers maintained their superiority in Scotland, defeating East Fife 3–0 in the final of the Scottish Cup and then securing the Championship by a single point from Hibernian within the space of two weeks. As club football wound down for the season, Struth had other things on his mind. A week before the Rangers Sports, on 29 July 1950, he was admitted to the Victoria Infirmary with a serious but undisclosed illness. The newspapers reported that he planned to attend the official opening of the Ibrox Sports, but we have no record of whether he actually made the event.

By August, Struth's ill-health forced his return to hospital when it was tended by the hospital consultant, Dr Alexander Miller. By this time it was known that he had problems with his leg. Miller was an orthopaedic surgeon who had operated on many of the players throughout his career and was well known to the Rangers Manager. He considered that Struth's leg would have to be removed and on Saturday 26 August 1950, the Rangers boss's leg was shaved and rubbed down with iodine in the pre-operative procedure. His courage and resilience were evident as he issued a final instruction to the surgeon before sliding under the anaesthetic. 'Help yourself, Sandy', he called to Miller before heading to the theatre. When Struth returned to Ibrox, he had to contend with his disability and this caused him some anxiety, despite finding some humour in an exchange with former Ibrox star, Tommy Muirhead. 'Look what they have done to me', Struth said. Muirhead replied, 'Aye, and I mind the time when you would have kidded us into going out and playing like that.' Struth laughed in acknowledgement, saying, 'so I would, and ye always came back.'

It was a light-hearted moment that the two shared, but it belied the real concerns that the manager had with his disability. Relying on Jimmy Smith and Joe Craven to carry him up and down the marble staircase to and from his office was demoralising. Gamely he battled on with his crutches, but it was not easy for a man who was now in his 74th year. He confided, 'We've had many a joke with an injured player, offering to knock them [crutches] away, but, it's different when you really have to use them yourself.'

Bill Struth reached a crossroads in his health in 1950 and on the playing field, Rangers' fortunes also dipped. None of the major domestic trophies ended up at Ibrox by the end of season 1950-51. The drought continued into the following season as Hibernian once again took the title, while the nearest Rangers came to some tangible silverware was a defeat by Dundee in the League Cup Final. At Ibrox, there was increasing concern for the welfare of the manager. In the months following his spell in hospital, Struth dipped from public life. The day-to-day business affairs of the club were handled by Bailie John Wilson and J. Rogers Simpson. Indeed, although Struth met Billy Simpson on his arrival at the club, some ten weeks after the operation, the Rangers manager had never seen his expensive acquisition play. Instead, Bailie John Wilson and fellow director George Brown travelled to Linfield to watch the lively young centre-forward.

The early fifties had been a period of disappointment on the football field for Rangers as they suffered barren seasons in the first two years of the decade. Although new players joined the club, there was unrest among the fans as the team failed to impress. It led to one fan writing to Struth, lamenting the quality of some of the new players while lambasting the club for failing to sign the winger and inside-forward he believed to be required. The impassioned letter spoke of the disdain that many fans showed at matches with boos and slow handclapping as the team failed to live up to the standards that they had once set.

At the end of the season, a wearied Struth wrote to his fellow board members suggesting that they appoint an assistant to

him. They declined his request, although the reasons are unclear. Perhaps they felt that he had all the assistance he needed
with trainers Jimmy Smith and Joe Craven. However, these
men were dedicated to the playing field and Struth's roles were
much wider. His fellow directors shared much of the responsibilities in player acquisitions, but they were busy men
themselves and were not always available. Instead, the club was
effectively run by Struth and his director/secretary Rogers
Simpson. At 75, the Rangers manager was clearly pressured,
but his plea fell upon deaf ears and he battled on.

On New Year's Day 1952, Rangers easily trounced Old
Firm rivals Celtic 4–1 at Parkhead. Ordinarily, this would
have been a cause for some celebration among the Rangers
directors and manager. However, as Struth was leaving the
Celtic directors' box, he tumbled down the stairs and was
rushed to hospital. Later in January, he was admitted to the
Victoria Infirmary. Struth's health continued to wane and in
February he was again admitted to the Victoria Infirmary,
reportedly after some internal bleeding.

Struth's illness worries continued and in January 1953, he
was again admitted to the Victoria Infirmary, this time with a
gangrenous toe. Gangrene is most commonly found in the
elderly, but can also be associated with diabetes or injury.

Struth, ageing and debilitated, found the rigours of management increasingly problematic, although Rangers ended their
short-lived championship drought in season 1952–53. They
completed the double by adding the Cup in a fraught final
against Aberdeen that went to a replay.

By now, Struth was regarded as the great statesman of
Rangers and in recognition of his contribution he was given a
portrait in oils, presented to him by the Lord Provost of

Glasgow, Mr Thomas Kerr, following a special lunch on 15 May 1953. The portrait remains today in the Ibrox trophy room. On being given the painting, Struth delivered his most famous speech, capturing the ideals of the club and those attached to it. He famously said:

> I have been lucky – lucky in those who were around me from the boardroom to the dressing room. In time of stress, their unstinted support, unbroken devotion to our club and calmness in adversity eased the task of making Rangers FC the premier club in this country.
>
> To be a Ranger is to sense the sacred trust of upholding all that such a name means in this shrine of football. They must be true in their conception of what the Ibrox tradition seeks from them. No true Ranger has ever failed in the tradition set him.
>
> Our very success, gained you will agree by skill, will draw more people than ever to see it. And that will benefit many more clubs than Rangers. Let the others come after us. We welcome the chase. It is healthy for us. We will never hide from it. Never fear, inevitably we shall have our years of failure, and when they arrive, we must reveal tolerance and sanity. No matter the days of anxiety that come our way, we shall emerge stronger because of the trials to be overcome. That has been the philosophy of the Rangers since the days of the Gallant Pioneers.

These are stirring words that have inspired and continue to inspire those who hold Rangers as their club. Struth knew that he could not continue as the Boss for much longer. Perhaps his speech set out the roadmap for his successor. Continuity in the management seat was the furthest thing from his mind when he was again admitted to hospital in October 1953, which the *Bulletin* reported to be his third time in hospital that year.

Struth and Rangers found solace in the Sports Day through the early fifties, by which time crowds of between 40,000 and 50,000 were attracted to Ibrox. No matter the performance of the team, the event remained one of personal pride for the Rangers boss. He had worked diligently through the years to build the reputation of the competition and he had seen some of the finest athletes in the world appear on his track. They included Paavo Nurmi, the great Finnish middle- and long-distance runner, who won nine Olympic gold and three silver medals and also set 22 world records. Nurmi had come to the stadium in the twenties. Eric Liddell was, of course, another of the celebrated runners who appeared at the ground during Struth's time at Ibrox, and many more giants of the sport pummelled the track, including Sydney Wooderson, the great English athlete who once held the world record over a mile and, but for injury, may well have taken the gold medal in the event in the 1936 Olympic games.

Struth cajoled them all to come to the Rangers Sports, lifting the profile of the event to great standing. Indeed, the growing prestige of the competition made the recruitment of athletes easier as the years went on. He had travelled the globe seeking the best and enticing them with stories of the great crowds back in Scotland. He would regularly travel across the Atlantic at the end of the football season to visit America and talk to the top athletes in person. It was also common for him to travel to events in England, and he could often be found at White City Stadium, in London. The *Sunday Post* of 17 July

1949, for example, reported him visiting the stadium, hoping to attract top-notch athletes, such as British runner E. McDonald Bailey and the Americans Joe Barry, Alan Paterson and Don Findlay. He rarely failed to get his man and they generally showed great devotion to him.

The bond that Struth built with the athletes was highlighted in a story that the great Scots endurance runner Ian Binnie later recounted. He had accepted an invitation from Struth to compete in the Rangers Sports in the early fifties, but later discovered that the event clashed with a GB international meet, due to take place in London. Late one night, Binnie received a call from Jack Crump, secretary of the Amateur Athletics Association, who pleaded with him, saying, 'England needs you.' As far as Binnie was concerned his word was his bond and he advised Crump, 'I am Scottish and my mince is getting cold.'

Binnie proceeded to race at Ibrox and as he was preparing to leave the hallway, he heard Struth call out his name from the top of the marble staircase. The Rangers boss thanked him for keeping his promise and, in gratitude, presented him with a key to the ground. He told Binnie that, providing the players were not using the track, he could use it any time. Binnie said, 'It was the best track in Scotland then, and the greatest gift any athlete could have had.'

Later in the year, Rangers finally completed a project that Struth had initiated many years earlier. In December 1953, the club unveiled its new floodlights in a challenge match with Arsenal. Rangers lost the match by two goals to one in front of a crowd variously recorded between 70,000 and 80,000. White-cord nets were used for the first time at Ibrox in a game that was played with great cordiality, aided no doubt by the fact that the players shared the same base at Turnberry prior to the match. The good spirit continued after the final whistle when Willie Thornton received a presentation from the Rangers Supporters Association. The good humour and plaudits masked the real feelings of the Light Blues legions. A few days later, the team travelled to Dumfries, 8 points behind Queen of the South, although with four games in hand. Rangers were desperate for the victory that would keep them in touch in the title race, but a poor back pass from Woodburn opened up the opportunity for the Palmerston side to get their first-ever win over Rangers in the Borders town. As the fans left the ground, they hurled abuse at the Rangers directors, pleading for the board to sign good forwards.

Unrest among the fans towards the end of 1953 was becoming increasingly vitriolic and public, precipitating a banner headline in the *Glasgow Herald* in December, which simply read: 'Affairs of Rangers Football Club'. That gave no hint of the context of the article, but the piece provided column space over several days to many fans who had written of their frustration with the club. The team was languishing deep in the First Division, attendances at Ibrox were dropping as the fans' tolerance was eroded by defeats by Stirling Albion, Partick Thistle, Dundee, Hearts and Queen of the South. One fan commented that in the previous two years he had 'seriously contemplated deserting the ranks'. Another spoke of the 'most shameful and ineffaceable deterioration in [the club's] history'. However, the hardest criticism was reserved for the board. One correspondent wrote that 'Rangers are suffering from the most dreaded of all business afflictions – division of rule, craving of personal power and disharmony on the board'. Never before in Struth's reign had the club been subjected to such harsh and persistent criticism. Indeed, much of the focus was Struth himself, referred to in one letter as the 'grand old man'.

If one fan thought Struth was 'grand', another suggested that 'the rot set in when another man was forced out of the club – a man who knew the game from A to Z and who was endowed with a pleasant personality as well as a keen business brain.' Clearly alluding to James Bowie, the writer even suggested that he should be invited back to the club.

Amid the rising criticism, Struth and his fellow directors remained silent. The tone of the letters written by some fans in disappointment at the team's performances suggested that they had long been supporters of Bowie. However, regardless of any loyalty they held for the former chairman, there was every justification for criticism. The final straw for many had been that 2–1 defeat at the hands of Queen of the South, which effectively killed off any aspirations that the Light Blues had of retaining their title. By the time they lost 6–0 to Aberdeen in the semi-final of the Scottish Cup, the pleas for change were endemic.

For most of the fans, the success the side had attained in the fifties had masked an underlying problem in the team. Rangers' success had been built upon its 'Iron Curtain' defence, with any flair in attack limited to a precious few players. Many lamented that the side were a shadow of the great sides of the past. More importantly, the voices for change were becoming increasingly audible and, while Struth's name was never mentioned in the press, he was clearly the main target of criticism. Ironically, when Bowie had called time on Struth's career six years earlier, to the chagrin of the Rangers manager, it precipitated the upheaval that signalled the end of the chairman's tenure at

Ibrox. Now, Bowie's supporters were at the forefront of the challenge to Struth. This time, they would not be defeated by proxy – indeed, the majority of fans believed that change was needed.

Following defeat in the Old Firm fixture on New Year's Day, Rangers achieved some stability on the field with wins in the next three fixtures. Then, on 23 January 1954, they faced East Fife at Bayview, where they had failed to record a victory in their previous two visits. Despite going in at the interval one goal up, the Light Blues slid to defeat when the Fifers scored twice early in the second half. The result was not heralded as a shock in the press, as the media focused on the two main title challengers, Hearts and Celtic.

A beleaguered Bill Struth thought through his position over the weekend and then, worn down by criticism and illness, wrote a letter on 26 January 1954 to his fellow members of the board. It echoed a plea he had made to them in 1951. He wrote:

> Mr Chairman and Gentlemen,
>
> I would like once again to bring to your notice the fact that the time has come when I feel I will have to take things easier.
>
> Could we not appoint an assistant as soon as possible, with a view to his taking over the position as Manager at the end of the Season?

When he wrote previously in 1951, the board had turned down his request, suggesting that Struth continue. Perhaps their decline of his request was a gesture of support for the ageing manager. This time, there could be no doubt that Struth should go – the team was a shadow of the great sides he had nurtured in the past thirty years. More important, however, was the ill-health that had weakened him physically and mentally. Struth wanted an assistant, but the board had already decided that the time had come to replace the legendary Rangers boss. On Struth's advice, the board moved to sound out the man he had identified as his successor six years earlier – Scot Symon. The former Ranger had acquired great experience with East Fife and Preston North End in the intervening time.

Willie Maley, commenting in a Rangers publication, offered some support to his beleaguered friend. He said:

I hope [that] he may be spared for many seasons yet to run the great club he loves so well and for which he has done so many years of great work since he rose from the trainership of the Bully Wee Clyde to the high position he now occupies with the Rangers FC whose place in our national game is not surpassed by any club in Britain today.

However, the parties had agreed that the manager should vacate his chair at the end of the season. It was sensible timing in that Symon was in no position to replace Struth at that time. He was already looking forward to the biggest match in his managerial career – the FA Cup Final scheduled for 1 May. He had taken the Lancashire side to Wembley for the first time in sixteen years and his focus was very much on the job at hand.

Defeat in the Scottish Cup semi-final at the hands of Aberdeen in the middle of April, followed by confirmation that the title was lost, hastened Struth's exit. The Aberdeen defeat, in particular, highlighted that the sands of time had finally caught up with Bill Struth. Aberdeen actually finished ninth in the Championship, and the fact that they were able to inflict such a humiliating defeat was alarming. Harry Andrew writing in the *Sunday Express* commented:

> They have been troubled all season with patchwork teams and unwise gambles with half-fit players. Their weaknesses were pointed out but they have closed their eyes to the trouble. Now they have to face a day of reckoning.

The match-day programme for the next home match after the 0–6 defeat had a message from the club directors to the fans. It read:

> We shall go forward grimly determined to restore this famous old club to the position it must hold in the world of soccer. That is our duty; none will shirk from it come what may. Evidence will soon be forthcoming. We cannot at the moment reveal our plans but the supporters will be informed once the results of our discussions have become known.

The final years

On 30 April 1954, William Struth formally surrendered his position as manager of Rangers Football Club. It was curious timing since Rangers were preparing to play Celtic in the Glasgow Charity Cup at Ibrox. Perhaps it lends some strength to the belief that the Charity Cup was the least important of all of the major trophies on offer. In fact, Rangers won the match against their Old Firm rivals, although this time Bill Struth was not there. He was not well enough to attend.

A few days later, the players and his fellow directors presented him with a TV-radiogram in the Blue Room at Ibrox, before they headed off on the liner *Empress of Scotland* for a tour of Canada. At this presentation, Lord Provost Tom Kerr described him as 'The Napoleon who never met his Waterloo'. Struth did not travel with the party – his days of travelling with the club were well behind him.

Although he had relinquished the role of manager, Struth continued to assist in the affairs of the club. However, by the summer of 1956 he was becoming increasingly debilitated and was confined to bed for many months. The Dallas family cared for him as he disappeared from public view and many doubted that they would ever see him at Ibrox again.

Rangers regained the Championship, which provided the old Boss with a lift, and plans were well in hand for the 70th Ibrox Sports, scheduled for 4 August. The weather was bright and warm, encouraging Struth to summon the strength to drag himself from bed, dust down his uniform and travel the short distance to the stadium. Inside the grandstand, very much 'home from home', he was comforted by the officials before taking up a position trackside. He watched a fine event alongside 20,000 spectators inside Ibrox, many intrigued to see the man who had been so instrumental in the success of the event.

There is no record of Struth ever returning to Ibrox. His condition worsened over the next few weeks. Finally, at 81, Bill Struth's body gave up the fight and he died at home at 27 Dalkeith Avenue, Dumbreck, on 21 September 1956. As if to symbolise the continuity of life at the club, Rangers and Celtic reserves battled it out at Ibrox. The next day 56,000 fans assembled inside Celtic Park to watch the first-team action in the sides' first Old Firm league clash of the season. The players lined up, ready to commence the contest, all of the flags were at half-mast, and the referee blew his whistle to signal a thirty-second silence. In a moving mark of respect from both sets of fans, not a sound was heard inside the ground as the players stood, heads bowed and each wearing a black armband.

Rangers won the match 2–0, which was a fitting send-off from the players for a man they revered. Struth was a colossus of a man from a bygone era and the news of his death stimulated tributes from friends and rivals far and wide, including the Celtic manager, Jimmy McGrory:

> He was one of the greatest figures in the game. To Rangers players he was always 'The Boss', although behind his demand for first-class discipline was a man who was always kind, considerate and generous to the players who worked for him. The Celtic players and the Celtic supporters will be distressed by this news.

Willie Maley offered his own personal tribute to Struth, lamenting that:

> [his death] robs me of a friendship of many years' standing – years in which he and I were prominent figures in the game we both loved. A strong silent man who knew the game of football . . . he coached and advised with strong measures which brought great results. He leaves behind memories of which the greatest might be proud.

Scot Symon offered his own words of tribute, saying:

> Mr Struth raised Rangers to a place of prestige and honour which it would be difficult to equal in the world of football. I think the highest tribute I can possibly pay to a great man is to say I have always tried – and will always try – to follow, as best I can, the magnificent example he has left behind.

A few days later, the funeral cortege left Ibrox church, headed down Copland Road, then along Edmiston Drive, past the stadium that had provided so many happy memories for the old manager. As it headed up Broomloan Road, then turned into Paisley Road West, the procession of cars following seemed almost endless. Hundreds lined the streets, including men in dungarees straight out of the shipyards, and women going about their everyday life, stopping to say farewell to a man they knew simply as 'Mr Struth'. Forty-two years earlier, Jimmy Wilson had been carried to the same resting place at Craigton Cemetery, and a similar procession had heralded the end of an era and signalled the commencement of another. Struth would be laid to rest, but there was uncertainty that a man of such stature could ever be replaced. At the cemetery, Struth's coffin was carried by six of his 'boys' – George Young, Ian McColl, Willie Rae, George Niven, Sammy Baird and John Little. His son William was on duty as one of the pall bearers.

Bill Struth's body lies in Craigton Cemetery, but his legacy remained enshrined in the Rangers that he left. He achieved his long-standing ambition to be a man of substance and there can be no doubting that he has been the most influential character in the club. His managership was driven by the ethos that the club was greater than the man. If anyone could challenge that notion, then ironically it would be Struth himself – or perhaps the club *was* the man.

REFLECTIONS ON BILL STRUTH

Greatness is easily conferred on celebrity sportsmen nowadays and it is certainly the case that the longer a character is dead, the 'greater' they can become in the minds of those who hanker for heroes. It is especially so at a football club, where fans and the media often reflect on the 'good old days'. It was a time when the grass was greener, the skies were bluer and everyone was happier – or so it would seem. In reality, life was far from that between the wars, but football did provide a welcome distraction, even during the period of world conflict. It is from this backdrop that heroes emerged in sport, especially when they provided the supporters with some cause for celebration.

Bill Struth gave the Rangers fans plenty to celebrate over the 34 years of his management. His sides won 30 of the 63 major competitions they entered and more than half of the Glasgow Cup and Charity Cup competitions. Even during the war years, his teams won 14 of the 21 competitions of substance. It is no surprise then that Struth was considered one of the Rangers 'greats' and in footballing terms it would be difficult to argue that he was not at least among the best managers that the country has seen. So, if greatness is defined by statistics, then Bill Struth was unarguably a great manager.

However, the story of Struth has shown him to be more than a mere football manager. Born and raised in rather humble circumstances, he was instilled with a determination to do better – to be something. The drive to succeed manifested itself on the running track, but found its way to the playing field where he was to find a rare talent – not in the routine of training, but as a leader of men.

In assessing Bill Struth it is important to strip away the 'wealth' of honours he collected through his lifetime and examine the real man and how he impacted on those around him. His early marital life was thrown into disarray with the birth of his son, but both Bill and Kate showed some true resilience to set that aside and rear young William in a harmonious family background. That there was no evidence of disharmony between the couple in the public record or within the family, suggests that in Kate, Bill found a very loving and probably tolerant wife. The smiles of the couple on holiday suggest that they were happy together, although Kate had to share Bill with one other love – Rangers Football Club. Was she any different from many other wives in this?

The tittle-tattle that surrounded his relationship with Alice Dallas in later years belies the fact that when he eventually shared a home with the Dallas family, he was already an old man, and Charlie Dallas also lived there. Perhaps too much was read into a relationship that was certainly born of a great friendship and perhaps nothing more. It would be wrong to speculate further, although many who were close to the club did at that time. Certainly, Alice's daughter Allison was quite shocked at any suggestion of impropriety between her mother and the man she called 'Uncle Willie'. However, in later years, he would become increasingly estranged from his true family.

Despite this, the true judgement of Bill Struth must lie with those who knew him, including the many players we have spoken with and those long since deceased who have left their tributes in the public record. Who better to offer judgement on the man than Willie Waddell, Willie Thornton, Willie Woodburn, Jock Shaw, Bob McPhail, Ian McColl, Billy Simpson, Adam Little, Johnny Little, Bobby Brown, Johnny Hubbard, and they go on. The overall consensus of these men, 'legends' in their own right, was that Bill Struth was 'a great man'.

While many talked of his fabulous career with Rangers, the few players who remain from that distant era warmly speak of a man who not only shaped their careers, but their very lives. Bob McPhail offered his own quite personal tribute, saying, 'I have no hesitation in saying that being a Rangers player under Struth made me a better human being. The discipline I learned at Ibrox stayed with me for the rest of my life.' That same influence extended to Mattha Gemmell at Clyde, whose esteem for Struth was such that he named his son after him. And then there were the newspaper men, such as his early autobiographer Harry Andrew, who listed him simply as 'immortal'. Even Jimmy McGrory, boss of great rivals Celtic, said he was one of the greatest figures in the game. The tributes through his career and when he died are lengthy and unanimous in their expression that he was a somewhat special man.

He was revered by his players and if a picture is worth a thousand words, the esteem in which he was held is reflected in the faces of those pictured in a photograph, gazing upon him at the Rangers dance, held towards at the end of his career. The words of Johnny Hubbard echoed the sentiments of his team-mates: 'Mr Struth was a great man. I learned a lot from him and I have a lot to thank him for. We knew what we could do and what we couldn't do with him, but we had huge respect for him.'

That Struth had enormous influence on those around him

at Ibrox is without question, but what of his legacies? His influence still looms large with Rangers Football Club and his famous speech has been glorified by disciples who acclaim his words: 'To be a Ranger is to sense the sacred trust of upholding all that such a name means in this shrine of football.' To many, Rangers is more than a club. It is a veritable institution – a religion, even – and Struth, while not one of the founding fathers, is idolised as the benchmark against which everything is judged. 'It would not have happened in Struth's day', 'Bill Struth would not have stood for that', 'Bill wouldn't have done that', and so on.

Every player must turn up at the ground in their club blazer and tie, and dress still remains important to those within Ibrox. However, perhaps his biggest legacy is the standard he ingrained within the broad term 'only the best is good enough for Rangers'. It has characterised the club's policies for years, aspiring to the highest standards on and off the pitch – often failing in both, it has to be said. However, when the standards do drop to unacceptable levels, the guideline is always in what would be expected at Rangers.

In researching this book, we have tried to reach beyond the honours and the results on the field of play. We have also tried to look beyond the popular façade embellished for superficial studies of a man who deserves more. Instead, we have tried to reach deeper into his background in order to understand Bill Struth, the man. What we have found is a man who had an enormous influence on all who came within his sphere and further. He was a man who had enormous ambition and aspirations. He was driven to be a gentleman of some respect, while never seeking the limelight. In that sense, he could not be considered to be egotistical. Indeed, rather than being selfish, much of our research has shown him to be a man who was happier helping or guiding those around him.

He was also considered a fair man and on the occasion when he stole away with the prize money at Porthcawl, his conscience and sense of 'doing what was right' pushed him into leaving the officials with ten times what he had 'won'.

What we found was a man who was not a god, and would not claim to be one. However, he was a great man by his actions and his deeds, quite apart from the honours he acquired at Ibrox. There were undoubtedly some misjudgements in his personal life, but these were simply that – he never showed any signs of malice. To different people he is different things; fans laud his successes and former players reminisce on his strict management. But in seeking words to best sum up Bill Struth, we found them in a casual comment from Johnny Hubbard. Looking quite misty-eyed in a quiet moment of reflection, he said, 'Mr Struth was a nice man – very caring. I couldn't say any wrong of him.'

There is little more we can add.

MATCH RECORD

	P	W	D	L	F	A
League	975	646	198	131	2325	960
Scottish Regional League West	30	22	4	4	72	36
Southern League	180	133	25	22	528	186
Scottish Cup	139	101	21	17	353	110
League Cup	70	45	10	15	161	70
Glasgow Cup	96	63	19	14	210	96
Glasgow Merchants Charity Cup	72	52	8	12	160	68
Summer Cup	18	13	2	3	51	24
Victory Cup	8	6	2	0	20	4
Scottish Emergency War Cup	7	5	2	0	17	7
Southern League Cup	50	42	5	3	132	39
Coronation Cup	1	0	0	1	1	2
Empire Exhibition Cup	1	0	0	1	0	2
St Mungo Cup	1	0	0	1	1	2
Glasgow Dental Cup	2	1	0	1	6	2
Lord Provost Rent Relief Cup	3	3	0	0	7	2
Friendly/Tour/Benefit matches	137	84	27	26	364	185
Total	**1790**	**1216**	**323**	**251**	**4408**	**1795**

Note: These results include all matches up until 30 April 1954, when Bill Struth relinquished the position of manager.

HONOURS

League Champions (18)
1920/21, 1922/23, 1923/24, 1924/25, 1926/27, 1927/28, 1928/29,
1929/30, 1930/31, 1932/33, 1933/34, 1934/35, 1936/37, 1938/39,
1946/47, 1948/49, 1949/50, 1952/53

Scottish Regional League Western Division
1939/40

Southern League (6)
1940/41, 1941/42, 1942/43, 1943/44, 1944/45, 1945/46

Scottish Cup (10)
1928, 1930, 1932, 1934, 1935, 1936, 1948, 1949, 1950, 1953

Scottish League Cup (2)
1947, 1949

Scottish Emergency War Cup
1940

Southern League Cup (4)
1941, 1942, 1943, 1945

Glasgow Cup (19)
1922, 1923, 1924, 1925, 1930, 1932, 1933, 1934, 1936, 1937, 1938, 1940,
1942, 1943, 1944, 1945, 1948, 1950, 1954

Glasgow Merchants Charity Cup (20)
1922, 1923, 1925, 1928, 1929, 1930, 1931, 1932, 1933, 1934, 1939, 1940,
1941, 1942, 1944, 1945, 1946, 1947, 1948, 1951

Lord Provost Rent Relief Cup
1921

Summer Cup
1942

Victory Cup
1946